Masters

MASTERS

Portraits of Great Teachers

JOSEPH EPSTEIN

EDITOR

Basic Books, Inc., Publishers

NEW YORK

"Christian Gauss," by Edmund Wilson, from *The American Scholar* (AS: Summer 1952),
Volume 21, Number 3. Copyright © 1952 by the United Chapters of Phi Beta Kappa;
"Morris R. Cohen—Fifty Years Later," by Sidney Hook, from *The American Scholar*
(AS: Summer 1976), Volume 45, Number 3. Copyright © 1976 by the United Chapters
of Phi Beta Kappa, Copyright transferred to Sidney Hook; "Alfred North Whitehead,"
by Joseph Gerard Brennan, from *The American Scholar* (AS: Autumn 1978), Volume 47,
Number 4. Copyright © 1978 by the United Chapters of Phi Beta Kappa; "Teggart
of Berkeley," by Robert Nisbet, from *The American Scholar* (AS: Winter 1978–79), Volume
48, Number 1. Copyright © 1978 by the United Chapters of Phi Beta Kappa; "Nadia
Boulanger," by Suzanne R. Hoover, from *The American Scholar* (AS: Autumn 1977), Volume 46, Number 4. Copyright © 1977 by the United Chapters of Phi Beta Kappa,
Copyright transferred to Suzanne Hoover; "F. O. Matthiessen," by Kenneth S. Lynn,
from *The American Scholar* (AS: Winter 1976–77), Volume 46, Number 1. Copyright ©
1976 by the United Chapters of Phi Beta Kappa; "Arthur O. Lovejoy," by Lewis S.
Feuer, from *The American Scholar* (AS: Summer 1977), Volume 46, Number 5. Copyright
© 1977 by the United Chapters of Phi Beta Kappa; "Yvor Winters of Stanford," by
Gerald Graff, from *The American Scholar* (AS: Spring 1975), Volume 44, Number 2. Copy-
right © 1975 by the United Chapters of Phi Beta Kappa; "John William Miller," by
George P. Brockway, from *The American Scholar* (AS: Spring 1980), Volume 49, Number
2. Copyright © 1980 by the United Chapters of Phi Beta Kappa; "Hannah Arendt,"
by Peter Stern and Jean Yarbrough, from *The American Scholar* (AS: Summer 1978),
Volume 47, Number 3. Copyright © 1978 by the United Chapters of Phi Beta Kappa;
"Leo Strauss," by Werner J. Dannhauser, from *The American Scholar* (AS: Autumn 1975),
Volume 44, Number 4. Copyright © 1975 by the United Chapters of Phi Beta Kappa;
"C. S. Lewis," by John Wain, from the *American Scholar* (AS: Winter 1980/81) Volume
50, Number 1. Copyright © 1980 by John Wain.

Library of Congress Cataloging in Publication Data

Main entry under title:

Masters: portraits of great teachers.

1. Teachers—Biography—Addresses, essays, lectures.
I. Epstein, Joseph, 1937–
LA2301.M37   371.1'0092'2   80–68180
ISBN 0-465-04420-4

CONTENTS

Contents

CONTRIBUTORS

VICTOR BARNOUW teaches at the University of Wisconsin, Milwaukee. His books include *Culture and Personality* and *Wisconsin Chippewa Myths and Tales and their Relation to Chippewa Life.*

JEREMY BERNSTEIN, Professor of Physics at the Stevens Institute of Technology, is the author of, among numerous other works, *Einstein, The Analytical Engine, Experiencing Science* and *Hans Bethe: Prophet of Energy.* A Fellow of the American Physical Society, he has been writing about science for *The New Yorker* since 1960.

JOSEPH GERARD BRENNAN, Professor Emeritus of Philosophy, Barnard College, Columbia University, is at present Professor of Philosophy, Naval War College, Newport, Rhode Island. His latest book is a memoir, *The Education of a Prejudiced Man.*

GEORGE P. BROCKWAY is Chairman of W. W. Norton and Company, Inc. He is the co-author, with his wife, of *Greece: A Classical Tour with Extras.*

WERNER J. DANNHAUSER is a Professor of Government at Cornell University. He is the author of *Nietzsche's View of Socrates.* His articles and reviews have appeared in a great number of journals.

JOSEPH EPSTEIN is editor of the *American Scholar.* He teaches English at Northwestern University and is the author of, among other books, *Familiar Territory* and *Ambition.*

LEWIS S. FEUER is University Professor of Sociology and the Humanities at the University of Virginia. His most recent books are *Einstein and the Generations of Science* and *Ideology and the Ideologists*.

GERALD GRAFF, Professor of English at Northwestern University, is the author of *Poetic Statement and Critical Dogma* and *Literature Against Itself: Literary Ideas in Modern Society*.

ANTHONY HECHT, who won the Pulitzer Prize in poetry, is a member of both the American Academy and Institute of Arts and Letters, and the American Academy of Arts and Sciences, and is John H. Deane Professor of Poetry and Rhetoric at the University of Rochester. His most recent book is *The Venetian Vespers*.

SIDNEY HOOK, Emeritus Professor of Philosophy at New York University, is currently Senior Research Fellow at the Hoover Institution on War, Revolution, and Peace at Stanford, California. Among his books are *Pragmatism and the Tragic Sense of Life and Revolution, Reform and Social Justice*, and most recently, *Philosophy and Public Policy*.

SUZANNE R. HOOVER has taught literature at Wellesley College, Sarah Lawrence College, and the College at Purchase, SUNY. She is currently working on a book about how to read poems with a full awareness of poetic technique.

KENNETH S. LYNN is the author of *Visions of America*, which is dedicated to the memory of F. O. Matthiessen. *A Divided People*, his most recent book, was published in 1977.

ROBERT NISBET is Albert Schweitzer Professor Emeritus at Columbia University. His latest book is *History of the Idea of Progress*.

PETER STERN is a post-doctoral student with the Committee on Public Policy Studies at the University of Chicago. He

Contributors

has contributed to several journals, including *Interpretation, Political Theory*, and the *Political Science Quarterly*.

HELEN VENDLER teaches at Boston University and Harvard. She is the author of books on Yeats, Stevens, and Herbert; her most recent book is *Part of Nature, Part of Us: Modern American Poetry*.

JOHN WAIN is the author of *The Pardoner's Tale* (a novel), *Professing Poetry* (criticism), and *Samuel Johnson: A Biography*. His *Poems 1949–79* is soon to be published.

EDMUND WILSON died in 1972. He was one of the great American critics and writers of the twentieth century, and the author of such works as *Axel's Castle, To the Finland Station, The Triple Thinkers*, and *A Piece of My Mind*.

JEAN YARBROUGH teaches political philosophy and American political thought at Loyola University of Chicago. She has published articles in *Publius, Polity*, and the *Review of Politics*.

INTRODUCTION

ALTHOUGH I did not realize it at the time, the idea for this book first occurred to me, dimly, some twenty years ago. It was when I read, in *The Shores of Light*, Edmund Wilson's essay "Christian Gauss as a Teacher of Literature." I was much taken with this essay, written with Wilson's characteristic mastery, and thought at the time how fortunate Edmund Wilson was as a young man to have come across so beneficent an influence as Christian Gauss. Gauss himself did not write much, and what he did write does not reflect what must have been his superior intellectual quality. (Along with Wilson, F. Scott Fitzgerald and John Peale Bishop were among his students at Princeton.) I concluded that much of Christian Gauss's mental energies went into his teaching. Carried out conscientiously, conducted at a high level, conveyed with proper passion, teaching is an arduous task. Yet it is not often written about, except indirectly in memoirs or autobiographies, and even in them more by Englishmen than by Americans. Edmund Wilson showed that it could be written about, and extremely well.

Edmund Wilson's essay on Christian Gauss originally appeared in *The American Scholar*. When I became editor of that magazine, in 1975, I determined to acquire for its pages other essays on teachers. With the approval and aid of the journal's editorial board, we, the editors, inaugurated a series of such essays. This seemed a useful idea for a number of reasons. First, great teachers have left no record of their pedagogical accomplishments. The effect of their work has been rather like that of opera singers before the advent of recordings: there was, that is to say, no trace of their work beyond the circle of their auditors. It does not do to overemphasize the comparison, but there is a sense in which teaching, like opera, is a performing art. Not only must the teacher get up his subject, but he must get it across. There is many a tried, but no true, method for doing this: Socratic teasing, sonorous lecturing, sympathetic discussion; passionate argument, witty exposition, dramatics and other sorts of derring-do; plain power of personal example, main force of intellect, and sometimes even bullying. But these are all matters of technique and vary from one teacher to the next. What all the great teachers appear to have in common is love of their subject, an obvious satisfaction in arousing this love in their students, and an ability to convince them that what they are being taught is deadly serious. The essays in this book, in different ways, make this point and while doing so leave a record of some of the most impressive teaching performances of the past fifty years.

Another reason for these essays is that they bring out some of the best qualities in their authors. To write about a teacher who has been an important influence in one's life causes a writer to dig deep within himself not only to bring off a piece of persuasive intellectual portraiture but to ascertain the subtle nature of intellectual influence as it is passed on from teacher to student. The authors of the essays in this book were instructed to write "critical appreciations"—eulogies and testimonials were not wanted—and to be as autobiographical as they deemed necessary. To recall oneself as a student, still very malleable intellectually, under the sway of a teacher with a powerful mind, requires powers of exposition and introspection of the first order.

One wonders whether these great teachers can really have known with any precision the extent or the nature of their influence upon their students. For if a teacher teaches a nonscientific or a nonvocational subject—if he teaches, say, philosophy or literature or history, where proof of learning is not so easily or convincingly demonstrated, quite apart from influence—he cannot even be certain that his teaching has been effective. It is a frustration of the job, shared, one suspects,

Introduction

by the great and not so great teacher alike.

Nowadays many universities and colleges have instituted a procedure called "student evaluation." The way this works is that, at the conclusion of a course, students are asked their opinion—which is given in anonymity and confidentiality—of the quality of a teacher's preparation, the effectiveness of his methods, the usefulness of the readings he has assigned, and ways in which his course might be improved. These student evaluations, which came about as a result of the pressure in the late 1960s and early 1970s for greater student participation in university life, have in my view a negligible utility. They can catch out teachers who may be slackers, but beyond that they are not helpful and can even be inimical in abetting the confusion between popular teaching and good teaching. But however useful to administrators and department heads for determining who is falling down on the job, or to students in allowing them to blow off a certain amount of critical steam, to teachers themselves they are not much help. As a sometime university teacher who has been several times evaluated by my students, I must say that I have learned little from these evaluations. It is good to know that one's teaching is appreciated, of course, but even the most gushing student praise does not allay self-doubts about not being as good at the job as one ought to be. In fact, in my own case, the only aid I have received from student evaluations is the single sentence comment, "He jiggles the change in his pockets." As a result of this penetrating criticism, I now put all my change in my briefcase before stepping into a classroom.

The truth is that one cannot adequately evaluate a teacher until years after one has sat in his classroom, except in cases of inept or egregiously shoddy teachers. Proper evaluation can perhaps only be made after the spell of a powerful teacher has worn off, in the former student's maturity, when in tranquility he can recollect influence. Influence is subtle, sometimes accidental, often mysterious. It cannot generally be analyzed on a computer form in the last ten minutes of the last class of a course.

Introduction

To speak autobiographically again, I feel a certain envy for the authors of the essays in this book. Although I attended a great university—the University of Chicago in the middle 1950s—I fell under the influence of no great teachers. Great reputations there were in plenty at the University of Chicago at that time, and I attended lectures or courses given by a number of them: David Reisman, Christian Makouwer, Elder Olson, Richard McKeon. There were also some extraordinary moments—and perhaps for me the most extraordinary was when I was sitting in on a course in classical art, and the teacher, a Baltic German classical archeologist, who was a dwarf and a hunchback, concluded his explanation of the meaning of the Parthenon frieze by remarking: "Thus we see that the Greeks believed intensely in their gods, but that they also knew that these same gods could not be troubled to care about the fate of human beings." But no single teacher lit up the world for me in quite the way that many of the authors in this book describe their worlds as being lit up by their teachers.

The closest I came to anything of this kind was a course in the modern novel taught by Morton Dauwen Zabel, the literary critic and former editor of *Poetry* magazine. Zabel conducted something midway between a lecture and a discussion course, in which he himself did most of the talking, and did it sitting on a chair upon a low platform, the better part of the time rubbing his eyes. Neither I nor any other student could know it, but at the time Zabel's sister, with whom he lived, was dying a slow and painful death, and he must have been up the better part of most nights attending to her. I suspect Zabel was not a brilliant teacher, yet even in this fatigued state he seemed to me impressive. What impressed me, I think, was that he was a man who lived for literature, who seemed to know most of the important literary figures of the age, and who, even in his dog-tired condition, gave off the rich aroma of the literary life. Regrettably, Morton Dauwen Zabel died before I got around to writing to tell him how much sitting in on his course had meant to me.

Introduction

If I had to name a single teacher who exerted a strong influence over me, it would have to be a man in whose class I sat for eight weeks in fear and distaste. The course took place at a summer session at the now defunct University of Illinois at Navy Pier—or, as it was then called, Harvard on the Rocks. It was taught by a man with a strong Central-European accent, who was probably in his middle thirties and no more than an instructor in academic rank. His chief method, as near as I could make out, was to make his students feel inferior, and this he succeeded in doing without difficulty. The way he went about this was to suggest parallels to the books we were reading in his course; and when he discovered, predictably, that we had not only not read but in most cases had not even heard of the works he suggested, he would look upon us with a disgust best reserved for the lower species. Once he went round the room to ask each of us—we must have been twenty or twenty-five in his class—if we had ever read *The Rape of the Lock*; and when he learned that not one of us had, he looked to the heavens and muttered, "My Got, vat do ze do wit dir time!" Although I was never singled out for mistreatment by this man, I felt humiliated by my ignorance—and felt, too, that I never wanted to be exposed to such treatment again. This may seem an odd stimulus to reading—and an even odder mode of influence—but then few things are less predictable than the forms that influence can take.

From the other side of the lectern, the teacher's side, the most touching letter I have ever received from a student came from a young man writing from Rhodesia, where he was working as a stringer for *The Times* of London and other newspapers. He wrote to tell me how much a course of mine at Northwestern University had meant to him. He said that he was beginning to regret majoring in English until he took my course in Literature and Politics, in which I had treated literature as more than a series of questions in analysis but rather with an interest in making connections to life through literature. He added that he was now writing stories, and enclosed two with his letter, which seemed to me very good. He ended by saying that he had said almost nothing in my course, and that I would probably not remember him at all. And the horror, to me, is that I did not remember him— and do not, after straining to do so, even now. I mention this not in self-congratulation but to show, again, how mysterious is the matter of influence between teacher and student.

The relationship between teacher and student, then, can be rich—and often thickened by complication. (How complicated has been best shown, in fiction, in Lionel Trilling's fine short story "Of This Time, Of That Place.") The bounds of this relationship have never been clearly defined, and probably never can be. Certainly, it is by no means bounded by the classroom—especially in the case of teachers and graduate students, where the relationship can easily blend into friendship. To Socrates, the relationship between teacher and student was characterized by love, spiritual love. Yet anyone who has taught for any length of time can, I suspect, sense the power he has over his students. This power is a sacred trust, never to be abused. Students can feel it too; and the better students will feel themselves simultaneously attracted to it and yet not wanting to be altogether dominated by it. There comes a time when the powerful influence of a strong teacher must, at least partially, be shaken off.

In the nature of this relationship, students frequently want more, and sometimes less, from their teachers than transmission of knowledge. Students will sometimes ask more from their teachers than their teachers are prepared, or in some cases temperamentally disposed, to give. Today, when professors as a group are deemed less formidable figures than they once were, a professor who is known to make himself accessible to students can expect late night calls from his students; can fill up his calendar with student lunches and invitations to coffee or drinks; and can be requested to stand in, all at once, as father-figure, therapist, and career and family counselor. A man I know, now in middle age, left graduate study when a famous teacher, whom he had gone specifically to

Introduction

Columbia to study under, advised him to undergo psycho-analysis. Was the teacher right so to advise him? Was the student wrong to be put off by such advice? Who can say? Lines need to be drawn, but not all teachers draw them in the same places. Here, too, guidelines are not self-evident. All that is evident—and as the essays in *Masters* make splendidly evident—is that the relationship between teacher and student can be of supreme significance.

A cynic, casting a cold eye over this book of essays on teachers, might conclude that a great teacher is a man or a woman who has been lucky enough to have had great students. Thus, running quickly down the roster of contributors to *Masters*, he could say that Christian Gauss was lucky to have had Edmund Wilson in his classes, Morris Cohen lucky to have had Sidney Hook, I. A. Richards to have had Helen Vendler, C. S. Lewis to have had John Wain, Yvor Winters to have had Gerald Graff, and so on—all students who have since themselves become notable as teachers and writers. He might, this same cynic, note that nearly all the subjects of these essays were associated with great universities, among them Harvard and Yale, Princeton and Stanford, Columbia and Chicago.

I do not think that either of these observations is more than a partial truth; yet as editor of this book, I must own up to my own failure in not procuring more essays on less famous teachers who taught at less august institutions. There are many schools notable for teaching excellence—Oberlin and Reed come immediately to mind—whose teachers are not equally noted for their publications. At DePauw University, in Greencastle, Indiana, for example, a man named Raymond Pence taught composition for more than forty years and exerted a strong influence over every student who sat in on his courses. Pence guaranteed results—listen attentively to him, he used to promise, and one would become a vastly improved prose writer—and delivered, it is said, unfailingly. Nor can there be any doubt that at lesser schools, including junior and community colleges, there are devoted men and women lighting intellectual sparks and setting the passion for learning aflame among their students. Everywhere the task of teaching is the same—this lighting of sparks, this setting aflame—and everywhere it is carried on differently. This is the inherent fascination of the subject.

I wish to acknowledge the help of the editorial board of *The American Scholar* in the making of this book. I wish also to acknowledge the help of three good friends, the editors of *The American Scholar*—Jean Stipicevic, Lisa McAuliffe, and Mary Elinore Smith.

JOSEPH EPSTEIN

Masters

1

Christian Gauss

EDMUND WILSON

WHEN Christian Gauss of Princeton died on November 1, 1951, I was asked by the Princeton *Alumni Weekly* to write something about his influence on my generation at Princeton. I sent the editor, who wanted a column, only part of what I had written in response to this request, and even of this he was able to publish only part. This has led me to try to put together a memoir that could stand as a more adequate tribute to a man whose importance to those students with literary talents or tastes who graduated in the early nineteen hundreds cannot be overestimated. We knew Christian Gauss at that time as head of the department of Romance languages, which was largely his own creation, and as teacher of two brilliant courses—in Dante and in French Romanticism—that had become extremely popular. He was not to become dean of the College till 1925. So I shall be mainly occupied here with his activities as a teacher of literature, rather than as an official of the University.

As a professor of French and Italian, then, one of the qualities that distinguished Gauss was the unusual fluidity of mind that he preserved through his whole career. A teacher like Irving Babbitt was a dogmatist who either imposed his dogma or provoked a strong opposition. Christian Gauss was a teacher of a different kind—the kind who starts trains of thought that he does not himself guide to conclusions, but leaves in the hands of his students to be carried on by themselves. The student might develop, extend them, transpose them into different terms, build out of them constructions of his own. Gauss never imposed, he suggested; and his own ideas on any subject were always taking new turns: the light in which he saw it would be shifted, it would range itself in some new context. It bored him, in his course on French Romanticism, to teach the same texts year after year; and with the writers that he could not get away from, he would vary the works read. With the less indispensable ones, he would change the repertory altogether. If Alfred de Vigny, for example, had been featured in the course when you took it, you might come back a few years later and find that he had been pushed into the background by Stendhal. Christian would have been reading up Stendhal, and his interest in him would seem almost as fresh as if he had never read him before. He would have some new insights about him, and he would pass these on to you when you came to see him, as he was doing to his students in class. I know from my own experience how the lightly dropped seeds from his lectures could take root and unfold in another's mind; and, in the course of writing this memoir, I have happened to find striking evidence of the persistence of this vital gift in the testimony of a student of Romance languages who sat under Gauss twenty years later, and who has told me that, in preparing a doctor's thesis, he had at first been exhilarated by an illusion of developing original ideas, only to find the whole thing in germ in his old notes on Gauss's lectures. But though his influence on his students was so penetrating, Gauss founded no school of teaching—not even, I suppose, an academic tradition—because, as one of his colleagues pointed out to me, he had no communicable body of doctrine and no pedagogical method that other teachers could learn to apply. If one went back to Princeton to see him, as I more or less regularly did, after one had got out of college, one's memory of his old preceptorials (relatively informal discussions with groups of five or six students) would seem prolonged, without interruption, into one's more recent conversations, as if it had all been a long conversation that had extended, off and on, through the years: a commentary that, on Christian's part, never seemed to be trying to prove anything in any overwhelming way, a voyage of speculation that aimed rather to survey the world than to fix a convincing vision. In his role of the least didactic of sages, the most accessible of talkers, he seemed a part of that good eighteenth-century Princeton which has always managed to flourish between the pressures of a narrow Presbyterianism and a rich man's suburbanism. It is probable that Christian was at home in Princeton as he would not have been anywhere else. He was delightful in the days of his deanship, in the solid and compact and ample yellow-and-white Joseph Henry house, built in 1837, where there was always, during the weekends, a constant going and coming of visitors, who could pick up with him any topic—literary, historical or collegiate—and pursue it till someone else came and the thread was left suspended. Though by this time so important a local figure, he seemed always, also, international. He had been born of German parents in Michigan, and German had been his first language. In his youth he had spent a good deal of time in France. He had no foreign accent in English, and, so far as I was able to judge, spoke all his languages correctly and fluently; but French, Italian and English, at any rate, with a deliberate articulation, never running the words together, as if they were not native to him. One did not learn a bad accent from him, but one did not learn to speak the Romance languages as they are spoken in their own countries. On the other hand, the very uniformity of his candid tone, his unhurried pace and his scrupulous precision, with his slightly drawling intonations, made a kind of neutral medium in which everything in the world seemed soluble. I have never known anyone like him in any academic community. He gave the impression of keeping in touch, without the slightest effort—he must have examined all the printed matter that came into the university library—with everything that was going on everywhere, as well as everything that had ever gone on. It used to amuse me sometimes to try him out on unlikely subjects. If one asked him a question about the Middle Ages, one absolutely got the impression that he had lived in Europe then and knew it at firsthand.

This extreme flexibility and enormous range were, of course, a feature of his lectures. He was able to explain and appreciate almost any kind of work of literature from almost any period. He would show you what the author was aiming at and the methods he had adopted to achieve his ends. He was wonderful at comparative literature, for his reading had covered the whole of the West—ancient, medieval and modern—and his memory was truly Macaulayan (an adjective sometimes assigned too cheaply). He seemed to be able to summon almost everything he wanted in prose or verse, as if he were taking down the books from the shelf. (He told me once that, in his younger days, he had set out to write something about Rabelais and had presently begun to grow suspicious of what he saw coming out. On looking up Taine's essay on Rabelais, he found that he had been transcribing whole paragraphs from it, his unconscious doing the work of translation.) He was brilliant at revealing the assumptions, social, aesthetic and moral, implicit in, say, a scene from a Romantic play as contrasted with a scene from a Greek tragedy, or in the significance of a character in Dante as distinguished from the significance of a character in Shakespeare. I remember his later quoting with approval A. N. Whitehead's statement, in *Science and the Modern World*, that, "when you are criticizing the philosophy of an epoch," you should "not chiefly direct your attention to those intellectual positions which its exponents feel it necessary explicitly to defend. There will be some fundamental assumptions which adherents of all the variant systems within the epoch unconsciously presuppose. Such assumptions appear so obvious that people do not know what they are assuming because no other way of putting things has ever occurred to them." Gauss had always had a special sense of this. But he was interested also in individuals and liked to bring out the traits of a literary personality. His commentary on a poem of Victor Hugo's—"Le Mendiant" from *Les Contemplations*—would run along something like this: "A poor man is passing in the frost and rain, and Victor Hugo asks him in. He opens the door *'d'une façon civile'*—he is always democratic, of course. *'Entrez, brave homme,'* he says, and he tells the man to warm himself and has a bowl of milk brought him—as anybody, of course, would do. He makes him take off his cloak—*'tout mangé des vers, et jadis bleu'*—and he hangs it on a nail, where the fire shines through its holes, so that it looks like a night illumined by stars:

> *Et, pendant qu'il séchait ce haillon désolé*
> *D'où ruisselaient la pluie et l'eau des fondrières,*
> *Je songeais que cet homme était plein de prières.*
> *Et je regardais, sourd à ce que nous disions,*
> *Sa bure où je voyais des constellations.* *

"This sounds impressive, but what does it mean? Not a thing. We have not been told anything that would indicate that the old man is full of prayers. It is a gratuitous assumption on the part of Hugo. That the cloak with its holes reminded him of a heaven with constellations has no moral significance whatever. Yet with his mastery of verse and his rhetoric, Victor Hugo manages to carry it off. I don't mean," Christian would add, "that he was insincere. Rather than live under Louis Napoleon, he went into voluntary exile—at considerable personal inconvenience—for almost twenty years. He lived up to his democratic principles, but he was always a bit theatrical, and he was not very profound."

I include such reminiscences of the classroom in the hope that they may be of interest in putting on record Gauss's methods as a teacher; for the work of a great teacher who is not, as Gauss was not, a great writer, is almost as likely to be irrecoverable as the work of a great actor. Not that

---

* And, as he dried this sorry rag, from which flowed rain and the water of the mudholes, it seemed to me this man was full of prayers. And I, deaf to what we were saying, gazed at the rough cloth, where I saw constellations. (Translation by William P. Kenney)

Christian was ever in the least histrionic, as some of the popular professors of the time were. On the contrary, for all the friendliness of one's relations with him outside class when one eventually got to know him, his tone was sober and quiet, his attitude detached and impersonal. This was partly due to shyness, no doubt; but the impression he made was formidable. He would come into the classroom without looking at us, and immediately begin to lecture, with his eyes dropped to his notes, presenting a mask that was almost Dantesque, and leveling on us only occasionally the clear gaze that came through his eyeglasses. When he made us recite in Dante, he would sometimes pace to and fro between the desk and the window, with his hands behind his back, rarely consulting the text, which he apparently knew by heart. In the case of some appalling error, he would turn with a stare of ironic amazement and remonstrate in a tone of mock grief: "You thought that barretry was the same as banditry? O-o-h, Mr. X, that's too-oo ba-a-ad!" This last exclamation, drawled out, was his only way of indicating disapproval. His voice was always low and even, except at those moments when he became aware that the class was falling asleep. Then he would turn on another voice—loud, nasal, declamatory and pitilessly distinct—which would be likely to begin in the middle of a sentence, for the sake of the shock value, I think, and in order to dissociate this warning from whatever he happened to be saying—which might be something no more bloodcurdling than a statement that André Chénier had brought to the classical forms a nuance of romantic feeling. When this voice would be heard in the class next door—for it penetrated the partition like a fire siren—it always made people laugh; but for the students in Gauss's own room, it seemed to saw right through the base of the spine and made them sit forward intently. When it had had this effect, it would cease. He was never sarcastic and he never bullied; but the discipline he maintained was perfect. Any signs of disorder were silenced by one straight and stern look.

Nevertheless, though Christian's methods were nondramatic, he had a knack of fixing in one's mind key passages and key facts. His handling of Rousseau, for example, was most effective in building up the importance of a writer whom we might otherwise have found boring. (In this case, he *has* left something that can be used by his successors, in his volume of *Selections* from Rousseau, published by the Princeton University Press—though, as usual with Gauss's writing, the introduction and notes have little of the peculiar effectiveness of his lecture-room presentation.) He would start off by planting, as it were, in our vision of the panorama of history, that critical moment of Rousseau's life which, since he did not include it in the *Confessions*, having already described it in the first of his letters to M. de Malesherbes, is likely to be overlooked or insufficiently emphasized (compare Saintsbury's slurring over of this incident and its consequences for western thought, in his *Encyclopedia Britannica* article): the moment, almost as momentous as that of Paul's conversion on the road to Damascus, when Jean Jacques, then thirty-seven, was walking from Paris to Vincennes, where he was going to see Diderot in prison, and happened to read the announcement that the Academy of Dijon was offering a prize for the best essay on the question, "Has the progress of the arts and sciences contributed to corrupt or to purify society?" Such an incident Gauss made memorable, invested with reverberating significance, by a series of incisive strokes that involved no embroidery or dramatics. It was, in fact, as if the glamor of legend, the grandeur of history, had evaporated and left him exposed to our passing gaze—the dusty and sun-struck Jean Jacques—the clockmaker's son of Geneva, the ill-used apprentice, the thieving lackey, the vagabond of the roads—sinking down under a tree and dazzled by the revelation that all the shames and misfortunes of his life had been the fault of the society that had bred him—that "man is naturally good and that it is only through institutions that men have become wicked." In the same way, he made us feel the pathos and the psychological importance of the moment when the sixteen-year-old apprentice, returning from a walk in the country, found for the third time the gates of Geneva locked against him, and decided that he would never go back.

Christian admired the Romantics and expounded them with the liveliest appreciation; but the Romantic ideal in literature was not his own ideal. In spite of his imaginative gift for entering into other people's points of view, he was devoted to a certain conception of art that inevitably asserted itself and that had a tremendous influence on the students with literary interests who were exposed to Gauss's teaching. Let me try to define this ideal. Christian had first known Europe at firsthand as a foreign correspondent in the Paris of the late nineties, and he had always kept a certain loyalty to the "aestheticism" of the end of the century. There was a legend that seemed almost incredible, of a young Christian Gauss with long yellow hair—in our time he was almost completely bald—who had worn a green velvet jacket;* and he would surprise you from time to time by telling you of some conversation he had had with Oscar Wilde or by describing some such Bohemian character as Bibi-La-Purée. It was rumored— though I never dared asked him about this—that he had once set out to experiment one by one with all the drugs mentioned in Baudelaire's *Les Paradis Artificiels*. He rather admired Wilde, with whom he had talked in cafés where the latter was sitting alone and running up high piles of saucers. He had given Christian copies of his books, inscribed, and Christian used to tell me, with evident respect, that Wilde in his last days had kept only three volumes: a copy of Walter Pater's *The Renaissance* that had been given him by Pater, Flaubert's *La Tentation de Saint Antoine*, and Swinburne's *Atalanta in Calydon*. And it was always Gauss's great advantage over the school of Babbitt and More that he understood the artist's morality as something that expressed itself in different terms from the churchgoer's or the citizen's morality; the fidelity to a kind of truth that is rendered by the discipline of aesthetic form,

---

* I learn from Mrs. Gauss, who has shown me a photograph, that the realities behind this legend were a head of blond bushy hair and a jacket which, though green, was not velvet.

as distinct from that of the professional moralist: the explicit communication of a "message." But there was nothing in his attitude of the truculent pose, the defiance of the bourgeoisie, that had been characteristic of the end of the century; and that that other professor of the Romance languages, Gauss's near-contemporary Ezra Pound, was to sustain through his whole career. How fundamental to his point of view, how much a thing to be taken for granted, this attitude had become, was shown clearly in a conversation I had with him, on some occasion when I had come back after college, when, in reply to some antinomian attitude of mine, or one that he imputed to me, he said, "But you were saying just now that you would have to rewrite something before it could be published. That implies a moral obligation." And his sense of the world and the scope of art was, of course, something very much bigger than was common among the esthetes and the symbolists.

Partly, perhaps, as a heritage from the age of Wilde, but more deeply as a logical consequence of his continental origin and culture, he showed a pronounced though discreet *parti pris* against the literature of the Anglo-Saxon countries. In our time, he carried on a continual feud—partly humorous, yet basically serious—with the canons of the English department. I remember his telling me, with sly satisfaction, about a visiting French professor, who had asked, when it was explained to him that someone was an authority on Chaucer, *"Il est intelligent tout de même?"* Certain classical English writers he patronized—in some cases, rightly, I think. Robert Browning in particular he abominated. The author of *Pippa Passes* was one of the very few writers about whom I thought his opinions intemperate. "That Philistine beef-eating Englishman," he would bait his colleagues in the English department, "not robust, as they say, but robustious, with his cacophonous slapdash writing—telling people that the good is sure to triumph! He is one of the most immoral poets, because he makes moral problems seem easy!" When I tried once to find out why Browning moved Christian to such indignation, he told

me a little darkly, that he had greatly admired him in boyhoo
and had learned from him "a lot of bad doctrine." He said
that the irregular love affairs in Browning were made to seem
too jolly and simple, and insisted that the situation of the
self-frustrated lovers of "The Statue and the Bust" had never
been faced by Browning: if "the end in sight was a vice,"
the poet should not have wanted to have them get together;
if he wanted them to get together, he ought not to have described their goal as a vice but, on the other hand, he ought
to have foreseen a mess. Christian would give one a dismaying
picture of a Browning offensively hearty, bouncing and booming in Italy, while the shades of Leopardi and Dante looked
on, as Boccaccio said of the latter, *"con l'occhio disdegnoso."*
The kind of thing he especially hated was such a poem as
the one, in *James Lee's Wife*, that begins, "O good gigantic
smile o' the brown old earth. . . ." Of Byron—though Byron's
writing was certainly more slapdash than Browning's—he
had a much better opinion, because, no doubt, of Byron's
fondness for the Continent as well as his freer intelligence
and his experience of the ills of the world. He accepted Byron's love affairs—he had nothing of the prig or the Puritan—
because Byron knew what he was doing and was not mislead-
ing about it. As for Shakespeare, though Christian was, of
course, very far from the point of view of Voltaire, there
was always just a suggestion of something of the kind in the
background. He knew Shakespeare well and quoted him often,
but Shakespeare was not one of the authors whom Christian
had lived in or on; and he always made us feel that that sort
of thing could never come up to literature that was polished
and carefully planned, and that knew how to make its points
and the meaning of the points it was making. He was certainly
unfair to Shakespeare in insisting that his characters all talk
the same language, whereas Dante's all express themselves
differently. For Christian, the great poet was Dante, and he
gradually convinced you of this in his remarkable Dante
course. He made us see the objectivity of Dante and the significance of his every stroke, so that even the geographical refer-

Christian Gauss

ences have a moral and emotional force: the Po that finds peace with its tributaries in the Paolo and Francesca episode; the mountain in the Ugolino canto that prevents the Pisans from seeing their neighbors of Lucca; the vividness of the scenes and the characters (he liked to point out how Farinata's arrogant poise was thrown into dramatic relief by the passionate interruption of Cavalcanti); and the tremendous intellectual power by which all sorts of men and women exhibiting all sorts of passions have been organized in an orderly vision that implies, also, a reasoned morality. No Englishman, he made us feel, could ever have achieved this; it would never have occurred to Shakespeare. Nor could any English novelist have even attempted what Gustave Flaubert had achieved— a personal conception of the world, put together, without a visible seam, from apparently impersonal descriptions, in which, as in Dante, not a stroke was wasted. He admired the Russians, also, for their sober art of implication. I remember his calling our attention to one of the church scenes in Tolstoy's *Resurrection*, in which, as he pointed out, Tolstoy made no overt comment, yet caused you to loathe the whole thing by describing the ceremony step by step. This non-English, this classical and Latin ideal, became indissolubly associated in our minds with the summits of literature. We got from Gauss a good many things, but the most important things we got were probably Flaubert and Dante. John Peale Bishop, who came to Princeton intoxicated with Swinburne and Shelley, was concentrating, by the time he graduated, on hard images and pregnant phrases. Ezra Pound and the Imagists, to be sure, had a good deal to do with this, but Gauss's courses were important, too, and such an early poem of Bishop's as "Losses," which contrasts Verlaine with Dante, was directly inspired by them. Less directly, perhaps, but no less certainly, the development of F. Scott Fitzgerald from *This Side of Paradise* to *The Great Gatsby*—from a loose and subjective conception of the novel to an organized impersonal one—was also due to Christian's influence. He made us all want to write something in which every word, every cadence, every detail, should perform a definite function in producing an intense effect.

Gauss's special understanding of the techniques of art was combined, as is not always the case, with a highly developed sense of history as well as a sense of morality (he admirably prepared us for Joyce and Proust). If he played down—as I shall show in a moment—the Thomist side of Dante to make us see him as a great artist, he brought out in Flaubert the moralist and the bitter critic of history. And so much, at that period, was all his thought pervaded by the *Divine Comedy* that even his own version of history had at moments a Dantesque touch. It would not have been difficult, for example, to transpose such a presentation as the one of Rousseau that I have mentioned above into the sharp, concise self-description of a character in the *Divina Commedia:* "I am the clockmaker's son of Geneva who said that man has made man perverse. When for the third time the cruel captain closed the gates, I made the road my home, and found in Annecy the love Geneva had denied. . . ."

With this sense of history of Christian's was involved another strain in his nature that had nothing to do with the aestheticism of the nineties, and yet lived in his mind with it quite comfortably. His father, who came from Baden—he was a relative of the physicist Karl Friedrich Gauss—had taken part in the unsuccessful German revolution of 1848 and come to the United States during the emigrations that followed it. The spirit of '48 was still alive in Christian, and at the time of the First World War, an hereditary hatred of the Prussians roused him to a passionate championship of the anti-German cause even before the United States declared war. Later on, when Prohibition was imposed on the nation, the elder Gauss, as Christian told me, was so much infuriated by what he regarded as an interference nothing short of Prussian with the rights of a free people, that he could not talk calmly about it; and, even when dean of the College and obliged to uphold the law, the American-born Christian continued in public to advocate its repeal, which required a cer-

Christian Gauss

tain courage in Presbyterian Princeton. It was this old-fashioned devotion to liberty that led him to admire Hugo for his refusal to live under the Second Empire, and Byron for his willingness to fight for Italian and Greek liberation. "Everywhere he goes in Europe," Christian would say of Byron, "it is the places, like the prison of Chillon, where men had been oppressed, that arouse him." When he lectured on Anatole France, he would point out the stimulating contrast between the early France of Sylvester Bonnard, who always wrote, as he said, like a kindly and bookish old man, and the France who defended Dreyfus, made a tour of the provinces to speak for him, and remained for the rest of his life a social satirist and a radical publicist. In the years when I was first at Princeton, Gauss called himself, I believe, a socialist; during the years of depression in the thirties, he gravitated again toward the Left, and, in *A Primer for Tomorrow* (1934), he made some serious attempt to criticize the financial-industrial system. In the inscription in the copy he sent me, he said that my stimulation had counted for something in his writing the book. But I was never able to persuade him to read Marx and Engels at firsthand: he read Werner Sombart instead; and I noted this, like the similar unwillingness of Maynard Keynes to read Marx, as a curious confirmation of the theory of the Marxists that the "bourgeois intellectuals" instinctively shy away from Marxist thought to the extent of even refusing to find out what it really is. Yet Christian had read Spengler with excitement—it was from him that I first heard of *The Decline of the West*—immediately after the war; and he never, in these later years, hesitated, in conversation, to indulge in the boldest speculations as to the destiny of contemporary society.

He was a member of the National Committee of the American Civil Liberties Union, and he made a point, after the Second World War, of speaking to Negro audiences in the South. On my last visit to Princeton when I saw him, in the spring of 1951, he talked to me at length about his adventures in the color-discrimination states: how the representatives of some Negro organization, under whose auspices he had been speaking, had been unable to come to see him in his white hotel; and how, as he told me with pride, he had succeeded, for the first time in the history of Richmond, in assembling—in a white church, to which, however, he found that Negroes were only admitted in the back pews—a mixed black and white audience. As he grew older, he became more internationalist. He foresaw, at the end of the First World War, and he often insisted, that nothing but trouble would come of creating more small European states; and, at the end of the Second World War, he was bitterly opposed to what he regarded as the development of American nationalism. He complained much, in this connection, of the intensive cultivation, in the colleges, of American literature—a cultivation that had been carried on, since sometime in the middle thirties, with a zeal that he thought more and more menacing to sound international values. I did not, on the whole, agree with him in disapproving of the growth of American studies; but I could see that, with his relative indifference to English literature, he must have acquired, at the end of the century, an extremely low opinion of American literature. He took no interest in Henry James and not very much in Walt Whitman. He told me once that Henry Ford had said, "Cut your own wood and it will warm you twice," not knowing that Ford had been quoting Thoreau. For Christian, the level of American writing was more or less represented by William Dean Howells, the presiding spirit of the years of his youth, for whom he felt hardly the barest respect. It was absolutely incredible to him—and in this I did agree with him—that *The Rise of Silas Lapham* should ever have been thought an important novel. "It wasn't much of a rise," he would say. Yet the "renaissance" of the twenties he followed—unlike Paul Elmer More—with sympathetic, if critical, interest.

Christian Gauss was a complex personality as well as a subtle mind, and one finds it, in some ways, difficult to sort out one's impressions of him. I want to try to deal now with the moral qualities which, combined with his unusual intellec-

Christian Gauss

tual powers, gave him something of the stature of greatness. In some sense, he was a moral teacher as well as a literary one; but his teaching, in the same way as his criticism, was conveyed by throwing out suggestions and dropping incidental comments. In this connection, I want to quote here the tribute of Harold R. Medina, the distinguished federal judge, from the symposium in the *Alumni Weekly*. It expresses a good deal better than anything I was able to write myself, when I drafted this memoir for the first time, the penetrating quality of Gauss's power; and it is interesting to me as describing an experience that closely parallels my own on the part of an alumnus of an earlier class—1909—who was to work in a different field, yet who had known Christian Gauss, as I had, not as dean of the College but as teacher of literature.

Of all the men whom I have met [Judge Medina writes], only four have significantly influenced my life. Dean Gauss was the second of these; the first, my father. From freshman year on, I had many courses and precepts with Dean Gauss, and during my senior year I was with him almost daily. He attracted me as he did everyone else; and I sensed that he had something to impart which was of infinitely greater importance than the mere content of the courses in French literature. It was many years after I left Princeton before I realized that it was he who first taught me how to think. How strange it is that so many people have the notion that they are thinking when they are merely repeating the thoughts of others. He dealt in ideas without seeming to do so; he led and guided with so gentle a touch that one began to think almost despite oneself. The process once started, he continued in such fashion as to instill into my very soul the determination to be a seeker after truth, the elusive, perhaps never to be attained, complete and utter truth, no matter where it led or whom it hurt. How he did it, I shall never know; but that it was he, I have not the slightest doubt. His own intellectual integrity was a constant example for me to follow. And to this precious element he added another. He gave me the vision of language and literature as something representing the continuous and never-ending flow of man's struggle to think the thoughts which, when put into action, constitute in the aggregate the advance of civilization. Whatever I may be today, or may ever hope to be, is largely the result of the germination of the seeds he planted. The phenomena of cause and effect are not to be denied. With Dean Gauss there were so many hundreds of persons, like myself, whom he influenced and whose innate talents he developed, that the ripples he started in motion were multiplied again and again. In critical times, I always wondered whether he approved or would approve of things I said and did. And this went on for over forty years.

"To instill into my very soul the determination to be a seeker after truth . . . no matter where it led or whom it hurt." I remember my own thrilled response when, in taking us through the seventeenth canto of the *Paradiso*, Christian read without special emphasis, yet in a way that brought out their conviction, a tercet that remained from that moment engraved, as they say, on my mind:

> *E s'io al vero son timido amico,*
> *Temo di perder viver tra coloro*
> *Che questo tempo chiameranno antico.* *

The truth to which Dante refers is his opinion of certain powerful persons, who will, as he has just been forewarned in Heaven, retaliate by sending him into exile—a truth which, as Heaven approves, he will not be deterred from uttering.

Another moment in the classroom comes back to me from one of Christian's preceptorials. He had put to use the issue created by the self-assertive type of romantic, who followed his own impulse in defiance of conventional morality and with indifference to social consequences; and he called upon me to supply him with an instance of moral conflict between social or personal duty and the duty of self-realization. I gave him the case of a problem with which I had had lately to deal as editor of the *Nassau Lit*, when I had not been able to bring myself to tell a friend who had set his heart upon contributing, that the manuscripts he brought me were hopeless. "That's not an impulse," said Christian, "to do a human thing; it's a temptation to do a weak thing."

I was struck also by what seemed to me the unusual line that he took one day in class when one of his students com-

---

* If to the truth I prove a timid friend, I fear to lose my life [to fail of survival] among those who will call this time ancient.

Christian Gauss

plained that he hadn't been able to find out the meaning of a word. "What did you call it?" asked Christian. "Didn't you call it something?" The boy confessed that he hadn't. "That's bad intellectual form," said Christian. "Like going out in the morning with your face unwashed. In reading a foreign language, you must never leave a gap or a blur. If you can't find out what something means, make the best supposition you can. If it's wrong, the chances are that the context will show it in a moment or that you'll see, when the word occurs again, that it couldn't have meant that." This made such an impression on me that—just as Judge Medina says he has been asking himself all his life whether Christian Gauss would approve of his conduct—I still make an effort to live up to it.

I love to remember, too, how Christian began one of his lectures as follows: "There are several fundamental philosophies that one can bring to one's life in the world—or rather, there are several ways of taking life. One of these ways of taking the world is not to have any philosophy at all—that is the way that most people take it. Another way is to regard the world as unreal and God as the only reality: Buddhism is an example of this point of view. Another may be summed up in the words *Sic transit gloria mundi*—that is the point of view you find in Shakespeare." He then went on to an explanation of the eighteenth-century philosophy which assumed that the world was real and that we ourselves may find some sense in it and make ourselves happy in it. On another occasion, in preceptorial, Christian asked me, "Where do you think our ideas come from—justice, righteousness, beauty and so on?" I replied, "Out of the imaginations of men"; and he surprised me by answering, "That is correct." This made an impression on me, because he usually confined himself to purely Socratic questioning, in which he did not often allow himself to express his own opinions. I felt that I had caught him off guard: what he had evidently been expecting to elicit had been either Platonic idealism or Christian revelation.

It was only outside class, and at secondhand, that I learned that he said of himself at this time that his only religion was Dante; yet it could not escape us, in the long run, that the Dante we were studying was a secular Dante—or rather, perhaps, a Dante of the Reformation—the validity of whose art and morality did not in the least depend on one's acceptance or nonacceptance of the faith of the Catholic church. Christian would remind us from time to time of Dante's statement, in his letter to Can Grande, that his poem, though it purported to describe a journey to the other world, really dealt with man's life in this; and we were shown that the conditions of the souls in Hell, Purgatory, and Heaven were metaphors for our moral situation here. The principle of salvation that we learned from Dante was not the Catholic surrender to Jesus—who plays in the *Divine Comedy* so significantly small a role—but the vigilant cultivation of *"il ben del intelletto."*

Some of those who had known Christian in his great days as a teacher were sorry, after the war, to see him becoming involved in the administrative side of the University. I remember his saying to me one day, in the early stages of this, "I've just sent off a lot of letters, and I said to myself as I mailed them, 'There are seventeen letters, to people who don't interest me in the least.'" But the job of the dean's office did interest him—though it seemed to us that it did not take a Gauss to rule on remiss or refractory students. He had never liked repeating routine, and I suppose that his department was coming to bore him. He made, by all accounts, a remarkable dean—for his card-catalogue memory kept all names and faces on file, even for decades after the students had left; and the sensitive feeling for character that had been hidden behind his classroom mask must have equipped him with a special tact in dealing with the difficult cases. His genius for moral values had also a new field now in which it could exercise itself in an immediate and practical way, and the responsibilities of his office—especially in the years just after the war, when students were committing suicide and getting into all sorts of messes—sometimes put upon him an obvious strain.

Christian Gauss

Looking back, since his death, it has seemed to me that the Gauss who was dean of Princeton must have differed almost as much from the Gauss with whom I read French and Italian, as this austere teacher had from the young correspondent in Paris who had paid for Oscar Wilde's drinks. The Gauss I had known in my student days, with his pale cheeks and shuttered gaze, his old raincoat and soft flat hat, and a shabby mongrel dog named Baudelaire which had been left with him by the Jesse Lynch Williamses and which sometimes accompanied him into class—the Gauss who would pass you on the campus without speaking, unless you attracted his attention, in an abstraction like that of Dante in Hell, and who seemed to meet the academic world with a slightly constrained self-consciousness at not having much in common with it—this figure warmed up and filled out, became recognizably Princetonian in his neckties and shirts and a touch of that tone that combines a country club self-assurance with a boyish country-town homeliness. He now met the college world, unscreened, with his humorous and lucid green eyes. He wore golf stockings and even played golf. He interested himself in the football team and made speeches at alumni banquets. Though I know that his influence as dean was exerted in favor of scholarships, higher admission requirements, and the salvaging of the Humanities—I cannot do justice here to this whole important phase of his career—the only moments of our long friendship when I was ever at all out of sympathy with him occurred during these years of officialdom, for I felt that he had picked up, a little, the conventional local prejudices when I found him protesting against the advent in Princeton of the Institute for Advanced Study or, on one occasion, censoring *Lit* for publishing a "blasphemous" story. One was always impressed, however, by the comprehensive and lucid way in which he seemed to have absorbed the business of the University.

We used to hope that he would eventually be president; but, with the domination of business interests on the boards of trustees of the larger American colleges, it was almost as unlikely that Christian would have been asked to be president of Princeton, as it would have been that Santayana would have been asked to be president of Harvard. Not, of course, that it would ever have occurred to anyone to propose such a post for Santayana, but it was somehow characteristic of Christian's career that the idea should have entered the minds of his friends, and that nothing should ever have come of it. There appeared in the whole line of Christian's life a certain diversion of purpose, an unpredictable ambiguity of aim, that corresponded to the fluid indeterminate element in his teaching and conversation. He had originally been a newspaper correspondent and a writer of reviews for literary journals, who hoped to become a poet. He was later a college professor who had developed into a brilliant critic—by far the best, so far as I know, in our academic world of that period— and who still looked forward to writing books; I once found him, in one of his rare moments of leisure, beginning a historical novel. Then, as dean, in the late twenties and thirties, he came to occupy a position of intercollegiate distinction rather incongruous with that usually prosaic office. Was he a "power" in American education? I do not believe he was. That kind of role is possible only for a theorist like John Dewey or an administrator like Charles W. Eliot. Though he was offered the presidency of another college, he continued at Princeton as dean, and simply awaited the age of retirement. When that came, he seemed at first depressed, but later readjusted himself.

I enjoyed him in these post-official years. He was no longer overworked, and he no longer had to worry about the alumni. He returned to literature and started an autobiography, with which, however, he said he was dissatisfied. In October of 1951, he wrote an introduction for a new edition of Machiavelli's *Prince*, and was pleased with it when he had finished. He took Mrs. Gauss for a drive in the car, and they talked about a trip to Florida. He had seemed in good spirits and health, though he had complained the Saturday before, after going to the Cornell game, when he had climbed to one of the top

Christian Gauss

tiers of seats, that he was feeling the effects of age—he was now seventy-three. The day after finishing his introduction, he took the manuscript to his publisher in New York and attended there a memorial service for the Austrian novelist, Hermann Broch, whom he had known when the latter had lived in Princeton. While waiting outside the gates for the train to take him back to Princeton, with the evening paper in his pocket, his heart failed and he suddenly fell dead.

One had always still expected something further from Christian, had hoped that his character and talents would arrive at some final fruition. But—what seems to one still incredible—one's long conversation with him was simply forever suspended. And one sees, now, that the career was complete, the achievement is all there. He has left no solid body of writing; he did not remake Princeton (as Woodrow Wilson in some sense was able to do); he was not really a public man. He was a spiritual and intellectual force—one does not know how else to put it—in a way that a man who does any of those other things may never achieve. His great work in his generation was unorganized and unobtrusive; and *Who's Who* will tell you nothing about it; but his influence was vital for those who felt it.

> *Chè in la mente m'è fitta, ed or m'accora,*
> *La cara e buona imagine paterna*
> *Di voi, quando nel mondo ad ora ad ora*
> *M'insegnavate come l'uom s'eterna. . . .**

---

* For in my mind is fixed and my heart knows the dear and kindly image of you as a father when, from hour to hour, you taught how man makes himself eternal. . . . *The Divine Comedy,* "Inferno," Canto XV.

2

Morris R. Cohen—
Fifty Years Later

SIDNEY HOOK

I

WHAT MAKES a great teacher? I believe it is the ability
to inspire in students a dedication to the subject of instruction.
The dedication may be expressed either in active pursuit of
the discipline or in an appreciation of its results. When we
look back on our schooling, we remember teachers rather
than courses—we remember their manner and method, their
enthusiasm and intellectual excitement, and their capacity
to arouse delight in, or curiosity about, the subject taught.
Different teachers affect different students in different ways.
But when students have been reached by their teacher, the
response is the same—respect, admiration, and a desire to
win approval. Sometimes a teacher's influence is strong
enough to override that of parents and peers.

Even more than an actor, a teacher is a sculptor in snow.
He is remembered only by the generations that have seen
him in action or felt the effects of his presence on those who
have sat at his feet. Great teachers are rare, and lucky are
the students who encounter them. But they are not always
great or original scholars. The popular assumptions that any-

Morris R. Cohen—Fifty Years Later

one who knows a lot about a subject can teach it effectively and that mastery in teaching inevitably develops with mastery of a subject are myths. The kind of teaching to which many students have been exposed in liberal arts colleges should have exploded those myths long ago.

One of the great teachers of the first third of our century was Morris R. Cohen of the College of the City of New York, where he taught courses in philosophy from 1912 to 1938. By conventional pedagogical standards, he would not be considered a great or even a good teacher. For he inspired only a few of his students to undertake careers in philosophy, and overawed the rest. Nonetheless his prowess as a teacher became legendary and his ideas a force in the intellectual community. Yet his classroom techniques would never have won him tenure in any public school system, and he himself confesses he was a failure in his early efforts as an elementary and secondary schoolteacher because he could not even control his classes. When he first began teaching philosophy at the college level, his manner, he says, was that of a "petty drillmaster." This proved so unsatisfactory that, lacking "verbal fluency," he adopted the Socratic method.

Although everyone praises the Socratic method, few really practice it. At its best a search for clarity in the quest for truth, it progresses by the sharpening of concepts and elimination of false hypotheses and notions. Primarily negative in impact, the Socratic method is ideally designed to undermine the dogmas, convictions, and assumptions that one has inherited from tradition and from the surrounding milieu without recognition of their alternatives or awareness of the grounds of belief on which they are founded. It is also effective in critically evaluating the challenges to tradition, the new revelations of popular religion or popular science, the glittering promises of reform and social salvation. It is particularly hard on the revolutionary fanatic who delights in discomfiting defenders of the status quo and is furious when the scalpel of analysis is inserted and twisted into the structure of his own beliefs.

The Socratic method is not illustrated at its best in the Platonic dialogues, which too often are prolonged monologues interrupted by leading questions from friendly stooges. It cannot be employed in disciplines, like the sciences or language instruction, that aim to impart knowledge or skills, and where the cumulative development of the subject matter is essential to mastery. When progress in a field of knowledge is measured by results, those searching, provocative, and unanswerable questions about fundamentals would be considered a pleasant irrelevance. Philosophy is the best, if not the only, study in which to practice the Socratic method, provided the teacher is not interested in lecturing or preaching or transmitting a body of doctrine. The Socratic method, skillfully used, can and should be a propaedeutic to a genuine liberal education: it gives students a feeling for evidence, an awareness of what follows from what, and it instills a healthy wariness of easy generalizations, a skepticism about "what everyone knows," and an intellectual distrust of panaceas.

There are subtle and crude ways of using the Socratic method in the classroom. The subtle way invokes the spirit of "let us reason together," discovers the problem in the course of a collective inquiry, and challenges not the student but the answers. It can never be completely painless because of the sensitivity of adolescents to the judgments—and, sad to say, sometimes the gibes—of their peers. But even when a student hazards an obviously wrong answer, a skillful and kind teacher can make him feel that he has contributed to the progress of the argument by helping to eliminate a false lead.

The crude use of the Socratic method is for shock effect. During the years I studied with Morris Cohen, until, almost a decade later, he began to resort more and more to lecturing, he would use it with devastating results in the classroom. If a problem was being considered, Cohen would deny it was a genuine problem. When he restated the problem, every answer to it was rejected as vague, or confused, or ill informed if not contrary to fact, or as leading to absurd consequences when it was not viciously circular, question-begging, or down-right self-contradictory. The students' answers, to be sure, were almost always what Cohen said they were while he dispatched them with a rapier or sledgehammer—and usually with a wit that delighted those who were not impaled or crushed at the moment. Cohen enjoyed all this immensely, too. There was no animus in this ruthless abortion of error, of stereotyped responses, and of the clichés and bromides that untutored minds brought to the perennial problems of philosophy. And although the students soon felt that whatever they said would be rejected, they consoled themselves with the awareness that almost everyone was in the same boat. When they were not bleeding, they enjoyed watching others bleed. Occasionally Cohen would let up on a student who had the guts and gumption to answer back; if, ignoring the laughter of his fellows, he insisted on his point in the face of Cohen's mounting impatience, that student was subsequently treated more gingerly. Or when Cohen had the answer to a moot point—an answer he was holding in reserve to trot out after he had gone through the class beheading one student response after another—he would occasionally skip the student who he suspected might supply that answer. Some of us who felt the call of philosophy and had avidly read Cohen's published articles could sometimes anticipate what he had in mind. He let us alone in class but we had our egos properly pinched in private sessions with him.

Cohen's class was often an exhilarating experience. We became logical hygienists and terrorized our friends and families, and especially other teachers, with the techniques, and sometimes the pungent expressions, that we picked up observing Cohen in action. His method was not merely a form of logic chopping, or splitting hairs pointlessly, or of talmudic exegesis with which many of his students had some familiarity. We acquired a salutary skepticism of authority in intellectual matters and were able to free ourselves of the hypnosis of the printed word in disputed matters. I recall a class in which Cohen asked us why Thales was considered the father of Western philosophy. "Because he taught that everything was made up of water" was the first answer, which repeated the words of the textbook. "Why should that make him a philosopher—no less a great one?" inquired Cohen. "What would you think of someone who announced that everything was made up of something else in the common world quite distinguishable from it—lead or zinc or paper?" It was agreed that he would have to be a fool or a lunatic, and since Thales was neither, the statement attributed to him was probably not meant to be taken literally. The upshot of the discussion left the student more impressed with Thales's contribution to geometry, not as a form of measurement, but as an exact logical science quite different from anything that preceded it. Students also acquired a realization that philosophy historically had embraced astronomy and other sciences, which led to a question as relevant today as it ever was: What is the relation between wisdom and knowledge, value and fact?

It was to be expected that Cohen's manner and method would periodically lead to the objection that he was merely negative and destructive, that he would rob a student of his faith, break his idols, and put nothing in their stead. Actually this was not altogether true. In the course of his unrelenting criticism, he revealed an amazing encyclopedic erudition that we all admired. It spurred many students to hunt up books they would otherwise never have read. Until smitten with a stroke in 1940, Cohen had a fabulous memory and, in his prime, an almost complete recall of the libraries of literature he had read. The range of his erudition was the despair of the most ambitious of us—history, biology, law, the physical sciences, comparative literature, theology and biblical criticism, not to speak of all the mansions of philosophy. He could suggest a bibliography for every topic or project, and all students, except those who were completely alienated by his devastating negativism, profited immensely.

Further, although Cohen was the personification of the naysayer, he gave his students evidence that philosophical thinking counted in all fields and disciplines; that intelligent doubt and skepticism did not arise out of ignorance but only on the basis of some knowledge; and that even though all definitions presuppose that some terms are undefinable, and all demonstrations assume some propositions that are indemonstrable, there are reasonable grounds for accepting what is undefinable and indemonstrable.

Where his teaching was concerned, Cohen resolutely defended his conception of the vocation of a teacher (at least on the undergraduate level) as a sanitation engineer sent into the world to free students' minds of intellectual rubbish. In a famous story he related quite often, a student reproached him for being merely negative. Cohen retorted: "You have heard how Hercules cleaned the Augean stables. He took all the dirt and manure out and left them clean. You ask me, 'What did he leave in their stead?' I answer, 'Isn't it enough to have cleaned the stables?' " None of us thought—or dared—to make what would have been an appropriate retort: "Of course! But Hercules was no philosopher! A philosopher, you have led us to believe, is full of—wisdom."

Looking back on those days and years, I am shocked at the insensitivity and actual cruelty of Cohen's teaching method, and even more shocked at my indifference to its true character when I was his student. I was among those who spread the word, in speech and writing, about his inspiring teaching and helped make him a legendary figure who was judged and admired for his reputation rather than his actual classroom performance. Only when I myself became a teacher did I realize that the virtues of his method could be achieved without the browbeating, sarcasm, and absence of simple courtesy that marked his dialectical interrogations. It is true that he inspired me. He was the first teacher to command my intellectual respect and the first to greet my opposition to America's entry into the First World War and my questioning of subsequent American foreign policy with anything other than the ferocious antipathy of my high school and City College teachers. Toughened as I was as a street brawler and political activist, I thoroughly enjoyed our give-and-take—although I almost always took more than I gave. But he needlessly hurt too many others in what was for him a form of theater. His religion, his accent, and his irascibility denied him an opportunity to teach in the graduate school of a great university. That is where he really belonged and where the challenge of mature minds would have enabled him to fulfill what he professed was his overwhelming desire—to pursue systematic philosophy. He compensated for the bitterness and deprivation of his lot by playing God in the classroom.

To his credit, Cohen acknowledged in later years that his way of giving students a proper appreciation of the depths of their ignorance left scars. He even related the comment of one student who, asked for an evaluation of Cohen's course, responded: "Justice Holmes said he envied the youth who sat at your feet. It is evident that he never took a course with you." Cohen spoiled the account by interpreting these lapses as an indication that he was "a hard and exacting taskmaster." He readily acknowledged that he deserved this reputation, implying that the great outpouring of "affection and esteem" from his students proved he could not have hurt them very much. One can, however, be "a hard and exacting taskmaster" without the show of irritated impatience and discourtesy that bordered on cruelty.

Although he was not above making a student the butt of a joke, the wit was so apposite and brilliant that it often deadened the victim's pain. Cohen was not a sadist. He did not mean to hurt anyone; and in the years when I could observe him closely, he was obviously unaware of how he affected students. One day a group of us were standing in animated conversation in the marble corridor of the college after an exciting hour with Cohen. After a while Cohen came along, obviously in fine fettle. Catching sight of us, he came over, turned to one of the students present, and said, "The trouble with you, A, is that you can't think." I can still see that student blanch at this sentence of doom pronounced before his peers. And I blush to think that, so great was Cohen's authority with us, we didn't hold this judgment against him but against the hapless victim. Yes, Cohen unwittingly left scars, and as I discovered when I ran into this student a decade later, some of the scars did not heal. It was all so gratuitous for a man who sincerely believed that he had respect for the personality of each of his students. His worst lapses may have occurred when he was plagued by ill health.

When he became aware that any of the students he came to know were in trouble or distress his manner was gentle and kind. Informed that the father of one of the members of our group had died, his letter of condolence was as effective as it was unexpected in sustaining the bereft student. And although my penchant for prolonged disputation with him, intensified as a result of his own teaching, vexed him sorely, especially when I myself began publishing and teaching, he sought, out of genuine personal concern, to dissuade me from taking heedless political positions that jeopardized my future and that of my dependents.

At a famous dinner for Cohen on the occasion of his twenty-fifth anniversary as a teacher at CCNY, all the notables in philosophy turned out to defend him against a rumored threat from the new president of his institution. When Cohen himself made an eloquent speech on his method of teaching undergraduates, he spoke of the service that philosophy can render in education by functioning as "a logical disinfectant."

It was a greater philosopher, Alfred North Whitehead, who remarked in another connection, "One cannot live on a diet of disinfectants"—especially in philosophy. Cohen was well aware that philosophy was vision, and that, at best, the purpose of logical techniques was to work out the details of the vision or to test its deliverances. The legacy of the great philosophers consists not in what they deny or reject but in what they see and affirm. Cohen, too, had visions and insights that, despite himself, shone through the dazzling intellectual swordplay of the classroom. He had great wisdom about the affairs of the world, despite his emphasis upon the virtue of professional detachment, and he had a moral courage that, in the perspective of academic behavior in our time, glows more strongly with the years. Wisdom was apparent in his writing and moral courage in his stance on various controversial issues.

His moral courage was evinced shortly after the First World War when he published his *A Slacker's Apology*—and to be a self-denominated slacker during that period was an invitation to some sort of violence. This moral courage was manifest in his criticism of the revolutionary fanaticism of those who had earlier shared his socialist ideals; in his persistent rejection, until the day of his death, of political Zionism as a form of tribalism—to the acute distress of many of his friends and admirers; in his struggle against the administrative tyranny of his own institution; in his gallant defense of Bertrand Russell, who was denied an appointment at the City College because of an ignorant magistrate and a cowardly mayor—and this despite Cohen's own original disapproval of the appointment; in his refusal to kowtow to, or be silenced by, some extremist students of the mid-thirties. I am sure that he would not have survived the academic life of the sixties. His unquenchable spirit of liberalism, his commitment to tolerance and academic freedom, his mordant criticism of all varieties of fanaticism would have enraged the student extremists and other barbarians of virtue who violently disrupted classrooms and libraries, seized and vandalized offices, and made a mockery of the freedom to teach, learn, and listen. Whatever else his colleagues and administrators would have done, Cohen would not have yielded.

The cultural climate of the country has changed so much in the last fifty years that it is difficult for even the middle-aged to recall the parochial atmosphere in which it was more hazardous to a man's career, especially in philosophy, to call himself an atheist than a socialist. Cohen, though, called himself an atheist and ironically claimed that most modernist Protestant theologians really did not differ with him. At the same time he had a profound sympathy and understanding for the symbols of religion, and contested the current Marxist vulgarization of its role in life as merely a soporific for the masses. In this as in some other social matters he reflected the influence of George Santayana, whose masterpiece, *The Life of Reason*, Cohen used as a text for more than twenty years in his course, The Philosophy of Civilization. The wisdom of *The Life of Reason* never stales on rereading. It was a book to which Cohen owed more than to any other.

What struck me about Cohen seemed just as true of Santayana. Despite so many theories that emphatically declare the opposite, there appeared to be no organic connection between either man's wisdom and his personality. Had Santayana met Cohen in his mature years, he would have detested him, not only because Santayana was an ill-concealed anti-Semite but because of Cohen's unqualified liberalism in the age of Mussolini, Franco, and Stalin, all of whom were Santayana's political heroes. To be sure, Santayana was scornful of Hitler, but because he was a German, not because he was a Nazi.

II

If one were to read contemporary American philosophy, one would hardly suspect that Morris Cohen had ever lived because there are so few references to him. This is somewhat surprising because Cohen's books are easily obtainable and the subjects he discussed, like the philosophy of law, history, and the scientific method, have moved into the center of philosophic interest. A fair number of his students have become professional philosophers, but they have not built on Cohen's work or even referred to it. Instead, they have developed on their own after initially transferring their allegiance to Dewey, Whitehead, G. F. Moore, and others. Herbert Schneider, Joseph Ratner, Morton White, Lewis Feuer, Paul Weiss, and, most distinguished of all, Ernest Nagel have been properly respectful but have not continued Cohen's work in any noticeable way.

Perhaps the chief reason why Cohen's intellectual light seems to have dimmed in American philosophy is that he was primarily a teacher of undergraduates. After all, it is in graduate school that students mature professionally, develop lasting interests, cluster around leading scholars, and become associated with schools of thought. The undergraduate experience is never specialized enough. Cohen boasted that he never sought disciples, but it would be hard to find systematic doctrines that one could identify as constituting a Cohenian philosophy. Despite his boast, it rankled when he observed his best students falling under the influence of Dewey (against whose views he thought he had immunized them) or becoming sympathetic to the logical empiricisms of Rudolf Carnap and Hans Reichenbach. For some years he was proud of Paul Weiss, who staunchly resisted both trends, but was scandalized when Weiss suddenly plumped for the existence of God.

The ambivalent feelings Cohen harbored toward Dewey may have arisen in part from disappointed expectations with respect to Columbia University. He once told me that Dewey, if he had really wanted to, could have arranged for Cohen to join the department of philosophy at Columbia. I asked Dewey about this, and it turned out that by the time Dewey had gotten to know Cohen well, he had dropped the reins of control in the department. The person who really barred Cohen from a post at Columbia was F. J. E. Woodbridge, Cohen's first graduate teacher in philosophy—perhaps more for social reasons than for any others. Cohen was a diamond in the rough, unpolished and argumentative; and in the critical years of Cohen's career, the brooding presence of Nicholas Murray Butler, the staid and ultraconservative president of Columbia, made itself felt, especially in philosophy.

There probably was another reason why Cohen was never called to the university post he deserved—a reason hinted at rather than stated directly: Cohen was an irrepressible talker. He outtalked everyone at every meeting in which an exchange was being carried on, and invariably insisted on having the last word. His talk was good, very good, but colleagues had difficulty getting their own words in. Students, of course, never minded this, but not all of Cohen's auditors were students. Then, too, Cohen was always the lion on social occasions, much to the distress of his hosts, who had invited other lions too. The historian J. Salwyn Schapiro, a colleague of Cohen's at CCNY, once bitterly compared Cohen to a member of a disadvantaged Harlem group whose exploits at the time were making the press. "He always brings his razor to a party!" he complained.

Other echoes of this reaction from Cohen's professional peers reached me at the New York Philosophy Club, which I was invited to join in the late thirties. The club was an organization of a select group of philosophers in the East, founded around the turn of the century by Felix Adler. Papers were read and discussed at the monthly dinner meetings, held at the Columbia Faculty Club. I was puzzled by its rule of procedure. After a paper was read in the late afternoon, the remaining time before dinner was divided equally among all the members for individual comment and criticism. Everyone spoke, even if he had nothing to say. The speaker then rejoined in a brief summary. There was little real give-and-take. When I inquired about the reason for this obviously unsatisfactory procedure, I was told that it had been adopted after Cohen joined the club and that it was devised as the only way to prevent him from monopolizing the discussion and turning it into a debate between himself and the speaker.

I suspect that in the early years, before Cohen mellowed, this may explain why those who were eager to have Cohen as a visitor to their campuses were not as enthusiastic about having him as a permanent colleague. This was a great pity. Earlier recognition in a university milieu would probably have resulted in the development of a more collegial *modus vivendi*, and a more systematic analysis of what he regarded as the perennial problems of philosophy.

Nonetheless, Cohen's intellectual gifts were so outstanding that he became a dominant figure in the cultural life of New York City. Not only was the range of his interests almost universᵃˡ, in contrast with the narrow technical concerns of most philosophers—concerns which Cohen never depreciated—but he was undoubtedly the most incisive and formidable critic of his time. He had an unerring eye for the weakness of any position, and since all positions on fundamental questions have weaknesses, Cohen always had something to say that was unfailingly right. There is more in the world than we can ever say about it, and Cohen, in addition to possessing a highly developed sense for contradiction and a superb dialectical skill, had a keen eye for what was left out, for what received too much or too little emphasis. He was death on the monisms and absolutisms and reductionisms of his time. Especially before an audience, he could easily silence, even if he could not convince, the psychoanalysts, behaviorists, dualists, Marxists, Spenglerians, technocrats, free-willists, necessitarians, Bergsonians, classic rationalists, Baconian empiricists, supernaturalists, anarchists, subjectivists, relativists, and natural law dogmatists who crossed his path. Dewey once remarked that the only thing he had against Cohen was his undue fear lest someone agree with him.

Cohen was incomparable as a judicial critic. If I ever wanted to find out what was wrong with a paper I had written, I would bring it to him. But as an interpretative critic he was quite unsatisfying, and sometimes unfair. Because of his passion for immediate clarity, he rarely helped in trying to find out what a person was attempting to say, to complete a vision of what had been only glimpsed or poorly expressed in assisting an idea struggling to be born. When I once told him how Dewey would make every student who raised a question feel he had said something deeply significant because Dewey would see so much in it, Cohen retorted that Dewey was contributing to intellectual delinquency. He would cheerfully admit that a good cause could be defended by bad arguments, but insisted that it was not his responsibility to establish that the cause was good. Occasionally, however, he would reformulate a position in a paradoxical way and argue for it with

Morris R. Cohen—Fifty Years Later

great ingenuity—for example, his view that the law is only and always what the judge says it is.

Morris Cohen was a critical genius wise enough to realize that the truly great philosopher must have creative vision and the power to embody it in detail. The secret sorrow of his life was that he lacked the creative gifts of so many thinkers to whom he felt intellectually superior. Those of his books that are still instructive consist largely of essays published at different times for widely diverse occasions and stitched together around some central theme. Only one, *The Meaning of Human History*, is a unified work, but it does not fulfill the promise that his vast knowledge of history and the social disciplines, and his deep reflection on human ideals, gave those who remember his remarkable course on The Philosophy of Civilization a right to expect. Its composition was delayed too long, and was completed and delivered by his son, Felix, as the Carus Lectures. The brilliant and pioneering text, *An Introduction to Logic and Scientific Method*, was essentially the work of Ernest Nagel, his ablest student, who to Cohen's disappointment repudiated Cohen's ontological conception of logic.

Although Cohen was aware that his forte consisted in criticism, suggestive generalization, and the discovery and posing of problems rather than in creative analysis, he was, despite frequent professions of intellectual humility, rarely inhibited by modesty. He claims to have coined a beatitude: "Blessed are those who are not modest: they shall not need any devices to call attention to themselves and their modesty." At the famous dinner in his honor in 1927, Cohen who was just forty-seven and had still to publish a book, was praised to the skies by some of the greatest men of the age. But Bertrand Russell, when invited to attend, didn't know who Cohen was (Cohen had met him once and may have written to him) and had even forgotten the occasion when I questioned him about it fifteen years later. He had consented to come for a moderate fee, and gave a clever talk on the basis of a hasty reading of some of Cohen's reprints that the organizing committee had left at his hotel. Einstein sent a cablegram and Justice Holmes a letter. Harold Laski sent a letter that was not read by Felix Frankfurter, the toastmaster, and Cohen once told me why: Laski had written that "among philosophical minds in America no one has done more penetrating or more creative work" than Cohen. Frankfurter, despite Cohen's urging, refused to read the letter in the presence of Woodbridge and Dewey. " 'Why won't you read it?' I asked him. 'It's true!' " It was, however, published in the tribute that contained the proceedings of the affair.

Cohen never responded kindly to criticism of his thought. Not that there was much criticism of it. I believe I was the only one who published an extended critical analysis of his basic philosophy, and he never really forgave me for it. Although urged by some of his students and colleagues to respond to it, for once he made no rejoinder. My piece was an article-review, written for the *Journal of Philosophy*, of Cohen's magnum opus, *Reason and Nature*, whose title was selected to contrast with Dewey's *Experience and Nature*. The editors of the *Journal* had sent the book to me at Cohen's request because on Cohen's fiftieth birthday, in 1930, I had published an encomium on his philosophy in the *New Republic* that Cohen praised as a masterly exposition of the *disjecta membra* of his thoughts. My article-review appeared in the first issue of the *Journal*, January 1932. In the first part, I paid him unmeasured tribute. In the second part, I was critical of some fundamental ambiguities in his conception of reason and logic in nature, his notion of invariance, and his use of the principle of polarity to dispraise life, experience, and novelty. The piece was respectful, in places flattering, and, compared with some of Cohen's critical onslaughts of others' views, rather gentle.

When I met Cohen a few weeks later, the first thing he said to me, in sharp tones, was, "I knew I shouldn't have given you an A in my course in the Philosophy of Science!"— which I had taken ten years before! Elsewhere I have related

Dewey's reaction to the review and Cohen's reaction to the news of it. It so happened that when Cohen rebuked me I had in my pocket a letter received that very day from John Elof Boodin, a philosopher whose metaphysical writings Cohen highly respected. In it he said rather extravagant things about the tone, the fairness, and the generosity of my criticism of Cohen. He concluded with the hope that someone would review his own books in the same way, saying he would then die content. But Cohen would not be mollified. He insisted that I had been unfair. "Boodin is pouring it on just to get you to write about him." After that we never met without heated arguments about almost everything—Hegel, Marx, Dewey, religion, politics. I was with him at Vassar when he had his first heart attack—fortunately unrelated to any argument—and helped in getting him medical aid.

III

Looking back at the end of a life which is now longer than Cohen's own, I find my memory of him stronger than ever, and pervaded with a sense of the continuing significance of his thought—thought worthy of attention that it is not receiving. The pettiness of the man falls away as an amusing incidence of his mortality. (I once suggested to him that he had been too harsh with Harry Overstreet, his long-suffering departmental chairman, whose divorce he had publicly and needlessly criticized, and that even philosophically he had underestimated him. Cohen remarked: "Don't misunderstand me. Overstreet's a big man. After all, it takes a big man to resign himself to living with a still bigger man under him.") In perspective, his wisdom was more important than his person.

In what did Cohen's wisdom consist? It is hard to say without making it appear rather banal. He was more of a moralist and philosopher of life than an original epistemologist or metaphysician. He knew what was important in human affairs, and yet he also knew that human affairs were not the only things of importance. He denied that man was the measure of all things. Aware of man's finitude and inescapable limitations, he warned of the dangers of cosmic egoism, of overweening ambition, and the easy optimism of both sacred and secular theologies. He recognized the reality and inexpugnability of evil. "There are whorehouses in the world and hell underneath them," he would remind students in the gay twenties when the country was on a speculation spree and everyone's prospects seemed rosy and assured. His favorite Hebrew prophets were Amos and Micah, who stressed justice and righteousness above the forms and rituals of conventions, which, he insisted, were themselves not to be despised. Yet he cautioned against the fanaticism of virtue, too. With an eye on those of us who believed that piecemeal reforms were inadequate, a compromise with the ideals of the good society, he would speak of the injustices that could result from the quest for absolute justice. He even criticized the moral extremism of Kant, who would rather permit the world to be destroyed than tolerate the unjust punishment and suffering of the innocent. He put things in perspective by reminding us that "we must all be prepared to suffer and be punished for the sins of others; otherwise we are not entitled to the benefits which we all do derive from the virtue of others." This was not, of course, a counsel to accept the remediable sufferings and injustices of the world but a consolatory reflection that made it easier to bear living in a world that contained so much irremediable evil.

Cohen had read too much history to be optimistic about man or to harbor any illusions about his inherent goodness. As a naturalist he was completely out of sympathy with any notions of original sin, but he recognized that, along with the possibility of rational reconstruction of self and social institutions, we had to take note of an element of intractability in human beings, a kind of perversity, or a will to illusion,

Morris R. Cohen—Fifty Years Later

that would almost ensure the presence of a pyromaniac in any Utopia. He was a firm believer in the objective existence of chance, in what the Germans call *die Tücke des Objekts*— the malice of objects. He would remark that jealousy and envy were natural to man—even to dogs—although their expression could be socially controlled. The upshot of all this was an unillusioned view of man as a "crooked stick" that brought Cohen close to the great ironists of human behavior.

Cohen's mind was always interesting to those whom he encountered. It had a quality of freshness and originality about it that stemmed from his challenges to what appeared to most people, in areas in which they were not expert, as plausible and self-evident. Einstein found his remarks about politics and history fascinating, and great jurists, respectful of Cohen's legal erudition, found his rejection of their popular notions of science stimulating. Every specialist seemed impressed by Cohen's illuminating observations about what was outside his specialty—even when he was annoyed that Cohen had invaded his own field.

The philosophic source of Cohen's wisdom seemed to grow out of his pluralism and his doctrine of polarity. That doctrine teaches that contrary elements or factors or forces are always present in every entity and situation; and all adequate explanations and solutions to problems depend not on reducing one principle to another but on finding the appropriate balance between them—like the use of both rule and discretion in punishing or rewarding or, to use Cohen's homely illustration, braking while driving downhill. In the doctrine's most general terms, principles that are usually taken as not only opposite to, but in strife with, each other, such as "immediacy and mediation, unity and plurality, the fixed and the flux, the ideal and the real, the universal and particular, the actual and possible, et cetera, like the north and south poles of a magnet, all involve each other when applied to any significant entity." Technically, the doctrine stems from Hegel's views on Essence; and, stated abstractly, it does not offer any guide to thought or conduct. It requires a wisdom that does not

derive from philosophy—and whose source we do not know—
to apply the principle of polarity.

The dexterity with which Cohen applied the principle of
polarity reflected his familiarity with concrete situations and
his wide reading. If he had read less he surely would have
written more, but his reading gave him a stock of information, examples, and anecdotes that made it risky to generalize
about anything in a discussion with him. There was no tincture of cynicism in his skeptical attitude toward all large
claims. For him skepticism was not the foundation of knowledge, but its crown. He was among the first to popularize
the fallibilism of Charles Peirce and to realize the devastating
significance of Roberto Michels's "iron law of oligarchy" for
any naïve conception of democracy. Many of his students
were indeed naïve, including the flaming radicals who were
drawn to communism by its rhetoric about "true" democracy.

Cohen was sometimes wrong about facts. I once heard him
say that from what he remembered about the Russian *moujik*,
it was doubtful that a *moujik* would ever learn to drive a
tractor. But he was right about much more important things
in the Soviet Union, although even he, I believe, would have
been as shocked by the revelations of the horrors of the Gulag
Archipelago as he was by the grim details of Hitler's holocaust. He had always scoffed at the notion that to a liberal
there was any principled difference between fascism and communism. He had a crisp reply to those who tried to explain
the transformation of their dream of a Soviet Union into a
Stalinist nightmare on the ground of special historical, psychological, and political circumstances. They reminded him,
he said, of the retort of some Christian apologists to Gibbon—
that Christianity had not failed because it had never been
tried.

Morris Cohen was a liberal for all times and seasons, by
which I mean that his liberalism, like that of Spinoza, was
not tied to any set of doctrines or programs or party platforms.
He didn't like the expression "the open mind" because too
many people with empty minds, unable to distinguish be-

Morris R. Cohen—Fifty Years Later

tween the improbable and impossible or to avoid a simple fallacy of conversion, would boast of their open-mindedness. But the mind of the authentic liberal is open to the consideration of any or all ideas relevant to a problem. He is tolerant of dissenting opinion even when it is necessary vigorously to criticize mischievously false opinion. He is aware of how the issue looks to the other side or interest—even when it is necessary to rule against it. Cohen had that kind of open mind when he was writing on philosophical and social issues, but not when he was teaching undergraduates.

Although in educational matters and psychological insight Cohen lagged far behind John Dewey, he would admit that Dewey's faith in the use of intelligence, and its imaginative projection to widen the circles of shared human experience, was the true faith of the liberal. But since he was loath to agree completely with anyone, he would declare that Dewey seemed to underplay, if not to ignore, the darker sides of human nature. Reinhold Niebuhr persistently made the same kind of criticism of Dewey. When I once related the gist of the criticism to Dewey, he plaintively asked, in an idiom he rarely used, "Do I have to believe that every man is born a sonofabitch even before he acts like one, and regardless of why and how he becomes one?"

There was one emotional quality in Cohen's thought that he apparently developed after my student days. Perhaps it was dormant then, never openly expressed, but its presence in his autobiography is both strong and striking. This was his love of America—an America of which he had been an acidulous critic from the very first day he arrived on the lower East Side of New York at the age of twelve. In the light of the hopes and illusions the immigrants brought with them to these shores there was plenty to criticize in American life, especially in the eyes of those who dwelled in the slums and whose families worked in the sweatshops. There was the hostility to foreign ethnic groups, the active and sometimes illegal opposition to trade unions, the hysteria and occasional mob violence against social dissenters, not to mention the unhappy history of the treatment of Indians and Negroes. With all these things and many more, as a result of his observation and omnivorous reading, Cohen became quite familiar.

Looking back at American history, however, from the perspective of his harvest years in the late thirties, in a world made dark by the threat of totalitarian power, he was impressed by the achievements, the progress, and, above all, the promise of the American experience. He saw the future of liberal civilization bound up with America's survival and its ability to make use of the heritage of human rights formulated by Jefferson and Lincoln.

Cohen's vision may have been sharpened and refocused by his increasing concern about the fate of his own people. His emphasis became quite different. Without abating any of his criticisms of existing American shortcomings and evils, he saw them in proper proportion. America had given him and countless others a chance to make good that would have been denied them anywhere else. This was no invitation to complacency. The moral task was to give others a chance to make good too. Despite the roughness, cruelty, and externalism of American life, tremendous advances had been made in his own lifetime. The lot of the common man had been improved. The nation had recognized its social responsibility to the unemployed, the aged, the fatherless, and the homeless. There was a greater appreciation for the affairs of the mind—for art, letters, music, science. America was no longer an intellectual colony of Europe. To those who cried out, "Not enough! Not enough!" and to those who painted American society as the incarnation of evil, he would point out that if the rate of progress in the next generation was the same as in the past, their grievances, to the extent that they were legitimate, would be largely met. But a reasoned belief or faith in the processes of American democracy was required to sustain the élan of improvement.

Cohen was no nationalist; he knew that no one chooses the country in which he is born. And he looked forward to the rule of enlightened world law. Yet withal, and without

the slightest tincture of chauvinism, he was an American pa-
triot, and never more fervently than when the United States
was enbattled during the Second World War. For him, as
for Santayana, piety was "reverence for the sources of one's
being." It was an emotion naturally acquired, without ideological indoctrination or blinding. Those who went beyond rational criticism and reform and denounced America, either
from the standpoint of an impossibly perfectionist ideal or,
more often, as defenders of the foreign policy of the Soviet
Union, appeared to him to be violating the adage "not to
spit in the waters from which one has drunk." Although he
rarely made this explicit, he felt that those among his students,
and in Jewish circles generally, who lapsed into this hostility
à l'outrance were morally insensitive in disregarding the special
obligation that they, like himself, were under with respect
to America. Had this country not been an easily accessible
refuge and sanctuary to them or their parents, they and all
their kin would have perished in the ghastly brutalities of
the Nazi holocaust.

Cohen's reflections on the nature of piety extended beyond
mere loyalty to one's country: they embraced the very cultural
matrix in which we are nurtured. Toward the end of his
life, he wrote:

> None of us are self-made men and those who think they are,
> are generally no credit to their makers. The language in which our
> thinking moves, the ideals to which we are attuned in the formative
> years of our childhood, our habits, occupations, and pastimes, even
> our gestures, facial expressions and intonations, are so largely the
> social products of generations of teaching, that no man can under-
> stand himself and his limitations unless he understands his heritage;
> and it is very difficult to understand one's heritage, or anything
> else, unless one approaches it with a certain amount of sympathy.

The sympathy with which one approaches his heritage may
become stronger or weaker as one understands it. Cohen's
sympathy as well as his understanding of the American heritage became stronger with each passing year until his death.

That heritage, with its faith in human rights, in tolerance of intellectual differences, in equal opportunity, and in the *moral* equality of all human beings, is as much threatened today on a world scale as it was when Morris Cohen lived and taught. His thought has become part of the American heritage that we should study and take to heart.

3

Alfred North Whitehead: Plato's Lost Dialogue

JOSEPH GERARD BRENNAN

Abide with me: fast falls the eventide . . . —H. F. LYTE

I don't understand Whitehead.—EINSTEIN

"IN ten thousand years, men may go to the moon," the lecturer said. His topic was cosmology; the audience, a Harvard philosophy class. The lecturer was competent: he was Whitehead. True, his estimate erred a bit on the conservative side. Less than thirty-five years after that class meeting, two American astronauts walked on the moon.

That lecture, given in the fall of 1934, was part of Whitehead's course, Cosmologies Ancient and Modern. I had done my undergraduate work at Boston College, a small school in those days, and the variety of Harvard's graduate offerings in philosophy was a little bewildering. My program adviser, Ralph Barton Perry, told me that Whitehead was a great man, though rather difficult to understand. So I took down the great man's lectures in a kind of amateur speedwriting I had developed at the beginning of my graduate work so that I would not miss anything important. It was not hard to keep up with the old metaphysician's leisurely pace.

When he began the course, Alfred North Whitehead was seventy-three years old. He told us that he had been rather seriously ill in the spring, and that was why he did not come to class until the third week of the semester, leaving the opening classes to his assistant, Dr. Kaiser. When he finally manifested himself in the lecture room in Emerson Hall, Whitehead seemed frail, even a bit older than his years. He was not a tall man and walked slowly, shoulders a little bent. His kindly head shone bald and pink over a fringe of white hair. He wore a black suit of clerical cut, a high collar, and a cravat, often a rich blue. His gentle voice pitched high, his smile benign, he seemed like a benevolent vicar from a nineteenth-century English novel. Whitehead himself thought he resembled Mr. Pickwick.

After his late arrival in that October of 1934, Whitehead taught our course with energy and good humor and did not miss a class, taking over the desk where William James and Santayana had sat as his predecessors. His classroom manner was far more easygoing than the formal style of the public lectures from which he put together his well-known philosophical books. "When I'm lecturing," he told us, "I experience a curious mixture of being immensely at ease and stage fright." Whitehead offered his wisdom to us in the form of amiable chats. Some of his admirers claim that his students had the unique experience of being taken behind the scenes and witnessing the very process of creative thinking. I would not go quite that far, for in class he often paraphrased what he had written down in lectures recently published, but no one could deny the spontaneity of his reflections. He talked slowly, often pausing to gaze out the nearest window. From time to time it would occur to him to draw a diagram on the blackboard; that produced a slow getting-up from his chair, a protracted hunt for the chalk, and a wistful little complaint: "I do not understand why they should devise chalk the lecturer cannot *see.*" There was plenty of time for stories about

Alfred North Whitehead: Plato's Lost Dialogue

characters he had known in England—like Sir Richard Jebb of Trinity who, in a fit of abstraction, rode his bicycle into the river, or that other Cambridge don who, tipsy at a Bump Supper, tried to open his door with a matchbox, grumbling, "Damn the nature of things!"

To his summaries of philosophical doctrines that he regarded as suspect, Whitehead would append rueful exclamations like, "That's Epicurus!" or "That's Hume!" or, in the case of his former student and colleague Bertrand Russell, "That's Bertie!" Musing on Plato, he might suddenly utter a passionate little shriek, "READ the *Symposium!*" or *"For God's sake,* be clearheaded!" Whitehead divided philosophers into two classes, clearheaded and muddled. Aristotle was senior member of the first class, and Whitehead included himself in the second. "There is a danger in clarity," he would say, "the danger of overlooking the subtleties of truth."

Graduate students were invited to Professor and Mrs. Whitehead's weekly open house at their apartment on Memorial Drive, where wit and hot chocolate were dispensed, but I was too terrified to go. I contented myself with an occasional word from the great man after class in Emerson Hall. One day I went up to his desk at the end of the hour to retrieve my term paper, a wildly romantic interpretation of Plato's *Timaeus.* On the cover sheet Whitehead had inscribed an *A* and had added in his small, neat handwriting, "Very interesting." As I was ducking away with my paper, he stopped me and asked where I had done my undergraduate work. On hearing that I had studied at Boston College with the Jesuits, his gentle clerical face lighted up. "Ah, yes. All the world knows and admires the Jesuits. But, oh, dear me! You must be frightfully shocked at my muddled philosophy. Your teachers were such clearheaded men, and I am in perpetual *terror* of clearheaded men." He smiled benevolently. Sometimes I wondered whether behind that smile, back of that persona of amiable sagedom, there might be another Whitehead. I had read somewhere that Nietzsche said, "Every profound spirit wears a mask." What, if anything, lay under that benign exterior? What was he like, I wondered, that Other Whitehead? Clearly, Whitehead enjoyed himself at Harvard. At sixty-three, ten years before I took his Philosophy 3b, he had retired from his post of Chief Professor of Mathematics at the University of London's Imperial College of Science and Technology to come to Harvard as professor of philosophy. He came attended by immense, though mysterious, prestige—co-author with Bertrand Russell of Euclid's elements of mathematical logic, *Principia Mathematica;* author himself of books on universal algebra, the philosophy of science, and the theory of knowledge—one of only three for whom Gertrude Stein heard her genius-bell ring. He had even written a treatise on relativity that suggested a need for certain changes in Einstein's doctrine in terms that the relativity theorist himself was reported to have had difficulty comprehending. Whitehead wrote his three metaphysical books in his American years. *Science and the Modern World* came from the Lowell Lectures at Boston in 1925; *Process and Reality* was made up of his Gifford Lectures, delivered at Edinburgh in 1928; *Adventures of Ideas,* of 1933, he put together from lectures at Bryn Mawr and elsewhere. By the early 1930s, like Henri Bergson at the College de France twenty years before, Whitehead at Harvard had become an institution. Looking back now, I find it hard to describe the atmosphere of reverent awe that surrounded the philosopher in those days. Of course his own unique genius was the major factor. But the Emersonian heritage of lecture worship, surviving in New England well into the twentieth century, made a favorable environment for the Whiteheadian organism. Prominent Boston citizens turned out for the philosopher's Lowell Lectures, and the older ladies of the audience wore their legendary headgear. ("My dear, we don't *buy* our hats; we *have* our hats.") Lucien Price of the *Boston Globe* wrote retrospectively: "How quietly, how gently this great light rose over Harvard. The sky begins to shine with the white radiance of eternity. . . ." He added that he associated Whitehead with the finale of Brahms's Fourth Symphony, a comparison that must have puzzled the philosopher, who told us

Alfred North Whitehead: Plato's Lost Dialogue

modestly, "I'm not musical myself, but my wife is."

Whitehead's Gifford Lectures in Edinburgh did not receive the acclaim accorded him by American audiences at his public lectures here—a reception understandable in view of the arcane "philosophy of organism" expounded in them and published later as *Process and Reality.* According to his biographer, Victor A. Lowe, Whitehead's Giffords were a fiasco. The previous Gifford lecturer had been Sir Arthur Stanley Eddington, an old spellbinder who held an audience of six hundred fast to their seats from the beginning to the end of his series. Whitehead began with the same number, but only half a dozen endured to the close. According to Lowe, Sir Edmund Whittaker, Edinburgh's distinguished mathematician, attended the first lecture and later remarked to his son that if he had not known Whitehead well, he would have suspected that the lecturer was an impostor, making it all up as he went along.

But Whitehead's classroom lectures were entirely enjoyable. There were forty or fifty Harvard men in our Philosophy 3b that autumn of 1934, most of them first-year graduate students like me. Occasionally three or four Radcliffe students would come to sit in on a lecture, but Whitehead mildly disapproved of this practice. One day a Radcliffe visitor installed herself in the first row right under his nose and sat smiling eagerly up at him. "By the by," he mused plaintively, pausing to gaze out the nearest window, "if there are any persons present who are not registered members of this course, perhaps they might sit another time toward the back of the room, where I cannot see them." He told us that he once asked an officer of an English college why smoking was prohibited there; the ban seemed unreasonable. "But, Whitehead," the official replied, "there must be *some* rules!" This, Whitehead observed, was an expression of the ultimate fact that there is a morality and an immorality. True, all questions of morals are passing rules for passing social systems. "But there is a *fundamental decency,*" he added. "The notion that something is the right thing to do is more fundamental by far than a code of morals." Obviously he regarded the regulation that

Radcliffe students should stay on their own turf as a passing rule, and indeed it soon passed.

Whitehead offered his Cosmologies course separately at Radcliffe in the early 1930s, although not that particular fall. Ellen Griswold recalls that she took Philosophy 3b with him in Radcliffe's Longfellow Hall in 1931–1932. "He is so dear," she wrote to her parents at the time. "That is the only word for him." Once she and her friend Justine encountered Whitehead as he was trying ineffectually to dismount from a shoe-shine stand in Harvard Square, against the wishes of a bootblack who wanted to snap the metaphysician's shoes to a higher gloss. Whitehead improved the occasion by asking the young women about their plans for the upcoming Columbus Day holiday weekend. New York? Ah, but he was too old for that. New York always seemed to him to be burning things up. In New York City he felt like wax under the flame of a candle. God bless my soul, and so forth.

But those who knew Whitehead more than casually were aware that his celebrated air of modest ineffectuality concealed a wily sharpness. Early on, Russell had noted Whitehead's "shrewdness enabling him to get his way on committees in a manner astonishing to those who thought of him as abstract and unworldly." Tressilian Nicholas, former bursar of Trinity, recalls his first sight of Whitehead at Cambridge; even then he seemed ancient, sage-like:

It was at a College Meeting in 1913. . . . The question before the meeting was whether any pressure should be put upon undergraduates to attend services in the College Chapel, in those distant days a battleground between the "clerical" and "anticlerical" parties in the College. The discussion culminated in a particularly violent speech by the philosophy professor James Ward, denouncing a clerical Fellow which he considered cynical. I wondered what would happen next, when an elderly Fellow of benign appearance and mellifluous voice rose to his feet and began a miniature filibuster with a series of unexceptionable remarks having no obvious connexion with the resolution under discussion which he continued until passions died down. The resolution was at once put to a vote resulting in an overwhelming defeat for the clerical party and the matter

Alfred North Whitehead: Plato's Lost Dialogue

has never been raised again. I recognized a junior mathematical Fellow and asked who it was who had saved the situation. He replied "Oh, don't you know that was A. N. Whitehead, the man who discovered what numbers mean?"*

The first part of Whitehead's course was very much taken up with Plato's numbers. Our teacher held forth with enthusiasm about the insights of the later dialogues and held up to us the ideal of a new *Timaeus,* a cosmological adventure that would unite mathematics and the Good. He wanted to achieve in his own philosophy, he told us, something he thought Plato had accomplished in his: to separate out of the welter of existence a definite number of ultimate cosmological factors—a procedure that John Dewey down at Columbia thought was the philosophical sin against the Holy Spirit, although he did not believe in the Holy Spirit. To Dewey, Whitehead's method of singling out "general features" of our experience and allegedly using them to explain the particularities of that experience constituted precisely the wrong way to go about philosophizing—a misconception inherent in Western philosophy, according to Dewey, since the days of Whitehead's beloved Plato.

Of his large books, Whitehead, in the year of our course, was closest to *Adventures of Ideas* of 1933. In Part II of that work ("Cosmological") he discusses what he calls Plato's seven main notions: the Forms, the physical elements, the Soul, Eros, harmony, mathematical relations, and the Receptacle. The cosmological factors Whitehead offered us for consideration are all (except Eros, which appears in the *Symposium*) to be found in the fable of the world's creation in *Timaeus.* God—or his helper, the Demiurge—makes the universe in a way analogous to that of an inspired sculptor, gazing at a fair model (the Forms) and working out of an inchoate matrix (the Receptacle) that is at once matter, space, and motion. Whitehead has said that all philosophy after Plato consisted of footnotes to him. In his own books that we read, the God

* Letter by Tressilian Nicholas to Ellen Griswold, Nov. 2, 1976.

of his metaphysical writings seemed rather like the Platonic Demiurge; his "Eternal Objects," deficient though they might be in actuality, were Plato's Forms somewhat Aristotelianized. The Whiteheadian principle of Interconnectedness has some link to the Platonic Receptacle, although it is perhaps more proximately derived from the Absolute Idealism that filtered into Whitehead's metaphysics via F. H. Bradley. Plato's Eros, the current in the universe that oscillates between the divine and the mortal, seems to perform a function in Whitehead's cosmos that he calls the essential Creativity in the nature of things—although toward the end of *Adventures of Ideas* he says that Eros is involved in the Primordial Nature of God: that is, God as the entity ultimately responsible for Reality being as it is and not otherwise.

To Plato—the author of the early and middle dialogues, at least—the paradigm of what is really real is the pattern-world of Forms, the immutable Ideas. Here Whitehead parted company with his Greek predecessor. For our teacher was a loyal son of his century, and to him reality was not unchanging Being but Process and Becoming. The world moves ever on into a newness. In his lectures to us, as earlier in *Science and the Modern World*, he claimed that transition, the *passage* of things, is an all-pervasive fact, inherent in the very character of what is really real (that sometimes came out "weally weal"). So he was delighted to point out to us that in the *Sophist* Plato seemed at last to acknowledge that Being Itself could not be static; it had to be dynamic, must contain within itself the principle of motion and life. Repeatedly, Whitehead called our attention to the passage in the dialogue which Benjamin Jowett translates, "I hold that the definition of being is simply power *(dunamis)*." Whitehead may have got onto the passage while discussing Plato with Professor James Haughton Woods, whose course in the later dialogues I took just before Whitehead's and which Whitehead himself had sat in on a few years earlier. Professor Woods told our little class that Whitehead "made a good deal" out of this passage, which Woods said was a very odd one and was thought by

Alfred North Whitehead: Plato's Lost Dialogue

some scholars to be a Stoic interpolation in the text. F. M. Cornford later gently scolded Whitehead for accepting Jowett's translation of the passage, not realizing that Plato said "a mark of real being" rather than "definition of being." Cornford, too, thought the passage peculiar, pointed out that the construction of the Greek is obscure and difficult, and drew the moral that even a profound thinker like Whitehead may be misled by a translation.

For our course with him, Whitehead asked us to read the *Timaeus* and A. E. Taylor's commentary on the dialogue. We also had to read Lucretius's *De Rerum Natura* and Cyril Bailey's book on Epicurus and the Greek atomists. He asked us to read some Descartes and Hume, Santayana's *Some Turns of Thought in Modern Philosophy*, and Lawrence Henderson's *The Order of Nature*. Of his own books, Whitehead suggested that we do *Science and the Modern World*, first turning to the chapter "The Romantic Reaction." He assigned parts of *Adventures of Ideas* and *Process and Reality*, then asked us to read the two lectures he had just given at the University of Chicago titled "Nature and Life," now included in *Modes of Thought*. Except for the chapter on abstraction, I had no trouble reading *Science and the Modern World*, and *Adventures of Ideas* made fairly smooth sailing. On the cover of "Nature and Life" I scrawled "Whitehead in a Nutshell," but *Process and Reality* was a tough nut to crack: nine categories of Existence, twenty-seven categories of Explanation. Why, the good Kant had only twelve! Besides, there were nine categoreal Obligations and three categoreal Conditions. To this day I find most of *Process and Reality* heavy going, and my favorite line from it remains: "Sometimes we see an elephant, and sometimes we do not. The result is that an elephant, when present, is noticed."

Late in the course, Whitehead moved from his meditations on Plato, Epicurus, and Descartes to his own metaphysical speculations. "I am now at the beginning of the construction of a metaphysics," he said in his twenty-second lecture. "There won't be much time to do it now at the end." Yet he had time enough to present something of his "Sociology of Nature," illustrating by chalk diagrams such typical White-headian entities as Occasions of Experience (". . . a *worried* region, here"), calling attention to the presence in the unity of *our* experience at the hissing of classroom radiators and the flapping of window shades. ("One of your number has just sensibly shut the window." I resumed my seat glowing with virtue.) With squiggles to indicate prehensive tentacles incorporating into unities of experience all data taken as rele-vant, these atomic diagrams looked like sketches for a mona-dology of the future, and indeed Whitehead told us that he wanted to produce a metaphysics that would have some of the characteristics of Epicurus and some of Leibniz. (Professor Woods told us Leibniz was "up to the eyes" in the *Timaeus.*) "But, dear me, Leibniz's monads have no windows. I rather think monads must have windows. Otherwise, how would they be aware of each other, even the low-grade ones—I want to know. Of course, you can always give God the job." To Whitehead, the cosmos was pervaded by a process akin to feeling; in his universe everything took account of everything else.

I did not take any of Whitehead's seminars. Apparently they were not as entertaining as his lecture classes. Victor Lowe says he found them rather boring. He remarks that Whitehead seemed to assume that every seminar student was a genius, and sat benignly through two or three long student reports each session. During the readings, Lowe and Paul Henle would sit in the back of the seminar room and play blindfold chess. But Lowe says that he perked up his ears whenever Whitehead spoke, adding that he owes part of his ability to understand his eminent teacher's metaphysics to the training he got in the back row of the seminar room.

A. H. Johnson took a different kind of seminar with White-head in 1936. He was asked to appear solo at the Whitehead apartment in Radnor Hall with prepared questions based on statements of his interpretations of Whitehead's theories and to offer criticisms set in the context of references to White-headian texts. Johnson would present a query like, "Is the

Alfred North Whitehead: Plato's Lost Dialogue

examination of human experience the source of your doctrine of the 'self-creativity' of actual entities?" Whitehead: "Yes." "Am I correct in saying that you apply the term *feeling* to (1) subjective forms, (2) data, and (3) complete actual entities?" Whitehead: "Yes." "Do you mean that a patch of red is a feeling and not the affective content which is felt?" Whitehead: "Yes." When the conscientious Johnson would ferret out some of Whitehead's notorious inconsistencies, the old metaphysician would blandly plead guilty. "Not quite satisfied with my own position here," he would note. "It is an inadequate and vague way of expressing an insight," or "I cannot settle the question," or "There is a danger here; I haven't been careful in formulating my ideas," or "A great carelessness on my part," and so on.

Whitehead was only one of a brilliant constellation of stars that made the 1930s the Silver Age of the Harvard Philosophy Department. Besides Perry and J. H. Woods the cluster included the old-line idealist William Ernest Hocking; C. I. Lewis, who took us through *The Critique of Pure Reason;* the irascible logician Henry Sheffer; and the incomparable Harry Austryn Wolfson. As a student in Wolfson's Aristotle seminar, I sometimes had to look him up in his Widener Library cell, stacked high with books, scrolls, and manuscripts in Greek, Hebrew, Latin, and Arabic. In Wolfson's own apartment, every available space was packed with books, and sometimes he forgot whether he had stowed a needed volume in the oven or the refrigerator.

Whitehead himself had moments when he was not quite sure where he had put things. One day in the early 1930s he had Professor James Melrose of Illinois to tea at the Whitehead cottage in Milton, "about 14 miles from Harvard Square," as the philosopher described it in a note to the visiting professor's daughter, from whom I have the account. It occurred to Whitehead that his guests might like to see the work in progress on a library addition to the house. So he led them outside, first carefully putting on Professor Melrose's hat, which he found in the coatroom closet and assumed was his own. After the excursion he returned the hat to the closet, but at tea's end, when he and Mrs. Whitehead prepared to accompany the guests to their car, he went there once more for his hat. This time Melrose had beat him to it and retrieved his lawful property. Whitehead reached up to the place where his visitor's hat had been, made a little exclamation of surprise, then trotted some distance to a spot where his own hat hung on a hook. It was clear to his guests that the author of *Process and Reality* did not realize there were two hats, but believed that his own had in some unaccountable way changed its place. This incident seemed partially related to what he told us in class while discussing Descartes's doctrine of continual creation of the world by God:

> Haven't you sometimes lost something around the house and looked for it for two hours and then found it exactly where it ought to be? We never think that the lost thing passed out of existence for two hours. Yet the direct evidence in favor of that assumption is rather large.

But Whitehead was never absentminded in the manner of certain other elderly Harvard scholars such as the English department's John Livingston Lowes, who in the autumn of his years would often give the same lecture twice in succession or forget to give one at all. As teacher, Whitehead remained ever conscious of his responsibilities to his students. Save for times of real illness, he did not miss classes. And although he may have made the same point more than once, it was always with a fresh illustration, often a funny one.

Consider a fact Whitehead repeatedly insisted on—the enormous advance made along the road of knowledge when some talented caveman first scratched his furry pate upon dimly perceiving something in common between a quartet of clouds and a quartet of mammoths. According to Whitehead, that was the first metaphysical insight, from which led the road to mathematics of the most practical kind. In another lecture Whitehead illustrated a similar claim by telling of a mother squirrel who brought up her babies in a nest near the fireplace

Alfred North Whitehead: Plato's Lost Dialogue

of a Whitehead summerhouse in Vermont. One day the mother squirrel decided that her offspring were big enough to move outdoors, so she carried them one by one to a flat rock outside. But when the last infant had been safely set down, the mother squirrel seemed distraught. Anxiously she ran back and forth several times between the empty nest inside the house and the rock outside where her children were waiting for her. Why was she so distressed? Because, said Whitehead, *she could not count.*

Whitehead repeated the same proposition to our class in the course of a mild polemic against positivism. He began by reading two passages, one from Morris Cohen's *Reason and Nature*, the other from Russell's *Freedom Versus Organization*. Cohen rejected as "vicious obscurantism" all efforts to describe "the indescribable," while Russell argued that the belief that metaphysics has any bearing on practical affairs constitutes a proof of logical incapacity. "Now suppose"— Whitehead turned on his most angelic smile—"that there were a primitive tribe of savages who could not count more than five; and suppose that some bold man of that tribe said, 'I wonder what is the relation of the stars to a flock of birds in terms of number.' Of course he wouldn't say it that way, but can't you hear the Morris Cohen of the period saying, 'I reject as vicious obscurantism all attempts to describe the indescribable,' and Bertie chiming in, 'The belief that metaphysics can have any bearing on practical affairs is to my mind an instance of logical incapacity'?" Whitehead did not like positivism, even in Lucretius. "I suggest that all these positivistic notions of Lucretius are complete and absolute *fudge!*" (strong language for him). "In his time hundreds of slaves were being crucified."

But Whitehead's stature clearly showed when he supported the positivist A. J. Ayer's candidacy for research student at Oxford's Christ Church in 1935. Ayer notes in his recent memoir, *Part of My Life*, that he had sent Whitehead the manuscript of two central chapters of *Language, Truth and Logic*, that small book which a few months later would crash like a brick through the dusty panes of British and American philosophy. Whitehead read the chapters and sent back his aye vote: "I am not in my own person a Logical Positivist. . . . But I cannot imagine a greater blessing for English philosophical learning than the rise in Oxford of a vigorous young school of Logical Positivists." Years later the grateful Ayer tried to call on Whitehead in his apartment near Harvard Square, but Mrs. Whitehead would not let him in because Ayer had a cold.

If in no other instance, Whitehead's greatness as a teacher is confirmed by the single case of his pupil Bertrand Russell, whom the old metaphysician once introduced to a Harvard audience at "Plato's Lost Dialogue"—a phrase I've always thought better fitted Whitehead himself. In 1898, at the age of nineteen, Russell sat for an entrance scholarship at Cambridge University. His examiner was Whitehead. Another candidate got higher grades than Russell, but Whitehead decided that Russell was the abler of the two, burned the grades, and recommended Russell, who received the scholarship. Subsequently Whitehead put up Russell's name for membership in that Cambridge super elite known as the Apostles, of which Whitehead and G. E. Moore were members. Some years later, Lytton Strachey and John Maynard Keynes joined the little clan, and the aura of the Apostles settled Holy Ghost-wise on the heads of the Bloomsbury group—the Woolfs, the Bells, and the rest. Whitehead read Russell's dissertation at Cambridge and, although he criticized it severely, passed it, remarking to his pupil that this was the last chance anyone would get to find serious fault with his work. Russell admired his Trinity senior's mathematical genius (he tells all this in his autobiography) and wondered at his hoard of historical knowledge. He was struck by Whitehead's clerical appearance, and traced it to his teacher's upbringing as the son of a Kentish Anglican clergyman. Russell claims that the vicarage atmosphere indelibly affected Whitehead's thought and surfaced in his later metaphysical writings. The collaboration of teacher and pupil in building that cathedral of deductive

Alfred North Whitehead: Plato's Lost Dialogue

logic, *Principia Mathematica*, is a fact too well known to descant on here. Russell's comments on his intellectual seniors are rarely unbarbed, but he had no reservations about Whitehead's pedagogy:

Whitehead was extraordinarily perfect as a teacher. He took a personal interest in those with whom he had to deal and knew both their strong and their weak points. He would elicit from a pupil the best of which a pupil was capable. He was never repressive, or sarcastic, or superior or any of the things that inferior teachers like to be. I think that in all the abler young men with whom he came in contact he inspired, as he did in me, a very real and lasting affection.

The collaboration on *Principia Mathematica* began about 1900, and Russell saw a good deal of Whitehead and his wife during the following years. If Russell's reminiscences of his senior colleague are trustworthy, it seems that the Other Whitehead really did exist. The decade before, Whitehead had spent years deeply absorbed in Roman Catholic writings, especially those of Newman, and at one time seems to have thought seriously of conversion to Catholicism. When he gave it up, he formed no tie during the rest of his life to any other religious denomination, apparently finding in philosophy what others found in faith. He and his wife had talked out the matter of religious commitment together, but Whitehead's decision not to convert did not bring peace to the philosopher or to his marriage, a union that seems to have suffered considerable strain in the early 1900s. Evelyn Whitehead must have been a lovely bride (they were married in 1890), and her husband was deeply in love with her. He tells how a London policeman once asked the Whiteheads' maid whether the beautiful girl he had seen letting herself into the house one night after a court ball was a real human or the Virgin Mary. Fifty years after their marriage Whitehead wrote that his wife's vivid life had taught him "that beauty, moral and aesthetic, is the aim of existence, and that kindness, and love, and artistic satisfaction are among its modes of attainment."

But in those days, it seems, things were not easy at the Whiteheads'.

By 1902 Russell had fallen out of love with his first wife, Alys, and began to confide accounts of his marital infelicities to Mrs. Whitehead. In turn she shared certain confidences and anxieties with him. She felt neglected by Alfred, says Russell, and frightened by his odd habit of running up tradesmen's bills he knew he could not pay. Russell furnished money to help them out, his generosity strictly anonymous. There were some doubts as to Whitehead's mental or emotional condition at the time. "Mrs. Whitehead was in perpetual fear he would go mad," says Russell. "I think, in retrospect, that she exaggerated the danger, for she tended to be melodramatic in her outlook. But the danger was certainly real. . . ."

According to Russell's biographer, Ronald W. Clark, difficulties compounded when the sympathy and sharing of confidences Russell got from Evelyn Whitehead turned the younger philosopher's gaze toward her as a possible object of his amorous attention. It appears that Mrs. Whitehead kept the friendship with her husband's junior colleague within bounds, no easy thing to do when Russell's blood was up— to put it only so. In any case, collaboration and friendship between the two men continued until the outbreak of the 1914–1918 war, when they sharply disagreed over attitudes and obligations. Russell went to jail for his pacifist activities while Whitehead lost a son shot down over France. Friendship between teacher and former pupil cooled, but never broke. To personal differences were added philosophical divergences. Of Whitehead, Russell said, "His philosophy was very obscure, and there was much in it I never succeeded in understanding." Russell saw the world in terms of clear-cut logical distinctions, while Whitehead concentrated on the interconnectedness of things. Russell expressed well the difference between himself and his old mentor when he said that he, Russell, saw reality as a heap of shot, while Whitehead thought it was a bowl of treacle.

Listening to Whitehead in class, we could count recurrent

motifs in our efforts to know something about that bowl of treacle—the need of philosophy to do justice both to the transient and to the abiding in experience, the oversimplicity of Aristotelian logic with its related metaphysics of substance and quality, at against the Whiteheadian scheme in which events are basic. Always he reminded us that philosophers tend to accept uncritically the presuppositions of the science of their day; unguarded belief in Newtonian physics, with its model of the universe as a great machine suspended in an absolute space-box, conditioned the epistemology of modern philosophy. The result, Whitehead warned us, was that Nature had been split in two, bifurcated into our perceptions and their supposed separate external causes, thus raising the hopeless question as to how we can know the second from the first. Whitehead recalled to us that in his own lifetime he had seen every presupposition of classical physics go by the board.

Today we can see that he overdid his anti-Newtonian polemic. Newton's laws helped put those men on the moon whose landing Whitehead did not expect for millennia. Recent work by neo-Newtonian philosophers tends to show that relativity theory enables us to dispense with some types of absolute motion but not all. Still, Whitehead's critique of sense-data epistemology was acute and needed, and it is interesting to see how continental phenomenologists reached similar conclusions. Working in part from premises not wholly unlike Whitehead's, they, like him, claimed that the task of philosophy is to give an account of experience in which no one dimension of it is given priority at the outset—experience as it actually comes to us in all its multidimensional richness, not thinned down to some colored-patch or mental-state abstraction designed to fit a special theory of mind misleadingly labeled "empiricist."

Strange that after Whitehead's early work on relativity, his interest in physics did not seem to keep pace with the dramatic advances in that science. The most brilliant work on quantum and wave mechanics was done in Europe after he left the Imperial College for Harvard. The attack on the atomic nucleus began in the early 1930s; the neutron was described in 1932; artificial radioactivity became a fact in 1934–1935, the year of our course with him. Yet Whitehead's references to quantum theory in his definitive metaphysical book *Process and Reality*, although wholly approving, are not sustained, and at least part of that approval seemed based on his satisfaction that physicists were now explaining chemical facts in terms that would have pleased Plato. In his last big book, *Adventures of Ideas* of 1933, there is only a single brief reference to quanta. Could it be that Whitehead's devotion to Plato actually led him unconsciously to repeat the pattern of the Platonic Socrates, who in middle life was absorbed in physical science but turned away from it in his old age?

In the *Phaedo*, Socrates says that when he was a philosopher of science earlier in life he found a book by Anaxagoras that said Mind was the cause of all things. Socrates was curious to see what the man would make of this wonderful notion, but was disappointed to find that Anaxagoras dropped it and instead explained everything in terms of external mechanical causes. "Might as well say," Socrates remarked to his students who had come to hear his last words before his death, "in answer to the question as to what brought me here to prison and execution (there now, Apollodorus, don't cry!), the muscles were pulling on the bones of my legs and making them move to carry me here. But you sensible lads know perfectly well that I'm here because I thought it right and just to accept the verdict of my fellow-Athenians and to die in a good cause."

The same distinction lay at the heart of Whitehead's philosophy, as he set it out to us in class and as we found it written in his books. You cannot hold that everything is ultimately explainable in terms of some sort of mechanism and at the same time maintain that human beings are self-determining organisms. Mechanical explanations are simply inadequate when we apply them to human action, which by its very nature is intentional and purposive. What Saint Francis and John Wesley did and why they did it cannot sensibly be ac-

Alfred North Whitehead: Plato's Lost Dialogue

counted for in terms of molecular interactions. No more can Franklin Roosevelt's New Deal, which promises to reform social and ecomonic life in the United States. (Things were hot in Washington in 1934–1935; we had not yet pulled out of the depression, and Whitehead, like Thomas Mann, admired Roosevelt as a Joseph the Provider, gifted with foresight.) Whitehead refused to admit that the brilliant successes of modern science required us to extend its method of objective nonteleological description to the whole of reality. To him, the simplest human experience precluded such extensions. What brought Alfred Whitehead to class in Emerson Hall was not just his muscles pulling on his old bones. Reality is not chopped into two fearfully unequal parts—one, a tiny fragment alive, acting with intent and purpose; the other, a blind run of mindless, aimless atoms, galaxies, universes. In a word, Whitehead was an antimaterialist. Yet he rejected Idealism too,

> *And God-appointed Berkeley that proved all*
> * things a dream,*
> *That this pragmatical, preposterous pig of a world,*
> * its farrow that so solid seem,*
> *Must vanish on the instant if the mind but change*
> * its theme.* *

So he was forced to construct his own world scheme, a cosmos in which all things and events are interfused and take account of one another, however dimly; a world in which a dropped book shakes the stars, where the abiding enters into the passingness of things, physics mingles with aesthetics and mathematics with the Good. The result of this metaphysical construction has had a mixed reception from critics. Some have been reminded of a splendid Gothic cathedral, others of one of those preposterous vehicles, elaborately curlicued, drawn by Emett for *Punch*. All have agreed that Whitehead's system was original. Six years after the philosopher's death

---

* From a poem by W. B. Yeats, "Blood and the Moon." See *The Collected Works of W. B. Yeats* (New York: The Macmillian Co., 1954), p. 233.

in 1948, Stephen Toulmin wrote: "In the history of recent
British philosophy, Alfred North Whitehead stands quite
alone. As a metaphysician, he had no direct ancestors, nor
any effective descendants. Admired by curious amateurs, but
ignored by most of his English colleagues, his great 'philosophy of organism' has already the air of a historical monument.
. . . Set beside it, the most esteemed works of the present
day look like prefabricated houses, or, at best, like neatly
turned out young factories."

At our last class, Whitehead read us some passages from
Process and Reality. They were about God. Whitehead had very
unfashionable notions about God. For one thing, he believed
He existed. He also used the masculine pronoun without self-
consciousness. Whitehead's God reminded me of Ford Madox
Ford's Tietjens fable in the novel *No More Parades*. There
Tietjens thought of the Almighty as a being remotely analogous to a great English landowner, a benevolent duke who
never left his study and hence was invisible, but knew all
about the estate down to the last deer on the farm and the
last oak. Christ is "an almost too-benevolent landsteward, son
of the Owner, knowing all about the estate down to the last
child at the porter's lodge, apt to be got around by the more
detrimental tenants; the Third Person of the Trinity, the spirit
of the estate, the Game as it were, as distinct from the players
of the game; the atmosphere of the estate, that of Winchester
Cathedral just after a Handel anthem has been played."

But Whitehead's God has two, not three, sides to his nature.
As Principle of Concretion, God is the cosmological factor
that elicits actuality from possibility, the agent responsible
for *this* crimp in the nature of things rather than some other.
In this, his antecedent nature, God is more conceptual than
actual, a supreme metaphysical paradox. For although God
is the Principle of Actuality, He is himself deficient in actuality. Conceived as the agent that elicits the actual out of the
boundless realm of the possible, God is not quite a "real"
being. In this respect, Whitehead's God is somewhat like Samuel Alexander's Deity which, as creative nisus, is responsible

for the emergence of all of the various levels of being in the cosmos, yet is itself not yet actual. But Whitehead's God also has a consequent or derivative nature. This is God as he is here and now, related to and affected by the world he has brought into existence. To this aspect of God we may trace abidingness. Though immanent in time, God is in one sense apart from time. It is the God who dwells in the world and in whom the world dwells, "the image," Whitehead read us from his book, "under which this operative growth of God's nature is best conceived, is that of a tender care that nothing be lost. . . . He does not create the world, he saves it; or more accurately, he is the poet of the world, with tender patience leading it by his vision of truth, beauty, and goodness."

Whitehead's theology may not have influenced the best minds for whom that subject is still a living concern, and the same might be said for his philosophy in general. Whitehead left no clear tradition, few intellectual progeny; hard-nosed philosophers have never taken much interest in him. Yet he *was* a great man, as Perry said, and an unforgettable teacher. In some way, hard to define, Whitehead influenced us all for the good. No one was ever the worse for taking a course with him, and most were better. If he did not inspire us to follow in his footsteps, he gave us all the sense of a unique presence, intellectual and personal. Even non-Anglophiles know that there is certain indefinable sweetness in English things. We find it in the gentle countryside of that land; the music of the madrigalists and Purcell; the poetry of Herbert, Wordsworth, Hopkins; the religion of Newman and the seventeenth-century divines. Whitehead had that sweetness, as well as strength. *Ex forte dulcedo.*

But at the end of that last class, there was something a little different. Whitehead, after he acknowledged the students' applause with a charming little nod and smile, remained seated at his desk looking out the window. His chauffeur, who came every day after class to call for him, waited tactfully in the rear of the room. I hung back, for I wanted him to autogr?_h my copy of *Science and the Modern World,* the sort of thing he always cheerfully did for students. But when I approached him he was standing up, staring unsmiling over the heads of the last departing scholars. (The desk in the lecture room in Emerson Hall was on a raised platform.) I heaved up my book before him, open to the title page, and made my request. Without looking at me, he took his pen and very carefully inscribed "Alfred North Whitehead" over his printed name, gave the book back to me, and once more stared gloomily over my head into space, mouth grim, eyes unseeing. His eyes—they were blue—seemed to look from caverns, and the light had gone out of them. It was the Other Whitehead.

4

Teggart of Berkeley

ROBERT NISBET

AT BERKELEY in the early 1930s, when I was an undergraduate, almost all student ratings, sober or beery, ranked Frederick J. Teggart among the outstanding teachers on the campus. That was a substantial honor then, for undergraduate teaching was taken seriously. No matter how illustrious one might be as scholar or scientist, the reputation for giving a good course, above all for being a stimulating lecturer, meant a good deal to the faculty and therefore to the students. The time hadn't yet come at Berkeley—or at any other university in this country, so far as I know—when teaching below the graduate level would be regarded as demeaning, would be stigmatized by faculty efforts to escape it, and when freshmen and sophomores would be consigned to the ministrations of the immature or incompetent. (What with the recently discovered economic importance of undergraduates to universities, that attitude may have come and gone. I hope so.)

Even, and especially, the introductory courses were taught by mature, often distinguished, scholars and scientists. Teggart's greatest fame as a teacher rested upon his introductory course, which he taught continuously from 1919 until his retirement from teaching in 1940. Freshmen in chemistry and physics knew the experience of being lectured to year after year by National Academy scientists. Scholars of equal distinction taught the beginning courses in history, geography, literature, zoology, and so forth. The rationale was then obvious: it was important that beginning students be put in direct contact with an active, learned mind, one whose luster could be expected to provide direct stimulus to the best students and leave some reflection in the work of all.

Such courses could be large—occasionally a thousand in Wheeler Auditorium; very often several hundred in just about every field, from art history to zoology. No doubt there were students in those courses who would have benefited from small classes, but I don't recall many complaints. Somehow, after high school, the air seemed freer and more invigorating in the large lecture courses. And there was the special kind of excitement that came from the knowledge that the individual you were listening to, and taking notes from, was an internationally renowned scholar or scientist. Better, it used to be said, to sit fifty feet from a first-rate mind than ten feet from a mediocrity. I well recall one poll of student opinion conducted by the faculty's Committee on Courses that yielded many more complaints about small classes than about the large lecture courses. Too often in the small classes, it was said, there was an obvious lack of real preparation by the instructor and undue reliance upon unstructured and uninstructive student discussion. Not many faculty members facing several hundred students would court the risk of being thought unprepared, inept, or dull.

The custom of student applause existed (it may still exist) at Berkeley. Such applause was standard at the end of a course, but you could tell from its volume and duration how much the course had been appreciated. More important in some ways, the same custom dictated that even during the term students should applaud an unusually good lecture. Any faculty member would have had to be singularly insensitive to be unaffected by such a reaction to a given lecture. For him, as for the actor, applause was at once reward and stimulus.

Lecturing at Berkeley in those years was definitely an art form, something one worked hard to perfect to the best of his abilities. Substance was of course crucial. No amount of platform presence could disguise emptiness of content. But given content and seriousness of purpose it was almost as important in the large lecture hall as in the theater or the pulpit to develop powers of expression that would be distinctive and effective. Students not infrequently sensed a dramatic finesse, or preacher's fire, in the lectures they heard. It was style as well as content that made Teggart's course popular and also respected.

I would not for a moment suggest that there weren't some poor lecturers at Berkeley. But I am convinced that had there not been the tradition of first-rate lecturing, and also the tradition of applause from the students, such lecturers would have been much worse than they actually were. Sometimes, no matter how assiduously an individual might strive for effectiveness before the large class, the results made it all futile. I was told in later years that the anthropologist A. L. Kroeber, the psychologist Edward Tolman, and the physicist Ernest Lawrence—all obviously titans—had at different times, before I reached Berkeley as a student, attempted to teach the introductory course in their respective fields, but with conspicuous lack of success. All three were, as the scientific world knows, notable teachers, but in other contexts. One can only marvel today, given the university setting we have come to know in America since World War II, that there was ever a time when scientists of the stature of Kroeber, Tolman, and Lawrence would have wanted, and would have been permitted by their departments, to teach beginning courses. But in the Berkeley of the 1930s, and other universities also, such courses were not held to be demeaning, and the status of a scholar or scientist was not measured by the degree of his liberation from contact with undergraduates.

Large lecture courses are in rather poor repute today. They have been, ever since the vogue of the "experimental" college or curriculum began in the 1950s; then smallness and intimacy in a classroom became ends in themselves, quite apart from their actual contribution to a genuine education. For many people today the "rap session" is held to be the very essence of a university education. There is certainly a place for small classes, an indispensable place in a good many instances. But I should not like to see the large lecture course disappear—so long as it is in mature, scholarly hands. There are gifted faculty minds whose light is brighter before several hundred students than it is before a handful; in these minds there lies, no doubt, a repressed desire for the stage or the pulpit.

Frederick J. Teggart was one such teacher. He had, in fact, been very active in amateur theater circles in San Francisco when he was young, and obviously enjoyed giving a good performance in his large course, although the mark of the preacher was also often evident. There were two settings in which I found Teggart superb as a teacher: the large class, where he could open up in spellbinding fashion, and his office, where conversations were sparked either by my questions or my manifest gaps in knowledge. I did not find him effective in his seminars—undergraduate or graduate. I was told by older members of the faculty that in earlier years he had been noted for his seminars, but this wasn't true in my time. There was a good deal more to be learned from him in the large class, even the third or fourth time around as a graduate assistant, than in one of his small seminars. But it was in his office—where I saw him often, inasmuch as I had volunteered to be his book runner simply to have extra opportunities for talking with him—that I learned the most from him.

Exactly two hundred students enrolled each fall in his introductory course—not, by Berkeley standards then, a large course, especially in the lower division. The number of students would surely have risen had Teggart been willing to give up 312 Wheeler, where for so many years he gave his Progress and Civilization course, supposedly to freshmen and sophomores, but in actuality also to a large number of upper-classmen, and even graduate students from all parts of the campus. But he wasn't willing. He liked the acoustics and the appearance of the room, and anyhow, as he once confessed, it was only a few steps from his office, where he spent nine or ten hours every day at work, often over weekends.

Teggart of Berkeley

There was something about Teggart's appearance and his manner of entering the lecture room and striding to the rostrum that silenced student conversation instantly. Never once did he have to wait a moment or two, as most of us do, for the chatter to cease and newspapers be put down. Not that he was in any way overbearing. He was simply the essence of academic man in his bearing, with a natural dignity that no one was likely to wish to encroach upon; not least, there was the appeal of his getting under way as quickly as possible in a lecture that students could expect would be important and eloquently delivered. Teggart was adamant in his refusal to allow his teaching assistants to take attendance, as was the policy in a few introductory courses: "They are in a university now, not a school, and academic freedom includes the freedom to cut class at will—provided they pay the consequences." The result was that those students who were present wanted to be there and wanted the action to start. He lectured with force, even passion at times. Clearly he believed that what he had to say was important, and he made it seem important. Once, in a campus newspaper, a student characterized Teggart's lecturing as having "evangelical zeal." I had expected him to snort dismissively at this, for he had roughly the same opinion of evangelism as had H. L. Mencken. But Teggart seemed to like this characterization and thought it accurate. He admitted that in his childhood, in Northern Ireland, he had heard his share of preachers "with fire in their bellies."

Teggart was, according to solemn, established student opinion, "one of the two most learned minds on the faculty" (the other being the redoubtable Max Radin in the Law School). When and how this remarkable judgment was formed on the campus I have no idea. But no one, at least in my student experience, seemed to doubt it, and we heard the statement often. Whether Teggart was actually one of the two, ten, or fifty most learned minds is of no consequence here. But I offer that bit of lore only as an indication of what in those years could impress students, even undergraduates. The time had not yet arrived when faculty members could achieve honor from presiding over some large and wealthy research institute on the campus, or make a name from the number of research grants publicly acquired, industrial or governmental consultantships held, or appointments garnered as secretary or director of something in Washington. There were but two sources of honor then on the campus—teaching and reputed learning, in that order.

In point of fact, Teggart was a very learned scholar. I have met no one since then who has approached him in range, diversity, and depth of knowledge. One need only scan his books to sense this, even his little footnote-free *Processes of History*, which Toynbee paid tribute to many years after its publication as one of the primary sources of inspiration for his own *Study of History*.

Teggart could unite his teaching and research more effectively than anyone else I have known. His current reading or investigation of some point in scholarly literature often came out in his lectures. I don't mean that each term's lectures were likely to be direct reflections of whatever he happened to be working on at the time. The course had a definite structure; major themes or emphases continued, albeit in altered form, from one year to the next. But Teggart had the insight to realize that students of any degree of maturity were likely to be interested in whatever genuinely interested him.

He lectured from brief, penciled notes on a single sheet of paper. I learned later, when I was his graduate assistant in the course, that he prepared these during the hour or two before his lecture. In some teachers this can make for thinness, anecdotalism, a preponderance of rhetoric over substance. It didn't with Teggart. He had remarkable powers of recall while on his feet, and he seemed to have no difficulty whatever in building his spare, telegraphic notes into sentences and paragraphs which, from both style and content, might have been prepared word for word in advance. I once asked him why, in order to save energy, he hadn't spent some early year typing his lectures for reuse. All he said was, "Never type your lectures; you and the students will both be their slaves."

His introductory course differed in one important respect from all others on the campus. They were introductions to a recognized discipline: history, economics, physics, and so forth. Teggart, however, because of his excommunication by the Department of History, had his own department, the Department of Social Institutions. It had been created by the regents in 1919 to contain his own teaching and research interests—interests that at least two other departments had found too heretical or irrational to make him welcome in their ranks. Teggart taught essentially Teggartism, a word he loathed but that had currency on the campus. Not that this term was always used with indulgence or respect. Teggart had his full share of enemies and detractors, and the word could come out as a sneer.

He knew this very well, and although it didn't seem to bother him (I think it actually pleased him, given his reclusiveness and his scorn for so much that others did in history and the social sciences), he would nevertheless caution students who indicated a desire to do graduate work under him. When, in the spring of 1936, I went up to his office to ask his approval for my Ph.D. work beginning the following autumn, he began by turning me down flatly, on the ground that no department in the country recognized him or his work and that I would never get a job. I persisted, though, and got his reluctant consent, but then only on condition that I develop a strong minor in some other department.

Just as his writings fall into intellectual history on the one hand and comparative social history on the other, so did his introductory course. He began each year with an arresting history of the idea of progress, an idea I hadn't even heard of before enrolling in his introductory course in 1934. I do not know when he first introduced the idea into his teaching, but I would guess by 1910, when he was still a member of the history department; for in that year a seminal article of his appeared in the *American Historical Review*, "The Circumstance or the Substance of History," in which much of the theme hangs upon the idea of progress. Certainly it played a large role in his teaching from 1919 on, the year he created his own department and first offered the course I was taking as an undergraduate. As far as I know, Teggart was the first in this country to build a course, even a curriculum, around the history of this idea, and he was also among the very first to appreciate fully its real importance and its wide and subtle influence in Western thought from the time of the Greeks.

He made his students see, as well as the readers of his articles and books, the several guises, so to speak, under which the perspective of progress had appeared in the humanities and the sciences—such guises as "social evolution," "developmentalism," and "historical growth"; each concept was utterly unrelated, as he used to emphasize strongly, to the kind of work that Darwin and Mendel had done in the nineteenth century; each in truth was but a manifestation of the master idea in Western thought: progress. He gave us a detailed history of the idea, but more than that he provided a highly critical assessment. When the last lecture on the history of the idea was completed at midyear, Teggart turned to comparative cultures and social institutions. We had been given a prophylaxis, so to speak, against the common fallacies that attended the presentation of world history, all emanating from the perspective of progress which has led—from Saint Augustine's *City of God* to H. G. Wells's *Outline of History* —to a compressing of the diversity of mankind through time into a single unilinear series of epochs and stages, with Western civilization invariably made the triumphant outcome of the series. Repeatedly, he had impressed upon us the enormity of such parochialism; in large part, he would argue, it was a consequence of historians' dedication, ever since Thucydides, to the narrative—the "first this, and then, and then, and then" approach. Such a form, he would tell us, is suitable to literature and religion ("everybody loves a good narrative; it relaxes"), but it is a totally inadequate means of presenting the true diversity, the plurality of mankind's history.

Teggart of Berkeley

History, I can hear him now, almost thundering, is not unitary but plural. The world is made up of many histories, many time frames, and it is sheer distortion of these histories to seek to put them all in a West-oriented, basically imaginary progression. If you wish to entertain and divert, by all means, he would say, construct narratives. It doesn't matter whether you call them fiction or history; the narrative approach is bound to reduce diverse material to fiction in some degree.

What the French historians of the *Annales* school today refer to, critically, as *l'histoire événementielle* —written history that is but a string of events, dates, actions, and their asserted causes—was anathema for Teggart. He had begun writing against this form of historiography as early as the 1910 article I referred to above. His *Prolegomena to History* (1916) carried his analysis and criticism further. It is his *Theory of History* (1925), though, that contains his most thorough and penetrating analysis of the frailties and inherent fallacies which attend all unilinear efforts to comprehend the diversity and plurality of historical data. The book is at one and the same time an attack upon the narrative in historical writing and upon the idea of social evolution in the social sciences. I respect what more recent writers, such as Karl Popper, have had to say about "historicism" (to borrow Popper's term), but quite apart from the fact that Teggart long preceded them, his *Theory of History* seems to me even now more profound and searching, more deeply aware of the issues involved, than any others I have read.

But even that remarkable work cannot convey the intensity with which he dealt in our class with the topics contained in the book. He was tireless in his criticisms of the narrative method and equally tireless in his insistence that the only worthwhile approach to historical data is, in the first place, rooted in selection of a bona fide problem and, second, oriented comparatively in space and in time. Only then can we do justice to the multitude of histories. We turn, when necessary, to the entire world, just so long as the question or problem we have begun with gives us guidance.

It was very probably Teggart's world orientation that the class enjoyed most in the course's content. He moved with such seeming ease and confidence from one civilization to another, past and present, in his highlighting of some problem. His comparative approach to world history was a heady experience for most of us, saturated as we were with conventional narratives, chiefly American and English, taught from the third grade onward. For the first time in our lives we were hearing—pertinently and excitingly—about China, India, Babylonia, Israel, Egypt, and many other civilizations of the past. Never, let me emphasize, did he speak in survey or travelogue fashion, which would have been deadly. He never brought up a civilization or culture, a seaport city, a trade route, a mountain pass, a river valley except as a means of casting light upon some problem. It was *histoire problème, histoire comparative*, that we were getting.

One of the more striking problems he would bring up year after year is that posed by the appearance within a single century of such widely separated founders of religions as Confucius and Lao-tze in China, Mahavira and Buddha in India, Zoroaster in Persia, Ezekiel and the Second Isaiah in Israel, Thales in Ionia, and Pythagoras in southern Italy. How, Teggart would ask, his voice rising in dramatic emphasis, are we to confront this astonishing phenomenon? As a true *problem*, warranting the most careful research? Or do we walk away from it as a—and his voice would ascend still higher, all stops pulled—*mere coincidence?*

For all I know, that extraordinary clustering *is* but coincidence. But after hearing Teggart on it, there couldn't have been many students in the class who were not ready to volunteer immediately for service in the assault upon *the problem.* Teggart never implied that he had any answers, but in the course of illuminating the problem we were treated to some enlightening lectures on the geographic and social mobility of Eurasia during the centuries preceding the Christian era: the migrations of peoples, invasions, wars, and other forces leading to the meeting of diverse cultures; the trade routes crossing Asia to Europe (which, Teggart would remind us, carried ideas and values as well as gems and fabrics); and the significance of what he called "idea systems" (a concept I find in Teggart's writing from 1918 at least; it is pretty much what the *Annales* historians today refer to at *mentalités*) and the consequences of their disintegration under geohistorical forces, and on the comparable military, political, economic, and social settings within which the prophets had lived. There was much historical geography in all this. Teggart had been deeply influenced by Sir Halford Mackinder's work, and the ideas of "Heartland" and "the geographical pivot of history" were conveyed to us.

Another of the problems Teggart liked to put before students was that of the sporadic, uneven appearances in world history of the great ages of intellectual and cultural achievement—such as the Athens of Pericles, the European twelfth century, the Age of Elizabeth, the Han dynasty in China, the Age of the Guptus in India, and so forth. A few words from the preface to Teggart's *Rome and China* will suggest the nature of the problem he was interested in:

The history of human achievement . . . displays extraordinary variations of advance and subsidence. How are the outstanding advances of men at different times and places to be accounted for? Think of ancient Egypt and Babylonia. How are the great periods of supreme attainment to be accounted for? Think of Sophocles and Shakespeare. How are the cessations of effort to be accounted for? Think of the old antagonists Greece and Persia. On these questions men have speculated and written many books. But no one has approached the questions with any semblance of the patient care exercised in the study of an atom of hydrogen, even though the systematic investigation of the problems hinted at lies well within the limits of possibility.

Those words were printed in 1939, but since 1919 students in Teggart's introductory course, and also in his upper division courses, had been hearing their message; even in senior and graduate seminars students had worked at the problem constituted by recurring ages by sterility as well as of efflorescence in human achievement. A. L. Kroeber, in his *Configurations of Culture Growth* (1944), dealt with the problem in some measure, but that book is more a set of tabular listings of fertility and drought than it is a work of explanation. Teggart, to me at least, affected to be unimpressed by the book, declaring rather extravagantly that, a quarter of a century earlier, students—*undergraduate* students, he trumpeted, carried away with the thought—had done better work in his seminars. To which I could only respond, mutely: a pity they never saw more light of day than they did. Teggart himself should have written the book, but his final fifteen years of scholarship before retirement were taken up with another project, a bold one: the study of certain correlations of events he had painstakingly found in the vast literature on Asia, Eastern Europe, and the Roman Empire around the beginning of the Christian era. His findings made up the substance of his *Rome and China*, published in 1939.

But well in advance of completion of that book, a good deal of the more exciting content had been made a part of his introductory course. I will not attempt even a capsule review of the aims and results of the book. It is more important to indicate briefly those aspects that found their way into his lectures at least a decade before its publication. As I have doubtless made clear by this time, Teggart was entranced by parallels or conjunctures among ostensibly separated histories. The notion that a relationship between Rome and China existed in classical times was, of course, not original with Teggart; nor did he, even in class, pretend that it was. What he had set himself to do was to convert a general realization into a series of verifiable connections extending from the borders of China to those of the Roman Empire. He wanted to show that precisely datable events in eastern Asia—military engagements, migrations, invasions, signal interruptions of trade routes across Asia—had demonstrable, verifiable, datable repercussions all the way from China's borders to that great area east of the Rhine and north of the Danube in which the Germanic peoples lived for so long, and from which they launched their historic invasions of the Roman Empire. What Teggart wanted to show beyond any reasonable doubt was that these invasions were not generated by simple tribal decision, or by insufficiencies of food supply, or by changes in the climate, but rather by a chainlike succession of events beginning in eastern Asia and terminating in the Germanic invasions of Rome. He sought to verify his conclusions, positively and negatively, either taking a given invasion of Rome and then working back to the precipitating event on China's border, or beginning with an event on that border and working across to the West, to discover whether in due time a significant invasion of Rome occurred. In the beginning, as I understood it, he had taken the whole period of the invasions for his study, but the sheer magnitude of the task, the vast number of histories which had to be examined, forced him to focus on a shorter period, one of a little more than a century.

How successful Teggart was in his bold and vast enterprise I cannot say. I admire his book, but for personal reasons I have never been able to enjoy it, to really read it. There is nothing felicitous about the style, given the plethora of compactly identified dates, peoples, wars, and place-names. Astute response to the book requires an immense interest in, and knowledge of, a substantial number of histories stretching from China to Rome. As I recall, there were relatively few reviews, which is understandable in view of the range and variety of knowledge required, and of these I can think of only a couple of genuinely favorable ones. Teggart was, I know, deeply disappointed by the book's reception. He had put such immense quantities of energy into it, and had such passionate belief in its importance, that he could not have helped thinking that a large and immediately responsive audience waited for its publication.

But putting aside the book itself, there was no mistaking the interest and response of students when he brought to the fore the larger and more easily assimilable themes of his research into the subject. He believed with all his heart that he had indeed approached historical data, for the first time, with the method of the scientist instead of that of the writer of historical narratives. And most of us in the class believed this too, though we would have been hard put to offer evidence for our belief. It is enough to say here that, irrespective of the validity and final assessment of the book, its contents, translated into the language of undergraduate lectures, made as much impression on students as did the other problems he dealt with.

As must surely be evident by this time, Teggart was keenly interested in, actually obsessed by, the possibility of a genuine science of history. He had acquired that interest as a youth, during the last third of the nineteenth century when history-as-science was very much in the intellectual atmosphere, especially in Germany. Early on, however, Teggart came to realize that what was meant by the word "scientific" when applied to history was nothing more than scrupulous use of documents and records, along with as high a degree of objectivity as could be reached. Such qualities do indeed belong in science, as in scholarship generally, but they hardly give distinctive identity to science. How, Teggart came to ask, can the historian work with his data in such a way as to achieve results comparable to those in the physical sciences? This was a question that students heard often in his course, and they also heard his answer: go to the data with a question or problem in mind, formulate a hypothesis, and, through repeated subjection of the hypothesis to relevant bodies of data—wherever they are to be found, in the past or the present—emerge with an explanation that will have the same probability that we now expect in a physical science and that can, moreover, be tested by others interested in the same problem. Such a procedure involves a method and an anticipated result utterly different from the simple, conventional narrative. It is evident that Teggart's opposition to the narrative sprang as much from his desire for a genuine science of history as from his recognition of the inescapably plural character of time and history in the world.

Some might think that in the course Teggart gave for under-

Teggart of Berkeley

graduates, students would have been better served by smaller, more directly manageable problems than those I have used for illustration here. I don't agree. The most important thing that can happen to any mind is that it be stretched, and the earlier in life the better. Once stretched, the mind will never retract to its original size. Teggart was an impressive stretcher of minds.

Like most vigorous and creative minds, Teggart had his quirks and paradoxes. Vocally, in the abstract, he was antifeminist to the core. But this philosophy notwithstanding, one of his earliest and most lasting appointments was a woman, Margaret T. Hodgen, who made a highly respected place for herself as teacher and scholar. No decision about the department was made without Teggart's inquiring into her views on the subject. Precisely the same respect governed his association with other women on the Berkeley faculty, of whom an uncommonly large number, at least by the affirmative action criteria of that day, held full professorships, all of them notable scholars and scientists. In his committee and other relationships with faculty women, there was never a trace of condescension or exaggerated masculine courtesy (the two are of course the same). But in principle he remained antifeminist so far as universities were concerned, and he was never reluctant to impress that principle upon me when the occasion arose in office conversation.

Needless to say, given Teggart's academic generation, he had other prejudices. He was the quintessential WASP, as were a great many faculty members in American universities before the late 1930s. In the privacy of his office he was quite capable of venting some of these WASP prejudices, but, as with women on faculties, they were pretty much in the abstract. In a decade of close association with Teggart, never once did I see any of these prejudices descend upon an individual, whether student or faculty. A man of prejudice, yes, but also a man of unvarying, unflagging academic honor.

Politically, he was a distinct conservative. Many thought this incongruous, given his rather notorious heresies in matters of teaching and scholarship. Perhaps it was incongruous, but we have learned that some of the most superbly creative minds in the arts and sciences have also been politically conservative, even reactionary. During the early years of my association with Teggart I was a rather ardent New Dealer. Teggart was anything but, and he never missed an opportunity to lay out Franklin Delano Roosevelt and all his works, for my benefit, I was not surprised that he supported Landon for the presidency in 1936 and doubtless voted for him, but I did find somewhat astonishing his prediction, just before the election, that Landon would win. Perhaps he trusted the *Literary Digest* poll.

He had a deep dislike of the military and of every form of regimentation or hierarchy springing from the military mind. His best known lectures dealt with the destructive impact, throughout history, of war and the military upon the family and other units of the social order. He frequently cited the steady decline of the Roman family and its *patria potestas* under the continuing buffets of military leaders, beginning with Gaius Marius and continuing through the Caesars, to illustrate this historical relationship between war and kinship. Yet notwithstanding all this, Teggart was one of the first on the Berkeley campus to see and call attention to the menace that Nazi Germany represented in the West and Japan in the East. Nor did he believe it incumbent on him to keep these views out of his lectures. He was no pacifist, no isolationist!

I have mentioned Teggart's extraordinary learning. There are, however, interesting and sometimes inexplicable gaps in the minds of all scholars, however erudite, and Teggart was no exception. I find it extraordinary today that he never referred to Vico in class or, so far as I can tell, in any of his books or articles. He could so aptly have placed Vico with Hume and Turgot in a chapter of his *Theory of History* that lauds these two for early insights into the pluralism of history and the necessity for the scholar to proceed from a concrete question or problem. But I never heard so much as a spoken

reference to Vico, and Teggart could be lavish in his praise
of others, especially if they lived in the past. Deeply read
though he was in the political and social thought of modern
Europe, he seems never to have read Alexis de Tocqueville,
to whom I had to find my own late way. The same holds
for Max Weber, Emile Durkheim, Georg Simmel, and Ferdi-
nand Toennies, whom I also had to reach on my own and
in whose writings he could have found, here and there at
least, valuable support for some of his own controversial
views.

He knew most of the major languages, including Greek
and Latin, and did work in all of them. But it was English
scholarship, particularly that of the eighteenth and ninteenth
centuries, that he admired the most. Germanic learning, despite the thousands of volumes it produced every decade from
the early nineteenth century on, Teggart chose to regard as
"imitative." Scratch a German thinker or scholar, he would
say, and you will usually find an English or Scotch mind.
Some of this disdain for German scholarship can be seen in
the long review he wrote for the *Saturday Review of Literature*
of Spengler's *Decline of the West* when it was published by
Alfred Knopf in this country. Teggart was not impressed
by the parade of learning that Spengler managed, barely managed—a parade that seems to have overwhelmed most American readers—and to this day I regard Teggart's assessment
as the soundest written in America. He was almost equally
critical of Toynbee's *Study of History*, beginning in the 1930s
when the first three volumes of that work appeared. As I
noted above, Toynbee, in one of the final volumes, cited Teggart's *Processes of History* as a formative influence on his thinking about comparative history. If Teggart was aware of this
impact of his book, he never mentioned it, and it assuredly
did not affect his negative judgment of the Toynbee volumes
he read before his death.

That points up another quality in Teggart that I thought
then, and still do, largely unfortunate: his almost total dismissal of any work (much of it very good) done by contempo-

raries which had at least some affinity with his own contributions. His outlook on what historians and social scientists were doing was dour, to say the least, and he could be as illtempered about some occasional favorable acknowledgment of his ideas that I might find in my reading as he could about any criticism of them. This generally dismissive attitude toward the work of others in the scholarly world was paralleled by a personal reclusiveness that became more and more complete during the years when I knew and saw a great deal of him. Before 1940, when Merle Curti (I think) was responsible for Teggart's being invited to present a major paper at the annual meeting of the American Historical Association, I don't think he had attended a single such meeting or any other conference since the creation of his department in 1919. When I recall his evident pleasure, his gratitude indeed, after he returned from that AHA meeting in 1940, it seems all the sadder that he had so completely cut himself off from the rest of the world. He had a great deal to give that could be given effectively only in contexts of personal give-and-take.

Teggart's aloofness from others, except for his immediate family, was almost total. There were faculty members who had been his friends from the time he had first come to Berkeley—William Popper in Semitic Languages, George P. Adams in Philosophy, Eugene I. MacCormac in History, others— whom he spoke of to me in his office with deep respect and affection. Only rarely, though, did he see them. And such friendship did not ever, to the best of my knowledge, extend to use of first names. I never once heard him called by his first name, even by those who had known and admired him for decades. There was something about Teggart that discouraged, that stopped dead, any overture based upon a desire for intimacy or for what Teggart would only have perceived as familiarity. Familiarity, he used to impress upon me, "doesn't *breed* contempt; it *is* contempt." Nor did he deviate from that principle. Even those he had known longest and most affectionately at Berkeley he never addressed other than by surname. Never in ten years of very close and congenial association did he use my first name in addressing me.

Not that he was in any way cold in spirit or manner. Far from it! Irish (he had been born in Belfast, Ireland, coming to this country with his family at college age), he exemplified most of the traits we commonly attribute to the people of Erin. Among these, inevitably, was capacity for fierce, volcanic anger when provoked by some enormity on the world scene or in academe. Even so, he probably controlled more temper in a month than most of us do in a year. His opinions and judgments tended, naturally, to be unqualified and set in marble. Of Teggart it used to be said that when he changed his mind the earth shook. He suffered neither fools nor foolish ideas gladly, and one always felt more secure entering his office when there was good and manifest reason for entering. Small talk was for others, not him, as I learned early on from my own (short-lived) indulgence in it. But if there was Irish temper and obstinacy, there was also Irish wit and humor. The first could be used cuttingly on occasion as I dare say most of us close to him had reason to know. But it took other forms too, with humor the only object. Sometimes I could hear his laugh half way down the hall from his office; he laughed as only those do who love laughter but find too few occasions for it in the world. And he had generous capacity for friendship; not easily begun, to be sure, but full and rich once it had begun.

5

Nadia Boulanger

SUZANNE R. HOOVER

TWENTY-ONE years ago, when I went to France to study music with Nadia Boulanger,* she was almost seventy. Although her face was lined, her hair white, and her low voice somewhat shaky, she was still strong—still, obviously, at the height of her extraordinary powers. My year with her began after my graduation from college in 1956, when I arrived at the American summer school of music and fine arts at Fontainebleau, an hour's drive southeast of Paris. There the Conservatoire Américain, founded by Walter Damrosch in 1921, holds its classes in the faded, damp, rambling, yet sumptuous palace, the present form of which was begun by François I. (Some indefinable *tristesse* that hangs about the palace prepares one for the discovery that it has been the scene of several portentous reversals: the revocation of the Edict of Nantes by Louis XIV in 1685; the abdication of Napoleon in April 1814 in the magnificent Cour du Cheval Blanc, with the baroque horseshoe staircase, where he bade farewell to his Old Guard before setting off for Elba; and Hitler's celebration, in 1940, of the fall of France.) We students were domiciled, dormitory style, in nearby hotels. Mlle Boulanger, whom the French have long treasured as a national asset, had a summer apart-

* This essay was written as a personal celebration of Nadia Boulanger's ninetieth birthday. She died on October 22, 1979, at the age of ninety-two. (S. R. H.)

ment in the palace, where she lived with her male cat, Natasha, and received students for private lessons.

Mlle Boulanger had agreed to give me lessons in conducting at the summer conservatory, although there was no such offering at that time in the school catalog. In addition, I was to attend classes in solfège, harmonic analysis, conducting, and vocal ensemble. Recently I had an opportunity to read a number of long letters that I wrote from Fontainebleau about my studies. The immediacy and idiosyncrasy of their detail brought the summer back to me entire, uncorked all the still pungent essences of those days. Once again I heard the robust and hopeful cacophony of student-made music issuing simultaneously from dozens of lesson rooms and studios, floating out from the palace to the formal gardens where I often studied, and mingling there with the landscape gardener's timeless, classical harmonies. Above all, those letters revived in me the exhilarating awareness of a specialized but close relationship between two very different people: a great and vigorous old woman who arose each day freshly to the age-old combat between darkness and light, and myself as a young woman. In the first of my letters I tried to capture some early impressions:

"You want to know what N. B. is like and how she teaches? I will try to give you an idea, if you will remember that she is difficult to describe calmly and succinctly. She is thin—beautiful, wise old face—her body unexpectedly energetic, moving brusquely and strongly. Large, powerful hands. She is usually dressed in a plain but elegantly tailored gray walking suit, one wide lapel of which bears the tiny carbuncle-rosette of the *Légion d'honneur*. Effect of classic simplicity. She speaks near-perfect English, with a heavy accent, of course.

When she addresses a class, she cannot remain serious for long: her temptation is laughter. At the same time, she is a fervent Catholic for whom all esthetic questions are ultimately, mysteriously, religious ones. Warm, direct, loquacious—I might say garrulous—can talk one under the table. Thinks twice as fast as anyone I've ever known; is equally the master of the abstrusest technique and the subtlest critical judgment, seeming capable of miracles of both. Aristocratic. I have had one private lesson with her—the next is tomorrow. She assigned me Stravinsky's *Dumbarton Oaks Concerto*, saying she knows it is too difficult for me. We were meant to have forty-five minutes together, but it turned into an hour and some more, during which time I don't think I said more than ten words."

I was too busy to describe the occasion fully in a letter, but I remember it well enough. I had entered her apartment in fear and trembling, as if descending alone in a diving bell to the ocean floor. Seeing me, Mlle Boulanger came forward and drew me into the room warmly, with a smile of real pleasure, as a friend—and then subjected me to a thirty-minute lecture on the absurdity of being shy. She interrupted herself at last, to ask whether I would, please, conduct something for her. As I stood up and she sank down attentively into a Louis XIV armchair, I realized suddenly that the next few minutes were going to be remarkably quiet. Well, then, I thought, I'll do something quiet.

"The second movement of the Brahms *Requiem*," I offered. (I had been studying it.) She nodded approval.

I raised my arm and began to inscribe in the air the spiritual shape of that music—a monumental funeral march, purified of anguish, that accepts, if sorrowfully, the knowledge that "all flesh is grass," as it looks forward with a lightening of the heart to eternal life.

After one full measure, my audience stopped me to inquire why I was using my left hand. I am left-handed, I explained. A pause, then an impatient gesture dismissing such a nonmusical, mechanical matter.

"Very well! It will confuse them for two minutes, but they will get used to it. Continue, please."

I began once more, in a deeply concentrated effort to weave into one fabric both the tender hopefulness of the music and its resigned sadness. Minutes passed in silence while I con-

Nadia Boulanger

ducted; she watched me, and we both listened to the same inner music. When it was over she seemed pleased, but took time only to admire the beat. It was strong, clean, and clear, she told me. Yes, she liked it very much.

In her later years, Nadia Boulanger has been known most widely as a teacher—of piano, organ, harmony, and especially composition. She is often described as the greatest music teacher of this century, still fully active today as she approaches her ninetieth birthday. Through her hundreds of American pupils, including Aaron Copland, Roger Sessions, Walter Piston, Virgil Thomson, David Diamond, Elliott Carter, and Roy Harris, and the thousands of pupils of those pupils, perhaps the strongest single influence on the quality of modern American music has been Nadia Boulanger's supreme sensibility. Earlier, however, her career was divided between performance and teaching.

It was in her conducting that Mlle Boulanger had made her greatest contribution as a performer, and because at that time I hoped to become a conductor, it was this that had drawn me to her. Many who have followed the unhappy story of Antonia Brico's struggle to be accepted as a conductor may not be aware that Nadia Boulanger was the first woman to conduct the Paris Philharmonic, the Royal Philharmonic in London, the New York Philharmonic, the Boston Symphony Orchestra, and the Philadelphia Orchestra—all before World War II.

That this record created as little stir as it did was probably due to her remarkable selflessness. Indeed, the most impressive characteristic of Nadia Boulanger as a conductor has been her sensitive use of herself as an instrument, a vehicle, for the music—never the other way around. The reviewer for the *New York Times* of February 12, 1939, made this point forcibly when describing a concert given by Boulanger at Carnegie Hall with the Philharmonic Orchestra, in which she participated in every selection either as conductor, pianist, organist, or choral director:

In whatever capacity she exhibited her talents this amazing artist moved with a like authority, profound understanding and skill. . . . When Mlle Boulanger, a nobly dignified but unassuming figure in white, first came on the stage she was greeted by the first of the many ovations that thereafter followed her endeavors throughout the evening. She conducted without baton, but nevertheless her every gesture was so sharply defined and significant that the results were admirable in precision, clearness of outline and tonal balance. She was completely the master of style in all that she touched, and her insight into the character and needs of the highly contrasted works she set forth was unfailingly deep and penetrating. . . . But despite Mlle Boulanger's amazing musicianship elsewhere, it was as director of her vocal group that she made a most unforgettable impression. For lack of space it is impossible to go into details here concerning the manifold beauties of the readings she and her splendid little aggregation of singers gave to the several great masterpieces of Monteverdi which formed the highlight of the evening's contributions. All those present will long remember the flowing line, the sensitive feeling and evocation of mood and atmosphere produced in such exquisite creations of the seventeenth-century master as the "Lamento della Ninfa" and the madrigal, "Lasciatemi morire."

Such was the example—and standard—that Nadia Boulanger set for her students. While Americans discovered her in the early twenties, more recently many of her students have come from Eastern Europe, the Near East, and Scandinavia. The reason is clear: her mission, as she herself seems to have understood it, has been to serve as midwife to cultures attempting to bring a rigorous native music. She seemed to know a student's own idiom before he knew it consciously himself and to know, before he did, what he could stretch himself to accomplish. Her quiet confidence in each of us enabled us continually to outdo ourselves. This was the miracle that unfolded in my letters.

For my second lesson I was uncertain exactly what to prepare. Mlle Boulanger had casually prescribed the *Dumbarton Oaks Concerto*, but my ability to realize even an uncomplicated score at the piano was still rather frail. I was just beginning to be able to find my way around in the special clefs; I was a poor sight reader and an indifferent pianist. When the Stravinsky score arrived from Paris I was deeply impressed by its difficulty. I began to analyze it, to see how it is built: the first movement in so many sections, exposition goes to here, development (with fugal subject), reprise, and so on. I studied its intricate rhythmic patterns. My next letter, written several weeks later, continues the story.

"When I arrived for my second lesson N. B. greeted me, settled herself at the piano, said 'OK—begin!' and waited for my upbeat. Consider the journey on which we were about to embark. Only ten measures out from shore one loses all sight of land: the time signature changes with virtually every measure for the next thirty measures! I stumbled. We stopped, repeated. I caught on. We went along for many pages.

" 'So—I find it goes very well. You will do it well. I thought at first we use it just for exercise, but you do it perfectly easily.'

"For the next lesson I had practiced beating it clearly. N. B. invited me to sit beside her at the piano on her left—I knew that meant trouble. The plan, she explained, was to work with just one (very complex) measure. She would play the cello part for that measure and I the double bass. At the end of the measure we were to begin it again in time, she playing the viola, I the cello; then she the violin, I the viola, and so on. (The French horns were resting.) Just after I came in with the (B-flat) clarinet, I broke down.

" 'So—what is the matter? You are not sure of the clef? Well, my dear child, don't look so serious. Laugh! Yes, you must laugh! But can't you see, it's *grotesque* that you should not be able to do this? Very well, don't worry about it. You will learn it, that's all.'

"And then a casual remark to the effect that I should learn the concerto by heart. And warmly: 'Good-bye. Please. Good-bye, my dear child.' (She thinks the 'please' here is very polite.) So for the next lesson I decided to memorize the outlines of the first movement—fifteen pages of score."

My life now became rather metronomic in the incessant

alternation between work in my small studio at the practice piano and all the other essential claims on my time, such as classes, meals, letter writing, and an occasional walk for exercise in the town or in the palace gardens designed for Louis XIV by Le Vau. The hours at the piano were filled with the righteous joys of hard work, and the intoxication of total immersion in a work of genius.

As a whole, the E-flat chamber concerto, like its creator, is both debonair and profound. In its vigor and closely knit *concerto grosso* style, it takes some inspiration from Bach's Brandenburg Concertos, as Stravinsky himself has said. Like the Brandenburgs, it often breaks out irresistibly into dance, as in the long, final, haunting, bolerolike section of the last movement. The overall feeling of the work is curiously touching, because it was written during the last stages of the fatal illness of Stravinsky's daughter Mika—by his own account "perhaps the most difficult period" of his life—yet it celebrates the triumph of life in its spontaneity, variety, and rhythmic, even sexual, vitality.

The first movement is lively and open, bustling and full. Both its beginning and its conclusion suggest the joyous ringing of bells, until the last few measures when the ringing breaks off and the music turns suddenly inward, then stops, suspended.

By contrast, the second movement seems intimate. It begins with a graceful, buoyantly witty, ingenuous, polymorphous-perverse motif, delicately reminding one of childhood, of resourcefulness and vulnerability. This free and inquisitive mood is overtaken at last by some strange spell or enchantment. Now the music, darkening, verges on the programmatic, suggesting, say, a scene in a ballet in which Beauty is lost in the forest. But just before uneasiness can modulate to fear, the original whimsical theme returns, this time in a sophisticated, mock-sentimental guise.

The last movement turns resolutely outward again, and has a fugal episode, like the first. But it is newly restless and driving, with troubling undercurrents of obsession.

Nadia Boulanger

The specific and visible musical body inhabited by these ideas is always ingenious and beautiful. Each instrumental part has its own life, its own speech, and yet reflects the large design. The basic musical materials of a few intervalic and rhythmic patterns are played with kaleidoscopically, like the smallest elements of a genetic code. My first task was to learn the design. The letter continues:

"I assigned myself three pages a day of the first movement. Late in the week I had to switch lesson time with someone, which gave me six days instead of seven. When I arrived at the lesson, N. B. asked, teasing, 'Do you know it by heart?'

" 'I think so—I hope so.'

" 'You do?' (Surprised.)

" 'May I play?' I asked.

" 'But yes, of course! *Superbe!*'

"I sat down at the piano—she sat right next to me. I played it through without the score, following the most important musical line, wherever it went, with my right hand. With my left hand I beat the measures as I played. N. B. had turned to face me, watching me like a hawk. In my peripheral vision I caught sight of her right elbow twitching in rhythm as I played. Now and then she shouted, 'The head! The head! No head!'

"When I had finished, she said gravely, 'But this is extraordinary—really quite remarkable. I tell you frankly I didn't think you could do this. It took courage. It was hard to do.'

" 'Now,' she said, motioning me to exchange seats with her, 'you must arrive to know what is going on in every part.'

"She began to play the 'inner' parts, shouting little offbeat pizzicati—'Hup! tup! twip!'— and the clarinet entrance, off-beat, a thirty-second note arpeggio, with her tongue, as if demented, and shouting 'Ta-a, ta-a' ('You must arrive to feel these syncopations'), and finally, at the climax of the section, playing with both hands, furiously, tapping her feet, shouting, she turned to me and punched me in the arm exactly on the strongest pulse, nearly knocking me off my chair—and continued with the decrescendo without missing a beat. *This is what I must arrive to feel*, she said. She is delighted, so pleased, it goes well, such a progress, et cetera."

The next days were spent learning the first movement inside out and backwards. Often, after working for a while at my piano, I took a box lunch from the hotel and struck out for the open fields beyond the palace gardens, where I passed the rest of the day lying on the bank of a canal built by Henri IV, studying my score and gingerly sharing my meal with the yellow jackets. Sometimes I worked with friends at an outside table at one of the cafés. The letter goes on:

"When I arrived for my next lesson, N. B. asked, 'What can you do?'

" 'I'll conduct the first movement for you and try to make sense of it.'

" 'Oh, very good.' She seated herself at the piano, waited for my 'departure,' and we were off—she playing, I conducting her without the score. (She herself conducted the first performance of the concerto in 1938 in Washington, D. C. She knows it by heart; indeed, she seems to have a note-perfect memory of practically every piece of music ever written.)

"The first movement is not only fast and energetic, but is also marked by the constant exiting and reentering of instrumental voices, and therefore requires constant cuing by the conductor. N. B. played not the most important melody line but only the fearfully syncopated accompanying parts, to confuse me. A couple of times I broke down under this treatment, but we plunged right in again and before long we had come to the end. More encouragement, and an assignment to begin the second movement.

"While not so heartily written as the first, the second movement is really more difficult because more subtle. A tiny particle of musical idea is delicately transformed, developed, changed minutely again and again. I memorized its outlines for my next lesson. I think N. B. knew I would.

" 'Do you know the second movement—a little bit?'

" 'I think so.'

" 'But not to play?'

" 'Yes, to play.'

" 'Oh, *superbe!*'

"I played it from memory with my right hand, beating with my left. This time she followed the score closely as I played and, sure enough, I had made a few reading errors, which she corrected. Once she stopped me to say, 'No, that is B natural, not B flat. He changed it back and forth many times, but I think his last feeling about it is B natural. Change it in your score.' (N. B. and Stravinsky are very close friends.)

"Again she seemed surprised and gratified. But the phrasing as I had played it was all wrong. It is light, proud, supple music. 'I know you will never be *coquette*, but move lightly, curtsy.' And she started to tell stories. How Paderewski had a way of helping a woman on with her coat that made her feel like a mother, a daughter, a sister, and a wife all at once. How one time Stravinsky, fallen in a heap on a chair after a concert, exhausted, had jumped up and clicked his heels when his mother entered the room, and remained standing for over an hour because she had forgotten to invite him to sit down. That a man kissing a woman's hand is a vulgar gesture when not done well—he must know not really to touch her hand with his lips—and if done well it is charming and elegant. Et cetera. She bade me a warm and rather excited good-bye.

" 'You will learn it all, I think. You will finish it this summer!' "

The summer was at its height. On Bastille Day I had been invited by a chambermaid who worked in my hotel, and who had befriended me, to join her and her family for the festivities. After a wonderful dinner, we had gone out singing and dancing through the town, which was in a state of carnival. I was beginning to feel a strong love for my new home. I had already experienced two of the most characteristic virtues of the French: their passion for excellence and their chivalrous hospitality.

By midsummer my letters had branched out to describe the classes as well as my private lessons.

"N. B. teaches the same thing in all the classes, taking the day's material as a *point d'appui* for inculcating the values she considers important.

"But conducting class is a little different. There she is all business, improvising impossible exercises for us that employ both hands and, often, both feet—and even speech. The idea is to practice the impossible until you can do it, and then nothing will ever again be difficult. Beat two while you count five; beat two while you count five and tap three. Using a distressingly uninfectious rhythmic pattern from Stravinsky's *Histoire du Soldat*, she has had us speak the pattern repeatedly while tapping every quarter note with one hand and beating the irregular measures with the other hand. Exercises in canon she considers particularly useful for attaining the independence of parts in ones mind, and for concentration. Once she asked Peter, a shy but good-humored Danish composer, to go to the piano and play 'In Dulci Jubilo,' first with one hand, then in canon with two hands, then singing, in three-part canon!

"Both in conducting class and vocal ensemble, N. B. discusses in detail the problem of the flow of the music. As the greatest danger is that of the deadening of the motion on the first beat, 'one must arrive to feel' the first beat as a springboard to the second. In Mozart, for instance, when there is an eighth-note rhythm, rest-ta-ta-ta, rest-ta-ta-ta, you may want to accent the first beat (that is, the *rest*), but then all will be lost. It is, rather, the first *played* note of the figure that must be accented slightly, and must not be late—if anything, make it a little too soon. Nor is the last beat ever long enough.

"Harmonic analysis class is similarly given over to fundamentals. While N. B.'s method here is quite traditional, her concepts are large. For example, she thinks in terms of modulation, or change of key, but places the pivotal point very early and understands the change as beginning far in advance of its accomplishment. As she says, 'When I first decide to go to Warsaw I am already a little bit there. [She happens to be going to Warsaw soon.] When I arrive and look back, I see that my journey really began when I decided I would go to Warsaw.'

"She started the first class by playing the first Prelude of the *Well-Tempered Clavier* as a progression of chords and asking, 'What is this?' When none of the answers suited, she said, 'It is a cadence. And so is a movement of a symphony. The genius, the style—that we cannot discuss here. We are here to discover the common materials and the ways they have been organized.'

"On the varieties of organization, especially nonharmonic organization, N. B. has said a great deal. When discussing melodic structure she instances Bach, whose asymmetrical melodic patterns have an unusual degree of vitality and motivity. She has remarked on the parallelism and registration of chords in Debussy that generate pattern and organization nonharmonically. Registration in general—the deployment of voices over the 'keyboard' (often in class she interrupts herself to call attention to *la disposition de cet accord*)—she considers a key stylistic element, used most strikingly, perhaps, in Beethoven's late piano works.

"And always much moral exhortation—as, for example, genius without character is nothing; character without genius is nearly everything. Untiringly, day after day, she preaches discipline and devotion. Make yourself do exercises in all things—such as harmonic progressions in every key at lightning speed, as the old masters of improvisation and figuration trained themselves to do. One must know by reflex action, without knowing that one knows, the name of every note one hears."

At one of my last lessons of the summer, Mlle Boulanger asked me whether I would be able to continue my studies with her in Paris during the coming year. My next letter expressed my joy and concluded the account of the summer. There were only two more lessons.

"By virtue of the natural rhythm of things, I now turned to the last movement of what has come to seem like my own private concerto. As usual, nothing specific had been assigned—it was all up to me, and I knew what had to be done. I began to be—if it can be measured so minutely—a little more casual about memorizing. I learned the last movement in three or four days, although it is longer than the others.

As before, I played with one hand while beating with the other. N. B. sat beside me, occasionally plinking one of the upper parts in the top octave or, leaning over me, ripping into the middle register with both hands and almost dislodging me from my seat—all while I played. I was sometimes knocked off balance figuratively, if not actually, by these sudden duets; and then a laugh from her, a simple nod, or a sotto voce 'Courage!' would send me on. Where my memory slipped, hers was always sure.

"The last lesson really rounded off the summer for me. I had decided that I would like to conduct the whole work from beginning to end; we had never considered more than one movement at a time. I worked, therefore, on the continuity. When I arrived at the lesson, N. B. asked simply, 'What are you going to do?' I said I would like to play and beat the whole concerto from memory, at the piano. That was, of course, what she had hoped I would do. So away I went— no pauses, no interruptions, and a minimum of stumbling. N. B. unusually quiet throughout.

"When I had come to the end, rather fatigued by the effort of concentration, by the nervousness I confess I was feeling strongly, and by the demands of the music itself, alternately vigorous and delicate, she said, 'Well, and tell me—don't you feel good?' I nodded yes (good that it was over).

" 'This is excellent. Superbe. I have never thought that you can do this. You have done a maximum this summer. I am so glad, you see, that you are going to remain for the year. Will it be possible for you to stay with me even longer? Another year, perhaps?' I indicated that I could not say now, but that at any rate I did not think it would be impossible.

Nadia Boulanger

" 'Well, and this is very good. I will see you soon in Paris, then. Meanwhile, have a good holiday, a good rest. Good-bye. Please.' "

Before that amazing summer ended, it held a special plea-sure for me: the opportunity to see my teacher conduct in public. The town of Fontainebleau was to celebrate its pa-tronal day of Saint Louis. According to her custom, Mlle Boulanger had prepared a musical mass to be performed by the conservatory students in the palace chapel, which at the appointed hour was filled to overflowing with townspeople and dignitaries. In one of my letters I described the occasion:

"We musicians, both chorus and instrumentalists, were crowded into the chapel's loft, a small balcony on one side of the nave that we shared with an eighteenth-century organ and some dormant bats on the floor. N. B. was with us, con-ducting, in her eternal gray suit and a large, floppy, black beret. Not too much contact with us—just enough; for the rest, slightly distant, as if at the same time listening for an answer, far off. Her religiosity is sometimes serene, sometimes spirited. This particular morning it was serene.

"At the end of the Sanctus I folded my music and then looked up again. N. B. had disappeared. Alarmed, I looked around, until I realized that she had dropped to her knees in prayer. She was the only one of a number of Catholics in the loft who had knelt to pray. When the little bell rang, she bounded to her feet again.

"The musical climax of the service was the *Salve Regina* of Fauré (who had been Nadia Boulanger's teacher), a quietly ravishing piece for soprano solo and instruments. N. B. was conducting in minimally—it more or less carries itself—left hand resting elegantly on her hip, right hand making small arabesques in three-quarter time, when suddenly the soprano lost her place. An expression of despair spread over the sing-er's face. One understood instantly its cause: the sensation of having let N. B. down.

"Still beating, N. B. took a step to the right, toward the girl. Then, smiling serenely, she took up the beat with her left hand as she laid her right hand gently on the soprano's shoulder and sang the music softly to her as it went along. The girl looked into N. B.'s eyes, smiled back, and in a moment or two resumed singing and continued without the score to the end."

During the next months I saw a great deal more of Nadia Boulanger, and later had the good fortune to be able to see her conduct at Carnegie Hall on her seventy-fifth birthday. And yet it is this memory of her in the chapel, conducting— so totally given to the music and the moment, and at the same time so close to her students—that will remain with me longest.

6

F. O. Matthiessen

KENNETH S. LYNN

TEACHERS of American literature who were born, as F. O. Matthiessen was, in the first years of this century, but who are still alive today, have seen the study of their subject move through three different eras. The first, which might be called the Era of Rediscovery, began with Van Wyck Brooks and H. L. Mencken around 1908; gathered strength in the 1920s and 1930s from the work of Lewis Munford, V. L. Parrington, Granville Hicks, Constance Rourke, and Newton Arvin; reached its most concentrated moment of excitement between 1939 and 1942, when Perry Miller's *The New England Mind*, Matthiessen's *American Renaissance*, and Alfred Kazin's *On Native Grounds* appeared in rapid and dazzling succession; and was finally organized into a triumphal march-past in the three-volume *Library History of the United States* (1948) by Robert Spiller and an all-star cast of contributors.

During these forty years, the historic prejudice of college English departments against making teaching appointments and offering courses in American literature was also challenged and overcome. When Matthiessen entered Yale in the fall of 1919, *Moby Dick* was shelved under "Cetology" in the university library. "It was hardly an accident," he later recalled, "that when I graduated from college in the early 1920s, I knew very little of our own literature except some contemporary poetry that I had read with my friends." That he started to immerse himself in American literature as a graduate student at Harvard a few years later was decidedly not because he was studying with George Lyman Kittredge, Irving Babbitt, and John Livingston Lowes, but rather because he had read, and been inspired by, a new book of Lewis Mumford's, *The Golden Day* (1926). Yet by the time Matthiessen returned to Harvard as an instructor in 1929, colleges all over the country were instituting new courses in American literature, and students were flocking to them.

The men and women who taught and wrote about American literature in this period took pride in their literary heritage. At the same time, they were severely critical of American authors, and even more critical of the society that had produced them. The paradox of the Era of Rediscovery is that it was born in the polemical attacks of Brooks and Mencken on a number of American literature's most important traditions and most gifted spokesmen, and was perpetuated by a younger generation of scholar-teachers whose attitudes toward the United States were tense with contradictions. The poignant dedication page of *American Renaissance* is a case in point. In thanking two friends "who have taught me most about the possibilities of life in America," Matthiessen affirmed a faith in the land of his birth in the teeth of torturing doubts.

Such contradictions made for brilliant books and moving lectures. However, there was a considerable psychological cost in living at such a pitch of intellectual and emotional ambivalence. The nervous breakdown that Van Wyck Brooks suffered toward the end of the 1920s was the shattering climax of his love-hate relationship with the American past. (Thereafter Brooks abandoned literary criticism in favor of literary nostalgia, having discovered that nostalgia was psychologically safer.) Matthiessen also suffered some sort of breakdown in the course of writing *American Renaissance*, and nine years after the book's appearance he jumped to his death from a hotel bedroom. In the course of the next quarter of a century, other professors of American literature decided that they too would rather sink in boundless deeps than float on vulgar shoals. ("Give me, ye gods, an utter wreck," cried Melville, "if wreck I do.") One way or another, the study of American literature became the means through which a shockingly large number of gifted teachers tried—and ultimately failed—to work out an accommodation with the world around them.

The personal urgency that marked the study of American literature before World War II carried over into the 1950s and beyond. Nevertheless, the appearance of *Literary History of the United States* at the end of the forties signaled the emergence of a more impersonal, more complacent attitude. Chapter by chapter, *Literary History* recalled the troubled discernments of the Era of Rediscovery. Yet the general lavishness of the enterprise, its comprehensive scope, its impressively detailed bibliographies, and some of its contributors' unalloyed confidence that American literature was destiny's darling—all reflected a new spirit that had emerged out of the global victory of American military power and the triumphant return to health of the American economy. In literary study, as in life, we had entered the Imperialist Era.

Extravagant claims about the importance of American authors now became the order of the day. Minor writers were hailed in terms previously reserved for major writers, while major writers were treated as if their achievements ranked with Goethe's or Shakespeare's. New editions of American authors were put forth, with elaborate textual apparatus that reeked of reverence in every variant comma. Graduate students produced doctoral dissertations with such astounding titles as "Rufus W. Griswold: The Major Phase," and hack writers struck it rich with coffee-table books about Scott and Zelda, "Mr. Papa," Mark Twain, and other delightfully colorful characters. This was also the era in which the New Criticism and an unspeakably vulgar porno-criticism came into fashion—and no wonder. For the refusal of the New Critics to be bothered with social questions, and the active delight that the porno-critics took in revelations of psychosexual maladjustment and suffering, perfectly suited the deadened conscience and casual brutality of imperial America.

Like most of their fellow citizens, teachers of American literature today have a very different view of the world they live in than they did ten years ago. Yet the surprising—and depressing—fact is that this has not inspired them to take a new and harder look at the subject they teach. Perhaps it is the frightening prospect of a collapse of the social order that causes them to clutch, as at a straw, at reassuringly familiar ideas about the American past. Perhaps they are also intimidated by the more mundane thought that if they retreat from the inflated estimates of the Imperialist Era they will not be able to justify the substantive importance of their subject to budget-conscious deans. But whatever the explanation for their behavior, one fact is indisputable: unlike teachers in a number of other fields, professors of American literature have not risen to the challenge posed by the current crisis in American values.

Unwilling to go through the painful process of reexamining their cherished assumptions about American literature, some professors have simply abandoned the field and are now investing their energies in such promising growth stocks as structuralism, women's studies, and film. Most professors, however, have met the challenge of the times by falling silent. They are still giving courses in American literature, but if writing is the sign of continuing mental activity, then they are no longer thinking about what they are saying to students. In the present era, the Era of Paralysis, the senior Americanist at a leading university on the East Coast has not published so much as a book review in the last nine years; precisely the same situation obtains at a leading university on the West Coast; and across the continent that separates them there stretches a chain of extinct volcanoes, most of which do not even have the dignity of being white-topped.

The prevailing silence, it is only fair to say, is not universal. Books on individual American writers and on general themes in American literature continue to be published every month of the year. For the most part, however, the authors of the

F. O. Matthiessen

individual studies have approached their subjects as if they were going to church, while the authors of the theme books have shied away from the disturbing implications of their material. The idea that American literature is a deeply flawed body of work which nevertheless can help us to understand the innermost propulsions of the American people does not have many genuinely serious advocates on college campuses these days.

In a time of caution and failing commitment, the need for strong models becomes acute. American scholars who want to break up the Era of Paralysis and restore our contact with our deepest sense of ourselves could do worse than to pattern their pedagogy after the whole-souled, risk-taking teaching of F. O. Matthiessen.

I first encountered Matthiessen in the fall of 1942, my sophomore year at Harvard, when I took his course in Shakespeare. I had come to college with the idea of studying English history and literature, and friends had advised me that Matthiessen's course was the best place to start. At the outset I was not impressed. A short, stocky man, largely baldheaded, and wearing rimless glasses, he looked to me like a grocer. His voice was hardly more commanding than his physical presence: it had a metallic quality, and went up and down the scale in a kind of singsong that I found annoying. Apparently the only hand gesture in his repertoire was a sudden downward motion, thumb-side down, palm open, followed by a lateral movement in the direction toward which the palm faced. That hand gesture, however, turned out to be symbolic of what I most loved about his teaching. For the downward part of the gesture was a cutting motion, as if he were trying to force his way to the axis of reality, and the sideward part was a revelatory motion, like the pushing aside of a curtain, which was always accompanied by fresh insights into the meaning of existence.

He achieved his revelations by a variety of methods. He was as closely concerned with the specific qualities of Shakespeare's language and dramatic form as were the close readers of the New Criticism. At the same time, he always began the consideration of a play by placing it in a broad historical and cultural setting, and at the end of every analysis he turned once again from text to context—for Matthiessen agreed with Harley Granville-Barker's dictum that great dramatic art is the working out, not merely of the individual alone, but of society as a whole. He agreed, too, with Granville-Barker's conception of Shakespeare's work as plays to be acted as well as read. *Translation* was the title that Matthiessen gave to the published version of his Ph.D. thesis, and the crossing of boundaries from one realm to another was an idea that appealed to him in many ways. The translation of printed pages into living gestures was certainly one of his main goals as a teacher of Shakespeare. To that end, he required us to memorize several hundred lines of poetry, and to show our mastery of them, not by writing them down in class, but by reciting the speeches he called for in private meetings in his office. The fact that this requirement took a great deal of his time casts light on his dedication to teaching. He was absolutely determined—as he often pointed out that Coleridge was—"to reinstate the Logos as a living power, to demonstrate in poetry itself the word made flesh." Having us speak Shakespeare to him was a part of that effort.

Matthiessen also spoke to us from the plays. While he lacked the theatrical skills of his friend and fellow Shakespearean Theodore Spencer, there was a marvelous inwardness in his rendition of the lines that soon made you forget the technical deficiencies of his voice. Kent was the role that he would like to have played on the stage, but in the classroom he also made a fine Edgar and a very moving Lear. Even in parts that were obviously not suited to him, Matthiessen managed to be effective, because he always spoke from inside the character. The same thing was true of his lectures. What gave his commentaries on the plays their extraordinary emotional power was his imaginative involvement with the men and women he was talking about. It was not simply that he brought to bear upon them an exciting combination of textual

F. O. Matthiessen

criticism and historical reflection; somehow he crossed over into their lives. Matthiessen once said of Sherwood Anderson that he had tried to awaken his readers to "the fellowship in living, the fellowship in life." A sense of fellowship with the people of Shakespeare's world suffused Matthiessen's lectures.

While I realized that his course had a personal signature that was utterly lacking in other courses in English which I was taking that fall, I did not understand that he often made Shakespeare the stalking-horse of his own thoughts and feelings—not until the day he lost his temper. He was lecturing on *Hamlet*, and had not finished what he wanted to say when the bell sounded. A student sitting to Matthiessen's left at once arose and began moving toward the aisle. Suddenly Matthiessen swerved, stabbed his right index finger straight at the student, and yelled at the top of his lungs, "Will you sit down!" For approximately the next two minutes, he was out of control. He had poured his whole being into this course, he raged, and we would not even extend him the courtesy of hearing him out. Finally, he calmed down and said he was sorry for yelling, but before dismissing the class he cried out as if in pain, "Hamlet had a temper, too."

Matthiessen's identification with Hamlet was no simple narcissism. One of his most critical observations about American literature was that American authors often fell short of greatness because of their inability to transcend themselves. There was a narcissism, even a solipsism, in the poetry of Allen Tate, for example, that reduced his broodings about the tragedy of southern history to mere autobiography. Matthiessen also criticized Edna St. Vincent Millay for her failure to go beyond the personal "I" to the universal "you." In talking about the prince of Denmark, therefore, he always tried to keep Shakespeare's intentions firmly in mind. The function of a lecturer, Matthiessen believed, was to express with as much intensity as possible whatever a literary artist believed. At the same time, however, he also felt that a lecturer could never reach a really burning intensity without personal risk.

Not until after his death did I realize that in his childhood Matthiessen, like Hart Crane, had witnessed painful conflicts between his father and mother; that his mother had finally withdrawn from the situation, taking young Francis Otto with her; that while he had dedicated a book to her, he had never once expressed a sense of indebtedness to his father; and that he had asked in his suicide note to be laid to rest beside his mother in a cemetery in Springfield, Massachusetts. If I had known or had had foreknowledge of these facts in 1942, I would have had a fuller appreciation of what *Hamlet* must have meant to him. But when he talked about himself and Shakespeare's hero in the same breath, even a naïve sophomore could sense how completely he had incarnated himself in the play. In the preface to *American Renaissance* he had asserted that the student of a work of art should not only take into account the influences that shaped it, but should also make use of what he brings to it from his own life. Clearly, what this man preached he practiced to the hilt. I walked out of the lecture hall that day with a new idea of what I wanted to study at Harvard: I wanted to study whatever Matthiessen taught.

Three years of army life intervened before I could carry out that resolve. In the spring of 1946, however, I switched from English to American history and literature, because most of Matthiessen's courses were in the American field. I also discovered that Major Perry Miller had returned to the Harvard scene. In addition to taking a number of courses from both of them, I had the great good fortune to do tutorial work with Miller in the spring of my return, and to write a thesis on Melville under Matthiessen's supervision the following year.

Some day I hope to write about my relationship with Miller, for in the long run his tough and profane intelligence meant more to me than Matthiessen's intensity. But in the stirring time at Harvard immediately after the war, when classrooms were filled to overflowing with the oldest, most experienced students the university had ever known, and cold-war disillusionments had not yet destroyed hot-war hopes, Matthiessen was the man I wanted to follow. For one thing, he made himself available to students to a degree that other professors did not. In the summer of 1946, for example, I took his course on modern American poetry. The swollen enrollment meant that it was no longer possible for Matthiessen to listen to us recite the poems he required us to memorize, and so we wrote them out in blue books. Yet he still managed to keep in touch with us. In addition to encouraging us to speak up during his lectures, he scheduled an extra, informal meeting of the class every Tuesday afternoon in his office in Grays 18. The stars of these informal sessions were two graduate students, Richard Wilbur and Laurence Holland, but undergraduates were also welcomed, and their often inchoate ideas were treated with respect. In spite of the increasing anonymity of postwar Harvard, Matthiessen created a community with his students.

Running through all his courses and tutorials in American literature was the historical conception he had taken over from the early Van Wyck Brooks and then modified for his own purposes—that American culture was split across the brow. Some Americans were the products of a tradition of learning and knowledge that went back through nineteenth-century Harvard to the Puritans, but other Americans were the children of a radical, know-nothing tradition born on the raucous and lusty frontier. Lacking the nourishment that they might have derived from one another, both traditions had eventually lost their vitality. The tradition typified by Mark Twain was filled with anxiety, a sense of dread, an exasperating inferiority complex, while the tradition typified by Henry Adams was consumed by "the Boston doubt." In our own time, the failure of belief had become the central problem of American culture. Novelists were turning in on themselves, because there was nothing else to believe in. Meter, rhyme, and other outside controls were being abandoned by poets in consequence of the view that poetry was now an end in itself, rather than a means to an end.

The question that bothered me every time I heard this analysis was why Matthiessen should have been immune to the rampant sickness he described. As he never wearied of telling audiences, he was a devout Christian and an ardent socialist. The very fact of his faith seemed to me to be a paradox, and its structure of ideas was certainly riddled with illogicalities. As a good democrat he wanted literary scholarship to be applied "for the good and enlightenment of all the people, not for the pampering of a class"; yet no elitist in all of Harvard was more scornful than Matthiessen of Granville Hicks's willingness to tailor aesthetic judgments to political measurements. As a believer in Original Sin, Matthiessen accepted the idea that man can never achieve self-realization inside history. At the same time, he hailed the Russian Revolution as "the most progressive event of our century," and worked side by side with Communists and fellow travelers in a wide variety of popular-front activities. When asked by students why a man who made common cause with Harry Bridges went around talking like T. S. Eliot, he generally said something not very helpful about being a socialist *because* he was a Christian.

Had Matthiessen's religious faith been earned, as Eliot's was, or was it merely willed, like Auden's? I have never been sure, but my guess is that Christianity was an order which had a powerful appeal to a man who hated his own disorder, but which never sustained him for very long. I also wonder about his political enthusiasms. During my undergraduate days I took his radicalism at face value and admired him for it; but afterward, in Austria, where we both spent the summer of 1947 at the inaugural session of the Salzburg Seminar in American Studies, I began to see that he could respond to ordinary people only if they played traditional roles. He wanted the good citizens of Salzburg and environs to drink the weak and watery white wine of postwar Austria, and was disturbed that they had Cokes whenever they could cadge them. He also could not understand why they tuned their radios to the popular music—"American jazz," he called it,

F. O. Matthiessen

in his 1920s vocabulary—broadcast by Armed Forces Radio. Had they forgotten that they were living in Mozart's birthplace?

Matthiessen passionately wanted a better life for the masses: there is no doubt that he had lived by this ideal ever since he had read R. H. Tawney's *Acquisitive Society* as a Yale undergraduate. But at the heart of Matthiessen's socialism was his own insatiable need for human contact. This is why the vulgarity of mass culture upset him. In his loneliness he wanted the masses to behave in ways that would make it possible for him to be at ease with them; if they refused to, he felt more alienated than ever. Thus, when he knocked on doors in Boston's West End for Henry Wallace's Progressive party or some other unpopular cause, he was most successful when he chanced upon an immigrant family that still clung to the old customs. Otherwise, the door was apt to be slammed in his face. Matthiessen did have one way of getting through to the native-born sons of the working class with whom he sometimes tried to make acquaintance in South Boston bars: by meeting their enthusiasm for the Red Sox halfway. Although he rarely went to Fenway Park, he was a fan. As soon, however, as Apeneck Sweeney switched to talking about the Bruins, Matthiessen was lost.

The multiple ambiguities in his beliefs made a number of thoughtful students suspicious of him. In fact, there were some who hated Matthiessen, as did quite a few of his colleagues on the Harvard faculty. Nevertheless, his improbable combination of ideals gave him great strength as a teacher. It was his habit in the classroom to turn questions of form and technique in American literature into larger questions about American life, and as a Christian and a socialist he was prepared to explore a wide range of social and moral problems. In Matthiessen's lectures, his sensitive readings of such works as Whitman's "Out of the Cradle," Hawthorne's *Scarlet Letter,* James's *Portrait of a Lady,* and Frost's "Death of the Hired Man" flowered into meditations on the meaning of democracy, the relationship of the artist to society, and the dignity of work, among other matters. The center of value in all his meditations was a vision of "man in his full revolutionary and democratic splendor," a phrase he had taken over from the nineteenth-century prophet of functional architecture, Horatio Greenough. When he talked about Melville or showed us Southworth and Hawes's magnificent daguerreotype of the shipbuilder Donald McKay, which he used as the frontispiece in *American Renaissance*, Matthiessen was able to make this vision come alive. But for the most part we were aware of it only as a ghost, in lectures that were full of ghosts.

Like many of his favorite American writers, Matthiessen was haunted by the feelings of loss and anguish they expressed. An almost unbearable undercurrent of personal suffering ran through his lectures at times. For example, in an analysis I heard him give of "Mr. Flood's Party" in the summer of 1946, he incorporated his own desolation within E. A. Robinson's, as he had good reason to do. Matthiessen and his most intimate friend, the painter Russell Cheney, had owned a house together in Kittery, Maine, an hour's drive or so from the Tilbury Town of Robinson's poetry. Cheney, however, had died in 1945, and in the summer of 1946 Matthiessen was trying to get used to living at Kittery without him. Listening to the sadness in Matthiessen's voice as he worked his way through the poem, I was sure that Eben Flood was not the only man who ever stood on a hilltop in the state of Maine, talking to himself, with only whiskey for company:

> *"Well, Mr. Flood, we have not met like this*
> *In a long time; and many a change has come*
> *To both of us, I fear, since last it was*
> *We had a drop together. Welcome home!"*
> *Convivially returning with himself,*
> *Again he raised the jug up to the light;*
> *And with an acquiescent quaver said:*
> *"Well, Mr. Flood, if you insist, I might."*
>
> *"Only a very little, Mr. Flood—*
> *For auld lang syne. No more, sir; that will do."*

F. O. Matthiessen

So, for the time, apparently it did,
And Eben evidently thought so too;
For soon amid the silver loneliness
Of night he lifted up his voice and sang,
Secure, with only two moons listening,
Until the whole harmonious landscape rang—

"For auld lang syne." The weary throat gave out,
The last word wavered, and the song was done.
He raised again the jug regretfully
And shook his head, and was again alone.
There was not much that was ahead of him,
And there was nothing in the town below—
Where strangers would have shut the many doors
That many friends had opened long ago.

By bringing his own life into works of American literature, Matthiessen clarified as well as intensified their meaning. Occasionally, though, he altered their meaning—and in my judgment improved them. I had never cared for the poetry of Carl Sandburg, ever since I had attended one of his readings in my high school days. With his hair carefully combed into his eyes and his pseudofolksy voice, he had seemed to me to be an all-American fake. Matthiessen agreed that the staccato effects of his poetry were not in the same class with the magnificent flow of Whitman. Nevertheless, he asserted that Sandburg's "Happiness" was a good poem, and he made me believe it—by dint of changing the poem's point of view to fit a conflation of his own memories. As the poem told it, Sandburg had asked famous professors to tell him what happiness was, and they had shaken their heads as if he were trying to fool them. "And then one Sunday afternoon I wandered out along the Desplaines river / And I saw a crowd of Hungarians under the trees with their women and children and a keg of beer and an accordion." I felt that the poet's attitude toward this scene was marked by Sandburg's usual off-putting heartiness, but Matthiessen's interpreted it differently, for personal reasons.

First of all, Matthiessen had spent part of his childhood in Sandburg country, albeit the river he remembered was not the Desplaines, but the Illinois. More important, the poem recalled for him one of the crucial experiences of his college years. Although he was deeply involved in the Elizabethan Club, the *Yale Daily News,* the *Yale Literary Magazine,* and other undergraduate activities, he had not been content, even then, to live his whole life within academic fences. Accordingly he had volunteered to teach English to a group of men at the New Haven Hungarian Club who were trying to qualify for citizenship. After the last session of the class, his students took their teacher down to the cellar, where they had been fermenting casks of Prohibition wine. Several glasses later, the stars seemed unusually bright as the young undergraduate walked back to the Yale campus. He had felt at home in the comradeship of these men. In "Happiness," Matthiessen viewed Sandburg's convival Hungarians through the mirage of a vanished happiness of his own, thereby endowing the poem with a wistfulness that considerably enhanced its appeal.

Since there was such a strong autobiographical element in his criticism, I was struck by Matthiessen's silence, in his lectures and tutorial conversations, on the subject of homosexuality in American literature. His comments on Whitman's interest in young male beauty were singularly guarded and inadequate, while the blatant case of Hart Crane obviously made him uncomfortable. The conclusion I drew from this at the time, and have subsequently had no reason to doubt, was that Matthiessen's own sex life was a guilt-ridden horror to him. So full of revulsion was he that he could barely pronounce the word homosexuality, let alone release his feelings through candid discussions of Melville's joke about "Devil's-Tail Peak and Buggery Island" and related matters.

But if he avoided the subject of homosexual love, he seemed eager to talk about death. Vachel Lindsay's suicide, Hurstwood's suicide in *Sister Carrie,* Poe's self-destructive impulses—such things loomed large in our tutorial conversations.

F. O. Matthiessen

In the note he left when he jumped from the twelfth floor of Boston's Manger Hotel, Matthiessen said that he did not know "how much the state of the world has to do with my state of mind." There was a good deal of speculation in the following days that his death had indeed been a political act, on the model of Jan Masaryk's defenestration. I myself cannot accept this view. Not only had Matthiessen been thinking about killing himself long before Czechoslovakia fell victim to the cold war, but I am convinced that he had long since decided on the way he would do it. For a certain scene involving Clifford Pyncheon in Hawthorne's *House of the Seven Gables* held his imagination in thrall. He referred to it often during my discussions with him about my thesis on Melville (Melville, too, was fascinated by the scene), and he wrote about it—in the present tense, significantly enough—in *American Renaissance:*

> Clifford has retrogressed until he is hardly more than an idiot, a spoiled child who takes a childish pleasure in any passing attraction that can divert him from the confused memories of his terrible years of gloom. But, occasionally, deeper forces stir within him, as one day when he is watching, from the arched window at the head of the stairs, a political procession of marching men with fifes and drums. With a sudden, irrepressible gesture, from which he is restrained just in time by Hepzibah and Phoebe, he starts forward as though to jump down into the street, in a kind of desperate effort at renewed contact with life outside himself, "but whether impelled by the species of terror that sometimes urges its victim over the very precipice which he shrinks from, or by a natural magnetism, tending towards the great centre of humanity," Hawthorne found it not easy to decide.

Nor do I find it easy to decide why Matthiessen jumped. Yet I believe that *The House of the Seven Gables* brings us closer to an explanation than does his suicide note.

Another popular theory about Matthiessen is that the golden day of his teaching was before the war. I will never agree to this. In postwar Harvard he was still the same teacher who had changed the direction of my life in 1942. Furthermore,

I believe that at the Salzburg Seminar in the summer of 1947 he reached the zenith of his career. A number of distinguished professors taught at Schloss Leopoldskron that summer— Alfred Kazin, Wassily Leontief, Benjamin Wright, Margaret Mead. But Matthiessen was the acknowledged leader. He worked harder and longer at getting to know the European students than did anyone else, and he gave a lecture at the beginning of the seminar and another toward the end that framed the experience for us all.

The first lecture was a speech of welcome, delivered in the garden of the Schloss. Somewhere in Matthiessen's childhood there was a garden that had spelled security to him, because it was associated with his mother. In an act of imaginative displacement, he had evoked this placid spot in the garden imagery of his first book—a biography of Sarah Orne Jewett dedicated to the memory of his mother, Lucy Orne Matthiessen. By the end of the book, however, he had worked past his nostalgia; fenced-in gardens were for pathetic, outdated people who were afraid to face reality. Standing in the garden at Schloss Leopoldskron, he spoke of perilous journeys across boundaries, and of the chance we had to create an international community. Near the end of the seminar, he spoke to us in the library, but once again he brought a garden and a perilous journey together in our imaginations, for his text was the fifth section of "The Waste Land": "After the torchlight red on sweaty faces. . . ." That is my best memory of Matthiessen, talking out of his American heart in the heart of Europe, just before the Era of Rediscovery began to die.

7

Arthur O. Lovejoy

LEWIS S. FEUER

WHEN Arthur O. Lovejoy returned to Harvard University as a visiting professor for 1932–1933, word quickly spread that the man who could make more distinctions than anybody else in the philosophical profession would soon be confounding the students. Here, too, was the only man who had taken to heart William James's warning against "the Ph.D. octopus." After thirty-five years of teaching, he was still without a doctorate, and it was known that he regarded most Ph.D. theses as "juvenilia." It was also recalled that he had been the founding spirit of the American Association of University Professors. One would have expected, therefore, that his experience with Harvard graduate students in philosophy would have been a happy one. Instead, it became clear in the fall semester that the *Zeitgeist* had placed Lovejoy at cross-purposes with the new generation. Yet his was the greatest rearguard action my friends and I would ever see, destined though it was, like all such actions, to defeat.

A man more committed to reason than anyone I ever knew, Lovejoy was impervious to ideological fashions; his critical spirit, elevated by his historical researches, seemed to dwell in a transtemporal realm. At Harvard, when he held a seminar, The Theory of Meaning, to analyze the new logical positivism that was attracting the current generation, most students disliked what he said and how he said it. The next semester, when he gave his great William James lectures on The Great Chain of Being, few of them attended. All, however, were aware of an intellectual power that had the inner moral resources to stand on its own, supported by neither sect nor school nor society.

The greatest tragedy that can befall a teacher, according to Einstein, is when he finds that his language, method, and problems have ceased to be those of the new generation of students, whose presuppositions he may find not only alien but willfully irrational. This indeed was Lovejoy's situation when he returned to Harvard at the age of fifty-nine. As a student of William James in the nineties, he had acquired a sense of the spontaneous, emergent, and unpredictable character of things—and, above all, of their pervasive temporal nature. He had joined with his own generation at the turn of the century in a revolt against absolute idealism. For several years he had scrutinized Josiah Royce's notion of a nontemporal Absolute, and argued that the Eternal was obsolescent, that the Absolute could not absorb the transient character of human experience; and if it did, would take on such a character itself. By 1930, however, Lovejoy had earned a reputation as (in Arthur Murphy's words) "the Edmund Burke of the epistemological revolution." His powerful book *The Revolt Against Dualism* was a culminating effort to show that when Russell, Whitehead, and Dewey tried to overcome or obliterate the distinction between mental and physical existents, their devices were specious.

But then in 1932 the terms of philosophic discussion began to change rather abruptly in the United States. At Harvard the first Cambridge University disciples of Ludwig Wittgenstein arrived, bringing the curious gospel that held all philosophy to be nonsense. The elder Harvard professors were appalled. Whitehead could not quite believe it when he heard one of them read a paper that was avowedly solipsistic; "impressionable young people" were being misled by Wittgenstein, a man who "has done nothing, except perhaps a little in logic," he said. It was hoped that Lovejoy, having dealt

Arthur O. Lovejoy

so devastatingly with the Girondins of the philosophic revolution, would deal equally with its Jacobins.

Lovejoy sat at the head of the table, his bushy hair almost all gray, with a white moustache and imperial, his eyes alert, occasionally squinting as if from too much reading. His voice was gruff and low, even monotonous, speaking in long, interminable paragraphs with parentheses within parentheses and brackets for digression, a bit haltingly to accommodate the semicolons, all the while twirling his cigarette holder to ease the strain and to replace the intellectual fog with a more congenial smoke. He invited and was pleased by discussion, but only one or two students had the temerity to speak as Lovejoy sat, with his notes scrawled in his large handwriting, and painstakingly analyzed the varied meanings of "verifiable" in the writings of Carnap, Schlick, Neurath, Wittgenstein, and the pragmatists. Each variety of "meaning" was pinned into its case with an appropriate label as if he were an entomologist lovingly affixing his taxonomy to his specimens. Unlike Edmund Burke, Lovejoy never resorted to any rhetorical, dramatic display. He began with the distinctions of common sense, the epistemology of the common man. He charted precisely how our thought-content in the present could refer to the past and future, and to other people's experiences ("transpersonal") as well as our own.

Yet Lovejoy, in 1932, found himself in a quandary. He had always taken it for granted that if he could show that a given view entailed a consequence that violated our minimal sense of reality, its proponets would repudiate it. He thought that if he could show that a particular theory led to solipsism, people would reject it as wrong; or that if it entrapped one in the notion, for instance, that the "person" to whom one was making love was a mechanical sweetheart without consciousness, the dogmatic trance would be shattered; or that if it led to our denying our present consciousness on the ground that only the movements of objects made sense, thereby leaving us incapable of thinking, the logomachy would be abandoned. The new generation was, however, prepared to accept the consequences that Lovejoy considered to be, as he put it, "preposterous." The single-minded young logical positivist would maintain unshakably that he was a solipsist (albeit of a "methodological" kind); the physicalist was nothing loath to make love to his physicalistic sweetheart; and the behaviorist blandly averred that he had no idea what Lovejoy was talking about when he referred to private thoughts or feeling-contents.

Several incidents took place that year and later in the mid-thirties, when Lovejoy was again at Harvard, that poignantly underscored the rift between the "critical realist" and the new generation of philosophic militants.

Lovejoy was an inveterate attender of meetings, at which he was also an invariable raiser of questions. At one session of the Philosophy Club, Henry Leonard, the talented and original symbolic logician, read a paper in which he scorned the propositions of traditional philosophy as nonsense. During the question period, Lovejoy suggested that since at least nine-tenths of what went by the name of philosophy was to be dismissed as nonsense, perhaps someone might investigate what kind of meaning the traditional philosophers intended— and take this as a starting point, rather than begin by closing the discussion. Leonard, tall, pale, with a highpitched voice, replied vehemently that the traditional propositions of philosophy were unverifiable and therefore meaningless. One felt that strong emotions of a nonlogical kind were at work; the segment of the *Zeitgeist* that diffused through the room in Phillips Brooks House had a foreboding quality. Lovejoy waived his reply, probably wondering why these young men were entering such a negative profession. At Johns Hopkins he urged his students not to seek a career in philosophy unless some "irresistible vocation" impelled them.

Then there was the meeting at which the famed biochemist, amateur sociologist, and historian of science, Lawrence J. Henderson, spoke. A recent convert to logical positivism, Henderson had come to the doctrine by his own unique path. Twenty years before, as a member of Josiah Royce's seminar,

Arthur O. Lovejoy

he had written a book, *The Fitness of the Environment*, which ingeniously collated scientific facts to suggest a new teleological argument for the existence of God. In the intervening time, however, he had sought new gods. In 1926, during the grim period of the Sacco-Vanzetti case, he was persuaded to read Vilfredo Pareto's multi-volumed treatise on general sociology. It caused such an intellectual upheaval in him that he derided his old Roycean days. Of all the teachers I had at Harvard, Henderson was the most outspoken admirer of Hitler and Mussolini as "empiricists." He scorned the political philosophers, even those who, like William Ernest Hocking, somewhat shared his political preferences. His face bearded, resembling Galileo whom he revered, his jaw thrust forward aggressively, Henderson walked the Yard with a cane with which he accented his steps, as if disciplining the earth itself.

The paper that Henderson read, "An Approximate Definition of Fact," blended his Paretian positivism into a loosely formulated psychophysical background. Lovejoy naturally proceeded to question Henderson about the realistic assumptions in the use of words such as receptor that were at variance with his professed positivism. Thereupon Henderson became ruffled, irritated, and impatient. His eyes flashing, he said loudly that he refused to enter into any discussion of words. Lovejoy was nonplussed by the intolerance and discourtesy. Since the paper itself was entitled, and purported to be, an "approximate definition," presumably some effort to make the definition more explicit was in order, and this inevitably involved discussing words.

Probably the most memorable meeting, however, was the great debate at Baltimore three years later (1935) between Lovejoy and Rudolf Carnap. This was Carnap's first appearance before the American Philosophical Association, and Lovejoy presented the counter-paper. Carnap expounded with simple clarity the principle of verifiability, explaining to the assembled philosophers why their many years' debate between idealism and realism was meaningless. Give us a method, he challenged, whereby we can test whether objects do or don't exist apart from perception; since none was forthcoming, one could only conclude that the controversy was meaningless. Carnap assigned the philosophers the residual task (for which they were scarcely qualified) of studying the language of science.

Lovejoy then read his counter-paper, and with more vigor and confidence than I had seen in him at Harvard. He was in his beloved Baltimore, his home territory. The audience, not large in those days, was still composed mainly of veterans of the thirty years' war between realism and idealism. He delivered with courteous straightforwardness and without rancor the arguments I had heard three years previously. Every scientist-experimenter, he noted, does accept other colleagues' reports as evidence of what they have observed. The physical theory of objects, whether large as the sun, or small as atomic particles, does (he continued) presuppose and explicate the distinction between physical reality and our psychological perceptions. Positivism has led to a solipsism out of keeping with the realism of ordinary men and scientists alike.

Afterward, there was an excited rush of commentators to the floor. We were witnessing the last stand of classical American philosophy. And for the next generation, metaphysics, apart from some existentialist outcroppings, was to suffer a desuetude. Carnap patently did not take seriously the objections of the metaphysicians; the *Baltimore Sun* reported next day that he refused to attend the session on Plato. He totally ignored Morris R. Cohen's reproach that his message was the old one they had heard from Ernst Mach, "the high priest of positivism." I had the feeling Carnap felt that if Mach were its priest, this was one church to which he and men like Einstein wouldn't mind belonging. But Carnap said he did want to answer Lovejoy's objections, which he regarded as serious. He never quite did, although some attempt to reconcile positivism with common sense was being undertaken in the form of a new emphasis on the "thing-language." Carnap still, however, refused to acknowledge metaphysics as having meaning, and annoyed some of his listeners by saying

Arthur O. Lovejoy

that it should be explained psychologically. He said he was not enough of a psychologist to do so, but he thought that dualism perhaps expressed an unresolved emotional conflict, whereas monism perhaps projected an emotion rendered dominant.

Lovejoy evidently felt that a sort of duplicity, a twofold theory of truth, was becoming fashionable among philosophers. A philosophy was becoming a stance rather than one's most sincere reasoned standpoint. When positivists cheerfully conceded that they were methodological solipsists, Lovejoy felt they didn't really believe what they were saying. How could anyone put forward as a methodological principle a tenet that their actions contravened every day?

Sad to say, Lovejoy's hopes for dispassionate, objective philosophizing ran counter to the chief lesson of his historical studies; the philosopher in him was at odds with the historian of ideas. Lovejoy had long maintained that the history of ideas was moved by a combination of temperamental, irrational motives availing themselves of logical "considerations." He admired the disenchanted seventeenth-century moralist La Rochefoucauld, who had said that the head was the dupe of the heart; and he thought that John Adams acted wisely in founding American constitutional theory on the perception that men's reasons were mostly rationalizations. In his classical articles on Henri Bergson, Lovejoy had held that the primary function of a philosophy was to initiate its adherents into a kind of Eleusinian mystery. Yet as a philosopher he wanted the fellow thinkers to transcend the sociological uniformities of the history of ideas. Like every thinker who has believed himself to be grasping a law of history, Lovejoy thought that his philosophizing could transcend the laws of generational fashion and the patterns of irrational temperament. Was he asking the impossible of his younger contemporaries?

Young philosophers want a distinctive, novel method that will enable them to solve the problems that have baffled their predecessors; hence the periodic manifestos that proclaim their respective master keys—that either phenomenological introspection, or the scrutiny of linguistic usage, or common sense rendered self-conscious, or the resolving of social problems, or logic is the essence of philosophy. Lovejoy, on the other hand, felt there were no master keys for philosophy. One could only adduce the "considerations" that seemed relevant to a problem, and the "considerations" could be almost anything—a scientific law, a logical presupposition, a necessary distinction, some notion of common sense, or a highly general principle. One weighed them all. Aware that such dispassionate "considerations" were only a partial source of people's philosophies, Lovejoy felt that a professional philosopher, if he stood for anything, had to study competing claims in order to rise above the mode, the vogue, and the emotional bias of his day. Two dispositions, he told his students, were at variance: the desire to edify and the desire to verify: "An eagerness to serve the spiritual needs of one's generation is a generous and noble thing; but it is a very different thing from an eagerness to probe an intricate logical problem to its obscurest elements and the nicest distinctions." He hoped philosophers might become sufficiently rational so that one would see the rare but admirable spectacle of "some once ardent champion of a philosophical revolution frankly repudiating the great discovery upon which the revolution was to have been based." But wasn't the illusion of philosophical revolutions the overriding reality in the history of ideas?

The main theater of Emerson Hall was only about half-full when Lovejoy gave the opening lecture of The Great Chain of Being. Although the philosophers lost interest rapidly as they got no intimation of a novel aggressive pronouncement, students of history and literature realized that a truly searching vision was at work. Lovejoy conveyed the sense of the collective human mind, struggling with certain basic axioms to which it tried to accommodate all it experienced, and with expressing its gropings consecutively in poetry, romances, philosophies, political ideologies, and scientific ideas.

Arthur O. Lovejoy

He conveyed it not vaguely but with clarity and an overwhelming documentation.

The drawback again was that there was a mark of the impossible about Lovejoy's historical method. He could preface some observation with the statement "after a lifetime of reading," but the graduate student, having no such accumulation of memories and notes, felt as helpless as a destroyer ordered to maneuver against a battleship. Also, those who aspired to original thinking—whether in criticism, political theory, religion, or philosophy—felt themselves disabled by Lovejoy's method of decomposing philosophies into their unit-ideas and tracing them through their combinations and recombinations. At the hands of this Mendeleev of the human mind, one's prized original ideas were reduced to a foreseeable entry in the Periodic Table of Human Ideas. Lovejoy's audience kept dwindling until his last lecture, when he spoke movingly in memory of William James. Although Lovejoy always kept his emotions under strict restraint, he openly venerated James for his Huckleberry Finnesque spontaneity, his restless, oscillating responsiveness to things.

Even among historians, however, there was an antipathy to Lovejoy's approach in *The Great Chain of Being*, and they could be as fearful for their craft as any trade unionist guarding against an interloper or a novel technology. Lovejoy was once invited to set forth that approach in George Sarton's seminar in the history of science. Sarton was not friendly. He had become a historian of science under the inspiration of Auguste Comte, and all his life, despite his vast erudition, Sarton remained a simple Comtist. He criticized Edward Gibbon, for instance, for having failed to recognize that the growth of scientific knowledge was a steady, irreversible force, making for progress and underwriting the creed of historical optimism. Sarton said at the seminar that Lovejoy's method of tracing unit-ideas through recombinations and recurrences violated both the Comtist linear principle and the unity of the individual scientist's contribution. Lovejoy seemed saddened, his face drawn. He replied that the proof of the pudding would be in the eating, but appeared too tired to point out that the "unity" of a thinker's work was often a fiction that disguised various independent elements, or even discordant ones, absorbed through various processes into its complex.

Most disappointing personally to Lovejoy was probably the fact that no intellectual discussion developed between Whitehead and himself while he was at Harvard. Lovejoy deeply admired Whitehead's *Process and Reality*, and when he gave the beautiful, principal address at the symposium in 1931 in honor of Whitehead's seventieth birthday, he characterized that book as "perhaps the most impressive and large-minded effort of philosophic synthesis since Hegel," combining "a large number of the great strains and major ideas in the history of Western thought" into a connected system that linked Platonic Eternal Objects with an emergent evolutionistic conception of the "principle of plenitude." Whitehead's work, in Lovejoy's estimate, "one of the great achievements in a speculative synthesis of the human mind," rethought the centrality of God as a final cause in terms of the latest researches in logic and theoretical physics, yet conveying a sense of "the intricate mystery of things." Himself a "poor specimen" (in Lovejoy's words) of the humbler, sceptical, piecemeal variety of philosopher, he still wished to raise questions, even concerning a book than which there was no "more faithful picture of the real world."

The Harvard Philosophy Club obligingly arranged a debate between Lovejoy and Whitehead midway in the academic year 1932–1933. What a momentous joust of ideas was envisaged! The room in Emerson Hall was filled; the Radcliffe girls came festive in their many-colored garments (for dresses were still worn in that era rather than drab, lumpenproletarian "unisexiforms"); idealists, realists, and positivists alike halted from poring over the pages of *Principia Mathematica* to attend the masters. The occasion, however, proved to be something of an intellectual fiasco. Lovejoy had covered the blackboard with numbered distinctions designed to show that White-head's notion of "prehension" did not abrogate the ultimate difference between the "mental" and "physical" poles of experience. Whitehead, with never a glance at the blackboard, propounded the place of perception in his panpsychist cosmology. When Lovejoy reminded him about the chart of distinctions, Whitehead replied in his good-natured sing-song: "Oh, I entirely agree with them," signifying willy-nilly to the audience that he was not concerned with such trivia.

Never much inclined to read or argue with contemporary philosophers, Whitehead was exclusively devoted to working out his own view of the universe; he had little interest in positivists, linguistic analysts, or critical philosophers. Nor did he think that Lovejoy's careful discrimination of meanings would much assist the philosophical imagination. Both he and Mrs. Whitehead had expected a great clash to occur at the annual fall reception of the Department of Philosophy, for its two great non-Ph.D. alumni, T. S. Eliot and Lovejoy, were to be the invited speakers. Lovejoy, wearing a grey frock coat that seemed to have been tailored in 1900, pleaded for philosophers to try to understand each others' terms of discussion, something Whitehead abhorred. Eliot said that he had proved a man could make a living without a Ph.D., and that in any case, he was not a philosopher. Both men were shy, not combative, and no battlelines over Babbitt's humanism were ever drawn.

Marxism meanwhile was being much talked about; it began around 1932, and by 1935 had made many converts among Lovejoy's students. That development deepened Lovejoy's sense of isolation. He was much troubled when an able young Hopkins colleague relinquished his academic career to become a Communist functionary. At least, said Lovejoy, his colleague was going to live by his doctrine rather than simply write about it the way the others did. He felt that young Jews especially seemed to need some political orthodoxy as a substitute for their lost religion. (Lovejoy for many years had been the only chairman of any major university philosophy department in the United States where a man's Jewish background was not a reason for exclusion.)

As the depression grew worse and the election of 1932 approached, Lovejoy vigorously opposed Herbert Hoover; he thought Hoover's speech about grass growing in the streets of New York if Franklin D. Roosevelt were elected was "scandalous." He wondered why young socialists hadn't acted as poll watchers to prevent votes being stolen from Norman Thomas, and said he had been a poll watcher once himself. He told of his work in the Maryland Civil Liberties Union to secure a change of venue on behalf of a Negro accused of murder. He disapproved, however, of the teachers' union that was later organized at Harvard, and asked how could professors hold on to their scientific detachment when they committed themselves to the labor movement? How could they serve as scientific analysts of the labor movement if the facts tended to embarrass their partisanship? He said he had learned a great deal from Eugene Lyons's *Assignment in Utopia*, and urged me to read it.

In 1937, Communist scholars published in their newly founded journal a symposium on Lovejoy's historical method as exemplified in *The Great Chain of Being*. Lovejoy responded with a page of trenchant writing that was probably the pithiest criticism of the Marxist historiography of ideas ever published. He readily conceded that the doctrine of the chain of being had often been used as an apologetic for stratified societies, but when Plato's conception of the world was said to have been caused by the characteristics of Athenian society, he still remained an "agnostic," for the fact was that "after all, nature, apart from society, has a tolerably hierarchical look," which was why Aristotle had been led in the first place to the idea of a scale of nature. In any case, said Lovejoy, "Mindreading seems to me a difficult and precarious art. . . . We *know*, from the texts, that this reason for the idea was present in the minds of these writers; we do not, I believe, know, from the texts, that the analogy of a hierarchical political order was similarly operative in the genesis of the 'princi-

Arthur O. Lovejoy

ple' of gradation. . . ." Unfortunately the Communists allowed Lovejoy only a page; otherwise he would have explored, he said, the "larger questions of psychology and of historical method." Thus we never had the benefit of his full analysis of these momentous issues.

Actually, of course, Lovejoy engaged frequently in what he called "mind-reading." His discussion of why people were attracted to Bergson's philosophy was as much a psychological inquiry into human motives as was his *Reflections on Human Nature.* He once remarked at the seminar that he had known the principal figures in the rise of behaviorism, Knight Dunlap and J. B. Watson, and both had told him that they experienced little mental imagery. Lovejoy wondered whether this impoverished experience might not be related to their readiness to exclude mental contents from their science. He also implied that the chief logical positivists were probably men whose personal lives were on a shallow emotional plane. Yet Lovejoy seemed to be arguing for a kind of "textual positivism" (as we might call it) in which one delineated the filiation of ideas but never knew what prompted the "ideators."

I have felt that Lovejoy preferred to avoid studying men's motives because he did not like what he saw of them; he turned "textual positivist" when he surmised that the thinkers were impelled by lowly and coarse motives. Historical materialism was unconvincing to him because it did not explain why his own generation had rebelled against philosophical idealism. Certainly no change in the American capitalist system explained why the idealism that had been the postulate of the 1890s was rejected within the next twenty years. And the one thinker in his time who tried consciously to articulate the philosophical counterpart to socioeconomic tendencies, John Dewey, seemed to Lovejoy to misdirect himself into the crudest fallacies. Why, then, had his own generation moved from idealism to realism? Had the distribution of psychological temperaments changed from what had prevailed among the generation of his teachers, Royce and Howison? Lovejoy never ventured an answer in his own autobiography.

What he would have thought of such novel methods as the study of the statistical frequencies of words and metaphors is an open question.

Through all the turmoil of generations, classes, parties, the world wars, and the contest between democratic and totalitarian societies, between capitalist and communist systems, Lovejoy remained the most imposing figure in the history of American academic freedom. His integrity was of a timeless kind that would not be subordinated to any political or tactical considerations. More than any other person, he was the prime mover behind the American Association of University Professors. It was characteristic of the man that at the outset of his career, at the age of twenty-eight, he was prepared to sacrifice his job simply and solely to protest what he regarded as a violation of academic freedom. Yet he refused to dramatize his role or act the academic prima donna; and above all he utterly rejected what he regarded as a leftist myth—that American capitalism was the implacable enemy of academic freedom. He rejected Veblen's view that the teaching of the social sciences in American colleges "reflect[s] unduly the interests and views of a single class." He argued not only that the greater gifts to American higher education have usually been "notably exempt from formal restrictions upon freedom of teaching," but that the privately endowed universities assured their faculties academic freedom more than did many state institutions. He felt that "at the close of the third decade of the twentieth century, freedom of thought and speech in universities is growing wider and less insecure."

I heard the story of the creation of the AAUP from Lovejoy himself in June 1960. During a visit to the east, I telephoned him in Baltimore, and he invited me to his lodgings. We had recently been in correspondence over some studies of mine in the history of ideas. He greeted me warmly after these many years, and then said, "I am now blind," having overstrained his eyes a few years back. He was thinner, had a heavier beard, and sat with a walking stick beside him, but still twirled his cigarette holder. He proudly showed me the

Arthur O. Lovejoy

new paperback edition of his *Essays in the History of Ideas*, although he said with some annoyance that the back cover misdescribed him as professor of philosophy at Harvard University when it should have been Johns Hopkins. We both knew that this was probably the last time we would talk together, and he seemed desirous, as I had never known him to be before, to talk of his past.

It all started, he said, when "I was fired at Leland Stanford" over the case of Edward A. Ross, the professor of sociology who was opposed to the immigration of Chinese. Mrs. Stanford was much offended because, as she said, her husband had been "very fond of the Chinese. It was not simply that he had used them as workmen to construct his railroad." Thereupon Ross was fired. A letter was then circulated justifying President David Starr Jordan; it was intended for the public, and every professor was invited to sign it. "I was then an associate professor. I felt that the letter implied that Ross was guilty of improprieties, when all he was guilty of was offending Mrs. Stanford. 'I shall write a letter to the *San Francisco Chronicle* about this,' I decided." At that time Mrs. Stanford was evidently in a highly emotional state. "My letter was published. I was fired the next day."

Lovejoy, as I knew from his long letter in Upton Sinclair's *The Goose-Step: A Study of American Education*, actually had already resigned his post, but then was told to cease teaching at once. (All others who resigned in protest, he wrote, were either unmarried or, if married, had no children.)

It was 1901. Lovejoy, twenty-eight years old, without a Ph.D., went looking for a job. Having heard of an opening at Washington University in Saint Louis, he went east to see its president. "I found him on a rowboat off an island in Minnesota. I got the job. The experience convinced me that an organization was necessary. When I got to Johns Hopkins, I felt the time was fair. I worked two years to get it organized. For political reasons, we decided to limit membership to full professors. When we first met at Hopkins, Bloomfield was chairman. Then it took me two and a half hours to persuade Dewey to accept the presidency." Lovejoy was a bit uncertain about the date, but there was in fact a formal organization meeting in 1914.

Then he described how the AAUP undertook its first investigation of an academic freedom case. "I was going to New York for the Easter vacation to see some plays. When the train stopped at Newark, I bought a copy of the *New York Post*. There was a report that there had been dismissals at Utah University, and that a professor of English had been removed from his chairmanship; there was an allusion to Mormon influence, and resignations in protest. An editorial said that perhaps the new AAUP would advise us as to the facts.

"I had only enough money with me for a week in New York. So, after dinner, I went out to Dewey's. He was already going to bed. I asked him if he would put up the money, and get it back from the Association later, so that I could go out to Utah. Next morning, Dewey got the money from the bank, and I went out to Utah. I tried to make that first investigation and report a model. I spent more time on cases for the next few years than on philosophy."

A strong exponent of the right of academic freedom, Lovejoy also insisted just as unswervingly that the professor had a corresponding duty to uphold academic integrity. If any professor violated that commitment, Lovejoy would not plead on his behalf. It is this principle of academic integrity that would have separated him as much from our latter-day latitudinarians as it estranged him in 1914 from the German professoriat, which he had once admired. When those professors commenced signing manifestos founded on lies, Lovejoy commented in his typical style—restrained, understated, and over-qualified—in words that might well be engraved on the walls of every university library:

We have at the same time formed certain conceptions of the intellectual and moral qualities reasonably to be expected from professional scholars, above all from leaders of the profession. It has seemed

Arthur O. Lovejoy

to us that professors ought to be scrupulous in their published statements of fact, careful in their examination of evidence, and moderately acute in their discrimination of the proved from the unproved, and the decisive from the irrelevant consideration. Scholars, we have felt, ought not to believe all that they see in the newspapers, even of their own country; in reading documents published in newspapers only, they should heed rather what the document itself proves than what the headline or the editorial comment says it proves; and they should not affirm "of their own knowledge" about matters in which they have no expert competency, and with which they can have had no first-hand acquaintance. We have gone so far as to expect that trained scholars, as a class, even in times of great popular excitement, will retain something of the critical faculty and manifest some detachment and coolness of judgment; that they will exhibit a greater ability than the average man to understand how a situation appears from a point of view not their own; that they will be less subject than other men to the more frenzied forms of national feeling; and that their public utterances will be characterized by some moral elevation and dignity, and a degree of restraint.*

To Lovejoy academic freedom did not authorize the university to organize itself into a center for political activism to reconstitute society. To him the scholar had been granted the privilege of the lecture hall, the mandated audience, and the leisure and materials for research precisely because, as someone not committed to the seeking of political power either for himself or his party, his findings would be available to all, and not partake of self-interest or partisan identification. The advancement of knowledge was thus the sole ground of the university: "It is, more distinctively, the chief organized agency for the advancement of science and the canvassing of new ideas. It is the outpost of the intellectual life of a civilized society, the institution set up on the frontier of human knowledge to widen the dominion of man's mind." Lovejoy's favorite metaphor for the scholar was that of the frontiersman penetrating the unknown; he repudiated the metaphor of the scholar and the scientist as revolutionists.

* Arthur O. Lovejoy, "Professional Landsturm," *The Nation*, Vol. 99 (1914), p. 657.

Evidently Lovejoy did not feel that the right of academic freedom should be extended to provide a defense for those practicing what he construed to be sexual immorality. In 1910, when he went to Johns Hopkins, he replaced James Mark Baldwin, a man of scientific reputation who had been found in a house of ill fame. Despite the sympathetic support of such men as Josiah Royce, Baldwin had been dismissed from his post. Nor would the subsequent statutes of the AAUP have protected him in his tenure.

In the last hour of our afternoon together, Lovejoy told me of his early life and family. He grew up in New England, and was descended from a long line of farmers in West Andover, Massachusetts; the earliest Lovejoy had immigrated in the 1760s. Lovejoy's grandfather had turned to business in Boston, a carpet establishment. Lovejoy's father, born in Boston, studied medicine at Harvard, but continued his studies in Germany and there married the woman who became Lovejoy's mother. She, however, died early. His father tried to practice medicine in South Boston but "couldn't stand it." He next tried to practice in Germantown, near Philadelphia, where he met and married Lovejoy's stepmother. Then he gave up medicine and moved to Newton, Massachusetts, where he later entered the low-church ministry, resigning from the Episcopal ministry to join the Reform Episcopal.

Lovejoy's father was of scholarly mind, and taught Hebrew to clergymen in Philadelphia. Arthur himself was raised on biblical literature. "I was the only child, the only one to take it out on that my father had," said Lovejoy, with a suggestion of acerbity. His father made him learn Hebrew, and Lovejoy said that he could still remember Genesis in Hebrew. He had learned German at home. Then the family had moved to Oakland, California, and he took the oral examination for admission to the University of California. Although, when asked to name the counties of the state he knew only Alameda, he was admitted nonetheless.

Many years later, I learned from Daniel Wilson's work that Lovejoy's young mother had probably taken her life with

Arthur O. Lovejoy

an overdose of a drug used to comfort her little child, and that the father, filled with grief and guilt, then renounced medicine to return to the family's traditional vocation for the ministry. Probably these events had much to do with shaping Lovejoy's character. Despite his fondness for the romantic poets, he exerted a careful discipline over his own emotions and avoided associations that might be disequilibrating. He felt that his friend John Broadus Watson had with his extramarital romance transgressed the ethics of the academy, and he approved Watson's dismissal from the Johns Hopkins University.

Lovejoy asked me about the Philosophical Union at Berkeley, where William James had launched the pragmatic movement in a celebrated lecture, and where Lovejoy himself had spoken several times. I told him that it no longer existed and that the philosophers were mostly discussing ordinary language. He replied wearily, "That's philosophy on its last legs." Then he said: "I can't understand how intelligent people can go in for ordinary language philosophy. It has been sufficiently damned by Bertrand Russell." In his view the Great Chain of Philosophies had evidently terminated; one wished one could have found out from him, as a historian, why. Late in the afternoon, a graduate student who was serving as Lovejoy's secretary arrived to read aloud several more pages of the books that Lovejoy was preparing and revising for publication. I said my farewell to the loyal scholar who, despite his blindness, was continuing his work.

As a graduate student at Harvard Lovejoy had "picked up" the idea of the historical tracing of unit-ideas from Wilhelm Windelband's newly translated *History of Philosophy*. It suited his modesty, his skepticism, as well as his broad interests, which ranged from the history of religion to the history of science and political ideas, and to literature as the chief avenue for the diffusion of philosophic ideas. I could never put together a coherent theory of his diverse interests. Once, at his rooms in Adams House where each weekend he would have an evening with his students, I asked him whether he had gone to hear Bergson lecture when he was a student in Paris. Lovejoy replied that he had not—he had been studying cannibalism at the time. I could not quite reconcile cannibalism with critical realism and the Great Chain of Being, and I knew too little of Freud at that time to probe for a nonlogical explanation. Indeed, even if I had known more, I would have felt that a component of integrity, a quirk of reason, had somehow emerged in Lovejoy, above and beyond the trammels of the irrational.

I once saw him sitting alone near the closing hour at the Faculty Club looking through the daily papers, and we got to talking. I asked him why he had become so much interested in the history of theology, since as far as I could see he held to no theological views. He replied that religious ideas had dominated those of most human beings during the course of their history, and that therefore he was interested in them. Probably, in his shyness, he preferred not to reveal his deeper motives. His early articles in theological journals occasionally hinted at a religious longing.

Drawn as he was to the doctrine of emergent evolution, and writing some of his most brilliant articles in defense of that theory, Lovejoy still felt that such thinkers as L. T. Hobhouse and Samuel Alexander had failed, from a logical standpoint, to attach a theistic basis or conclusion to the evolutionary process. He once remarked at dinner: "One may have strong emotions about certain things, but that has nothing to do with the cogency of the argument." For a brief period, as George Boas, his warm friend and colleague for many years, tells, he was a member of a Unitarian church and "used to pass the plate," but that didn't last long. He did say that "maybe there was Something out there, at the beginning or the end."

At Johns Hopkins, Lovejoy created a center for the history of ideas which, without subsidies or secretaries, exerted a tremendous influence on the world's scholarship. For example, a few years ago, Sir Isaiah Berlin, lecturing on romanticism, spoke of his delight at discovering Lovejoy's writings.

Arthur O. Lovejoy

Lovejoy declined a permanent appointment at Harvard in 1933 because, he told Boas, Baltimore was the only place where anyone called him Arthur! He was the conscience of American scholarship, and people are rarely on a firstname footing with their conscience.

8

Yvor Winters of Stanford

GERALD GRAFF

The young are quick of speech.
Grown middle-aged I teach
Corrosion and distrust,
Exacting what I must.
—Yvor Winters,
"On Teaching the Young"

I FIRST MET Yvor Winters in 1959, the year I began graduate school at Stanford. Since I was planning to concentrate on American literature, I was told that Winters would act as my adviser. Seated at the desk in his office, Winters was formidable in appearance: in his fifties, short and squat with a very large head, the face sunburned and the hair topped by a cowlick. His eyes looked coldly at and into you, as if to cut straight through your pretensions to your essential superficiality. His appearance, combined with bits of information (and misinformation) I had had of him before coming West, thoroughly cowed me, but I tried not to show it. I inquired casually about the course in the English lyric he was scheduled to teach the coming term, and when he asked me about my preparation for it, I did my best to convey that I was not to be dismissed as your typically callow first-year graduate student. After all, had I not, in my senior undergraduate year, taken a course in poetry taught by a poet-critic and man of letters no less distinguished than Winters himself? Was I not therefore *au courant* on the essentials of the subject? So I thought, and I began to describe this course and to expound some of Professor So-and-So's ideas. But Winters was unimpressed. "Mr. Graff," he sighed with a kind of weary patience, "I teach my course according to certain fixed critical rules. . . . And Professor So-and-So's rules are not *my* rules."

Although this incident had the initial effect of cowing me further, it also stimulated my curiosity. I ended up enrolling in Winters's course that term and other courses in subsequent terms. Soon I was reading and rereading Winters's writings, talking and arguing about Winters with other students, and in general, over the four years I spent at Stanford, finding my intellectual life pervaded by Winters and his concerns. I became, in short, a committed "Wintersian"—perhaps too much so for my own good, as will be seen later. But I want to talk about the qualities that made Winters a great teacher.

I had had enough contact with the professional intellectual world before coming to Stanford to know that Winters's remark about operating by "fixed critical rules" was unusual. None of my previous teachers had tied their hands by a set of "rules," much less "fixed" ones. Flexibility, adaptability, and a pragmatic readiness to regard all approaches and points of view as potentially valid responses to a text or a situation were the qualities of mind most of these teachers had seemed to exemplify. "Insights," as they were called, rather than anything so formulaic and systematic as rules or principles, were the constituents of which literary-critical intelligence seemed to be made. Each work of literature, you were given to understand, organized itself according to intrinsic norms peculiar to it. Insight was the faculty by which you intuited these norms in each unique instance and accounted for them in critical language. Questions about whether the work was good or bad, how it fit into any larger system of values or ideas, or why you were reading the work and what you were expected to get out of it did not often arise. Above all, you were not supposed to argue with a work of literature. In general, literary discussions seemed to take for granted some undefined set of assumptions that everybody present was presumed to understand and share. To ask what these assumptions were, to ask what literature was *for*, was a risk exposing you naïveté. There was a tacit understanding that you knew what literature was for—otherwise, what were you doing here studying it?

Working within these limits as an undergraduate, I felt I had learned a good deal about literature, but I had also been left uncertain about what I was doing—to a point beyond the necessary and healthy uncertainty that is a part of any education. Looking back, I can see that this feeling was a reflection of the growing confusion about literary study itself, and that my very personality mirrored the intellectual diffuseness and indeterminacy of both the social and the educational system. I was looking for a point of view—some framework of ideas more substantial than a collection of insights with reference to which I might locate myself. Winters's talk of "fixed critical rules" sounded rigid, all right, but honest and straightforward. Here, clearly, was someone who took a position—someone who told you where he stood, so that you had a chance to figure out where *you* stood.

Winters's best courses (in literature, that is; I did not take his courses in the writing of poetry) were his surveys of the English lyric and American poetry. These were lecture courses which enrolled both undergraduate and graduate students, usually in large numbers. In both courses the poetry was read and discussed in chronological sequence, permitting Winters to illustrate a theory of historical development. According to his theory, English poetry had reached a high point of excellence in the sixteenth and early seventeenth centuries, with such masters of the plain style as Gascoigne, Raleigh, Jonson, Greville, the Elizabethan song-writers, and certain poems of Donne such as the "Holy Sonnet" that begins "Thou hast made me." Then a great degeneration had set in, due chiefly to the influence of the associationism of Locke, the sentimentalism of Shaftesbury, and, in America, the pantheistic romanticism of Emerson. These influences had led to an overemphasis on sensory imagery and emotion in poetry at the expense of the rational "motivation" of emotion. With some notable exceptions, such as Charles Churchill's "Dedication" to Warburton, F. G. Tuckerman's "The Cricket," and the best poems of Emily Dickinson, the period from Milton to Swinburne was largely a poetic disaster area. The dissolution had reached its extreme point in the French symbolists and their imitators, who sought to do away with almost all rational content in order to intensify suggestion and nuance— a self-defeating enterprise in Winters's view. Nevertheless, the romantics and the symbolists had enriched the resources of poetry by extending the possibilities of imagery, suggestion, and connotation in new ways. In certain twentieth-century poets, who employed these romantic techniques while restoring rational philosophic content, Winters saw a poetic recovery. This poetry, which Winters called "Post Symbolist," was best exemplified in certain poems of Bridges, Valéry, and Stevens. In Winter's view, it surpassed even the best work of the Renaissance plain style in its richness, complexity, and depth of awareness.

Although formulated independently, this theory has certain affinities with Eliot's theory of "dissociation of sensibility," which, in turn, echoes such earlier theories of romantic degeneration as those of Schiller, Hegel, and other romantics. "Antiromanticism," which defines the romantic mood as a kind of sickness of the soul, was an invention of the romantic movement itself. Winters's theory has the advantage over these others in being worked out more clearly and in greater detail, and it gave his courses an overall coherence and cumulative drive that deepened their effect. These courses rehabilitated the study of literary history, which by that time had degenerated into such lifeless fact-mongering that many departments were giving up on it, replacing it with the close study of works isolated from any historical context. History as Winters presented it had a shape and a dramatic plot focusing on key issues of ethics, philosophy, and epistemology. For the first time in my experience, my disparate information about works, writers, and periods began to arrange itself within an "overview." What I had previously known as a mass of discrete data, a series of isolated events succeeding one another in the gratuitous and inexplicable "revolutions" of which literary history seemed to consist, I now began to understand as a process of development that obeyed a logic which could at least be discovered after the fact. I even noticed that my reading now began to stick in my memory, whereas previously, having no scheme that could give things significance, I had quickly forgotten most of what I read.

The fact that Winters's theory of history was highly debatable—indeed, for many students, wholly unconvincing—did not destroy its value: if you were not convinced by it, you were stimulated to try to correct and improve on it. If you rejected the valuations Winters placed on the historical phases, you might still find his description of them and his account of historical change extremely useful. And even if you rejected both the valuations and the descriptions, you were forced to become aware that some sort of historical process existed, that it had a determinate propulsion, and that certain issues could give it coherence. Moreover, this historical process was a living thing that would condition your own development for better or worse, depending on your ability to understand it.

On the other hand, Winters stressed that a grasp of historical generalizations was useless if you lacked intuitive sensitivity to the concrete texture of the work. It became clear at the outset that Winters respected the primacy of "insights" no less than any of my previous teachers, and that his "fixed critical rules" were no substitute for them. Donald E. Stanford, who studied in Winters's poetry-writing classes, has said that Winters "was *the* poet-critic of our time who combined an understanding of general philosophical ideas with a sensi-

Yvor Winters of Stanford

bility almost hypersensitive in its awareness of the most minute particulars of poetic style." This combination was
grounded in Winters's theory of the unity of form and content
in a literary work. "Unity of form and content" has long
been a slogan of modern criticism, but Winters managed to
spell out more satisfactorily than others what the phrase
meant. To him every literary work necessarily advances or
presupposes some "rational understanding," plausible or not,
of its subject, and this understanding "motivates" the emotions and valuations that the work communicates through
style and technique. Thus such devices as poetic meter,
rhythm, and syntax are more than mere tecnical apparatus;
they are a kind of spiritual grammar which, like a person's
characteristic gestures and facial expressions, reflects his
whole disposition toward the world. It followed from this
that literary form is "moral," in Winters's sense—a judgment
as to how the world is to be understood and dealt with. It
also followed that the teaching and study of literature are
exemplary acts through which your own personal "unity of
form and content" is tested.

All this is a complicated way of saying that Winters as a
teacher presented a model of intense, almost priestly, seriousness about literature. That trait in itself connected him with
many of the modernist writers and critics with whom he
was so frequently at odds—and with what has come to be
called the modernist religion of literature. But Winters's seriousness—free of the incense-burning and posturing that sometimes marked the more cultish precincts of modernism—was
distinguished by the passion with which it sought to discover
a rational justification for itself and by the stringent moral
and intellectual demands under which Winters placed the
creative imagination. The New Critics (of whom Winters was
a heterodox member himself) and many others in their wake
have interpreted the unity of literary form and content in
such a way as to divorce literature from belief, or at least
to set up highly equivocal relations between the two. The
truth or falsity of the work's meaning, considered with respect

to some outside reality, is said to be irrelevant to its literary value. A poem, it is said in a bit of folk wisdom which does not seem to have declined in popularity, "should not mean but be": it may "mean," but the meaning is "intrinsic" and does not apply to empirical reality. Winters, too, held that literature is a great deal more than mere statement, and he was more interested in meanings that are communicated through suggestion than those that are explicitly asserted. Yet for him the fact that literary meaning was embodied in complexities and indirections did not excuse you from addressing questions about the validity of this meaning as a view of life.

Thus Winters took the severe position that if you professed to admire a poet while being wholly out of sympathy with his ideas, you were either deceiving yourself—that is, accepting the poet's beliefs without owning up to it—or else failing to take the poetry seriously. I now disagree with some of Winters practical applications of this position, but I think in principle he was right. Literature appeals to its readers not merely as a series of intense experiences, mythical hypotheses, or adventures on the frontiers of the psyche, but as a mode of belief that solicits conviction. This is no less true of the literature of the Absurd and the Irrational than of the literature of traditional humanistic wisdom. The absurdist's wisdom may hold that experience is all conflict, ambiguity, and irresolution, but that is itself a view of the way things are and must accept responsibility as such. To issue the creative writer a certificate of limited liability for the view he presents may appear to express deep respect for literature, but it is actually patronizing. A kind of poetolatry pervades many areas of contemporary culture, both popular and academic, which rests on the condescending assumption that the poet and his productions are terribly fragile things, like the mechanical butterfly devised by the artist in the Hawthorne tale, which may shatter at the touch of criticism. This patronizing of creativity—in reality a patronizing of the self, which our world consoles for its miseries by making it unanswerable to external controls—only betrays the trivial position to which creativity has sunk. Winters, by making demands on writers even to the point of holding what they *say* to a test of philosophic credibility, felt he was merely acknowledging the importance of the craft. If making such demands necessarily reduced the number of works you could admire, something which to many minds will always seem a needless spoiling of the fun, there were more fundamental things at stake.

Winters's view was liberating because it showed how, without descending to philistinism, the stubborn common sense of the plain man might stand up against flashy but untenable literary ideas. It thus restored in the unsophisticated student a sense that his previously acquired knowledge, experience, and common sense might not be completely worthless. For example, Winters had little use for the theory—which has become even more popular recently—that one of the functions of literature is to supply "fictions" that make tolerable the inherent senselessness of life by imposing a humanly agreeable meaning on things. In his book, *The Sense of an Ending*, Frank Kermode speaks of literature as giving "fictions of concord" which, if only momentarily and precariously, reconcile us to the otherwise unbearable pointlessness of reality. We understand these fictional "paradigms" to be purely imaginary constructions, Kermode implies, yet we "make use of them" somehow as a means of ordering our experience—as if the usefulness of these paradigms were not vitiated by our awareness of their arbitrariness.

Winters was at once too shrewd and too naïve for such sophisticated credulity, as this ironic embrace of fictions may be called. He was shrewd enough to see the futility of trying to satisfy a hunger for metaphysics through ideas admitted to be fictional—a recognition that underlies his critique of the later poetry of Wallace Stevens. Winters would have agreed with the observation of the contemporary philosopher E. M. Cioran that "a value we know to be arbitrary ceases to be a value and sinks into a fiction. With fictions there is no way of instituting a morality, still less rules of behavior in the present." On the other hand, Winters was naïve enough to be shocked by the desperate lengths to which the longing for consolatory fictions could go. I recall one class in which he was lecturing on Hart Crane's *The Bridge* and came to the following lines:

> . . . *Medicine-man, relent, restore—*
> *Lie to us,—dance us back the tribal morn!*

Although he had certainly read these lines hundreds of times, Winters's face expressed genuine astonishment as he looked up from his text. "What a terrible thing to say!" he said. He meant that not only was it wrong to ask to be lied to, but it was terrifying that one should be driven to surrender one's intellectual integrity.

Winters's own poetics of rationality afforded little comfort. His critics are mistaken when they read his appeals to "reason" as attempts to reinstate a tidy universe of neoclassical certainties. Reason and intelligibility for Winters were precarious, always in danger of being overwhelmed by unreason. He never went in for the literary *machismo* that measures writers by the amount of disorientation with which they can claim acquaintance. Nor did he speak in what Theodor Adorno has called "the jargon of authenticity," the pretentious vocabulary of anguish perfected by those whose risky transactions with the Abyss frequently lead to academic fortune and tenure. Nevertheless, the dissolution of the ego, the encroachment of solipsism, and the inhuman indifference of the natural world are recurrent themes in his poetry. Winters's emphasis on reason, order, and control of the emotions was a counterforce which he set against his own powerfully romantic temperament. In Philip Rahv's rough-and-ready differentiation of American writers into Redskins and Palefaces, Winters lines up more closely with the Redskins than a cursory understanding of him suggests.

Winters followed the formal style of teaching—the written-out lecture delivered from an elevated podium and frequently consisting of lengthy passages from his own critical works.

Yvor Winters of Stanford

This way of teaching has come under fire recently—and often for good reasons. But it can be effective if the lecturer's reading of his material is clearly alive rather than simply a mechanical process. And it helps if he has the gift of departing from his text at intervals with pertinent and lively illustrations, anecdotes, and ad-libs. Winters had a distinctly low estimation of the dramatic and performing skills. "Actors," he once wrote, "are always unimportant and their qualities are unimportant, and it seems foolish to devote so much attention to them." Yet Winters was himself an excellent performer. He could hardly be unaware that the "corrosion and distrust" he was directing at established opinions and reputations shocked and discomfited a sizable proportion of his audience, and his style was calculated for such provocation. One of his most memorable performances for me was his polemical lecture on Emerson's philosophy in his course on American poetry. He had compiled a stack of Emerson quotations on large file-cards, which he read and proceeded to demolish in sequence. The effect was devastating. However strong your admiration for Emerson, it could never be quite the same after hearing Winters's lecture. But the climax came when Winters paused in his demolition momentarily and looked out at his listeners, as if anticipating their response. "Oh, by the way," he said, "please don't tell me that I'm taking Emerson's statements out of context. . . . In an Emerson essay, there *is* no context."

But I do not wish to put too much stress on the negative in talking about Winters as a performer. What made his lectures remarkable occasions were his readings of poems. All the intensity and passion of his commitment to the art of poetry came across in these readings, most especially when he read certain favorite passages, such as the final stanza of Stevens's "Sunday Morning." The first time I heard him read this stanza was in response to a student who had challenged him to give some example of poetry that passed his test. He recited it from memory, achieving an effect of extraordinary profundity:

She hears, upon that water without sound,
A voice that cries, "The tomb in Palestine
Is not the porch of spirits lingering.
It is the grave of Jesus, where he lay."
We live in an old chaos of the sun,
Or old dependency of day and night,
Or island solitude, unsponsored, free,
Of that wide water, inescapable.
Deer walk upon our mountains, and the quail
Whistle about us their spontaneous cries;
Sweet berries ripen in the wilderness;
And, in the isolation of the sky,
At evening, casual flocks of pigeons make
Ambiguous undulations as they sink,
*Downward to darkness, on extended wings.**

In an appreciation of Winters's poetry, Robert Lowell wrote that his poetry passed Housman's test—if you think of it while shaving you will cut yourself. This was the sensation Winters's reading of verse inspired. Even students whose ears in those days were attuned to the jazz-accompanied rhythms of the coffeehouses up in San Francisco were amazed at Winters's power.

Winters described his style of reading as a kind of "restrained but formal chant," a method he defended against more histrionic styles of "dramatic declamation." This defense of formal reading reflected the good dialectical principle on which Winters based his call for strict forms in literature: without a discoverable norm, deviations from the norm become meaningless. The self-conscious violence and disjunctiveness in much modern experimental verse fails to achieve its effect, he argued, since it establishes no norm which would make its departures significant. Winters stated his arguments in an essay called "The Audible Reading of Poetry" in his *The Function of Criticism:*

I have been told that this method of reading makes all poems sound alike, but this can be true only for those persons to whom

---

* Copyright 1923 and renewed 1951 by Wallace Stevens. From *The Collected Poems of Wallace Stevens.* Reprinted by permission of Alfred A. Knopf, Inc.

Yvor Winters of Stanford

all poems sound alike in any event, or for whom essential differences are meaningless. The virtue of the method, on the contrary, is that it gives each poem its precise identity, and no other method will do this. . . . The kind of reading which I defend is equally appropriate to a song by Campion or to an epic by Milton. Any poem which cannot bear the impersonal illumination of such a reading or which requires the assistance, whether expert or clumsy, of shouting, whispering, or other dramatic improvement, is to that extent bad poetry, though it may or may not be a good scenario for a vaudeville performance.

This stress on impersonality, which is fundamental to Winter's conception of proper reading, is another characteristic that links him, despite himself, to the literary generation of Eliot, Valéry, and Joyce. The disdain of high modernist writers for personal self-expression has come to be viewed as frigidity. But at its best, the attitude represented a kind of heroism, a transcendence of triviality. The paradox of these strategies of impersonality lies in the force and pungency of individual personality that they permitted to appear. Winters, in achieving his ideal of impersonal reading, read poetry like nobody else.

Those who got to know Winters personally—as I did to an extent in my last year—found him willing to set aside the authoritative manner he presented to his classes and to the readers of his criticism. This suggests there may have been an element of playacting in his public gruffness. He was often playful about his formidable reputation as a literary pugilist and outlaw. I use these terms advisedly, for Winters was a close follower of boxing, fond of analogies between the art of the ring and the art of poetry, and some people perceived a resemblance between his critical intransigence and the swagger of the western hero—or villain, depending on your point of view. This latter association was made more plausible by Winters's love of the American West. There was certainly a trace of the cowboy myth in many of the folk tales then circulating among Winters's students. According to one of the best of these stories, a crazed student, driven to a frenzy by a series of Wintersian dismissals of his literary idols, went to Winters's home and, on being admitted, produced a pistol and announced his intention of doing away with his tormentor. Winters, so the story goes, stared at the man coldly from his armchair, then said quietly, "Go ahead and shoot." Instead, the student launched a stream of insults and profanity. "Winters," he said, "you're the rottenest, lousiest, meanest, most inhuman son-of-a-bitch ever to hold a job in an American university," or words to that effect. Winters's glare never wavered. "I've known that for the last twenty-five years," he is said to have replied, draining his adversary of whatever may have been left of his resolve. I do not know if this incident actually took place, but the self-judgment is characteristic. I would like to think that Winters relished the drama of the showdown.

But finally, I believe, Winters would have preferred to forgo his role of the stern moral conscience of American literature. He paid for the rigor of his judgments with bitter isolation from the centers of literary prestige—no laughing matter to him. And there was a basic gentleness in his nature that went against his penchant for antagonism and contention. If he seemed eager for combat, it was not because it gave him pleasure but because he thought it his obligation to live up to the standards he had set himself, standards he believed to be impersonal, and I believe he was as hard in his judgments of himself as in those of others. As the lines I have used as my epigraph suggest, Winters exacted his "corrosion and distrust" because he "must," not because it gratified him to do so. This invocation of an impersonal imperative, which many of his enemies assumed to be mere fanaticism, was grounded in his view that only by aspiring to such an imperative can judgment save itself from self-indulgence. The point is, Winters accepted the consequences of his choice.

I do not want to imply that Winters had no defects as a teacher. Like many powerful minds, he tended to overwhelm a student's resistance, turning him into a duplicate of himself. I do not mean to say that he permitted no disagreements, which would be untrue; but you had to be tenacious to disagree with him, and to do so successfully you had to think through the issues as carefully as he had—a requirement few students could meet. When I began to have my own classes at Stanford, I found myself not only repeating Winters's theories and opinions, but aping his mannerisms, safe in the assumption, or so I imagined, that freshman students would not recognize their source. I copied the tone of studied weariness with which Winters introduced an adverse judgment, and the formula, "I confess I am just a bit *tired* of hearing, . . ." and so forth. Outside class, I made myself insufferable by detecting "the fallacy of imitative form" in my friends' literary tastes and behavior, and by offering triumphant predictions of eventual oblivion for their favorite contemporary writers. In my writing, too, I copied all the master's strokes, affecting a tone of authority without bothering to earn it and mistaking solemnity for seriousness. I recall coming home to the Midwest one summer with a long essay I had written, which I showed to an old friend. He was appreciative, but he could not help remarking that, judging from the tone of the piece, it might be entitled "Reflections at Sixty."

Winters's intense passion for paring things to the essentials, his impatience with what seemed of merely transitory interest, set an example of nobility that every student should experience but that he will imitate at his peril. "The important thing is not action in itself," Winters wrote in *The Function of Criticism*, "but the understanding of action. . . . Life is full of action; we can see it about us and read of it in the newspapers; we are too much involved in it ourselves. It is the raw material of generalization." This must be seen in context: a defense of the use of generalized language in poetry against the prevailing taste for a poetry of "immediate experience." But these statements do reflect a disquieting weariness with the concrete level of experience, a wish to get on to the loftier plane of the universals: "There comes a time in the lives of some men," Winters continued in the same passage, "when the spectacle is no longer informative but the theory is packed with meaning." Whether this attitude represents classic wisdom or a deadening embrace of finality depends on the use that is made of it. In Winters's defense, it can be noted that he was by no means alone among writers of his generation in disdaining the messy, confusing distraction of modern life—and also that he too, in his poetry, appreciated the necessity of dramatizing the contingent and inessential realm that he wished to transcend. But whatever the validity of the attitude, there has to "come a time for it," as Winters's own statement implies. It is an attitude, in other words, that no young person can adopt without succumbing to the most hollow posturing.

Edmund Wilson, in his dedication of *Axel's Castle* to Christian Gauss, paid tribute to his former teacher as "a master of criticism who has taught much in insisting little." Yvor Winters, it might be said, was a master of criticism—and of poetry—who taught much in insisting a great deal. Obviously, to regard Winters as a great teacher is not to suggest that his way of going about the job is the only right way. But I think that in our increasingly scrambled intellectual environment, teaching according to the mode of "insistence," without reduction or vulgarization, is more and more necessary. The fact that students no longer acquire the rudiments of an intellectual identity and a point of view from family, church, and other local institutions may initially stimulate them to intellectual rebellion, but the long-run effect is docility—docility to fashionable intellectual pieties. A teacher like Winters provides a model of critical dissent enabling the student to gain a perspective on the ideas that surround him.

Of course, a university or a department in which everybody was an Yvor Winters would probably be unbearable. But a university or a department without a Winters, without somebody who stands for the type of demands for which Winters stood, is certain to be sterile.

9

John William Miller

GEORGE P. BROCKWAY

JOHN WILLIAM MILLER taught philosophy at Williams
College from 1924 to 1960; and for the next eighteen years,
until his death on Christmas Day 1978, he talked philosophy
with his former students, for whom his house was always
open and to whom he wrote marvelous and marvelously voluminous letters, some more than a hundred pages long. Until
a few months before his death he had published only four
essays, one in an undergraduate magazine and all of them
more or less technical; yet he taught and left detailed notes
for vigorous and original courses in epistemology, aesthetics,
ethics, the history of philosophy, logic, metaphysics, the philosophy of history, psychology, and the state.

At one time he held the informal record of having the largest
number of former students doing graduate work in philosophy at Harvard, but he derived special satisfaction from his
continuing association with those who became historians, doc-
tors, lawyers, and businessmen. He said that history was the
history of thought; at the same time he felt that businessmen
were doing the work of the world and that one of the weaknesses of intellectuals—he thought they had many weaknesses—lay in their supercilious indifference to such matters.
He took pride in the familiarity with cost accounting he had
gained in his father's business.

The Williams senior class regularly voted him the teacher

"whose personality has influenced you most" and frequently "best lecturer." The yearbook was three times dedicated to him—once while he was a visiting professor at Minnesota, in celebration of his imminent return to Williams.

Miller was a tall, large-boned man of unfailing courtliness. A favorite word with him was "presence," by which he meant proclaiming one's thought in one's actions and accepting in one's thought the implications of one's actions. His own presence was powerful and immediately felt by all his students. He made none of the usual plays for popularity. His classes did not start with warm-up jokes, nor did he make regular-guy references to football games or house parties. He demanded decorum in his classrooms; if you slouched or put your feet up on the seat in front of you, he made a sharp impersonal comment on the meaning of courtesy. You didn't do it again.

Early in his career, he had the misfortune to find himself in competition with the senior man in his department, who wrote him several letters, which he preserved, of ambivalently avuncular advice on his teaching. From these it can be inferred that even as a very young man he made extraordinary demands on his students, and that they responded enthusiastically by following him to his office and to his home for long extracurricular discussions, often of matters barely touched on in class.

Anyone calling on him in his office or his home was greeted with a formal but warm handshake and an assurance of welcome. Almost immediately, with little or no small talk intervening, conversation would begin on a question that had been exercising him or his visitor. At appropriate hours something to eat or drink might be offered; in his younger days it could have been homemade wine. At the end of the session he would gravely thank the visitor for breaking up his "routine," when all around him piles of uncorrected examinations and term papers testified to his resistance to routine.

For him the method of philosophy was Socratic. One started where one was—local control, he called it—and proceeded to articulate the implications. Sophomore empiricists, of whom there were always many, were asked what they could possibly mean, on their premises, by "no" and "not": "Can you *see* no elephants?" Sophomore dogmatists, who were equally many, were led to understand the occasion of skepticism in the clash of dogmas. His senior logic course started with a question: "What sort of universe would a logical universe be?" He was perhaps happiest when some student, imbued with the pluralism of William James, replied, "A block universe." Then a dialogue would begin, eventually involving the entire group, which rarely exceeded ten or twelve in the prewar years when Williams mustered fewer than a hundred and fifty seniors. In a heady hour that frequently continued past the class-ending bell, students would be led to say and see that logic is inherently incomplete, implying continuums at both ends and so the possibility of, and occasion for, new discoveries. A logical universe would be similarly and—to use another of his favorite terms—constitutionally incomplete. Since logic, moreover, is a study in connections, a logical universe would be intraconnected and articulated—in short, very much like the universe we know and not a block universe at all.

To say that students were stimulated by such discussions would be a colorless understatement. I remember especially my first formal introduction to the idea of cause, which ended with Miller's writing on the board the conclusion that "Universal causation is the refutation of mechanism." For anyone like me, and indeed for most "literary" undergraduates of that day, who had hitherto learned quietism from Hardy or Housman, such a conclusion was shattering.

The demands Miller made of us were not merely intellectual. "There is," he said, "just one quality in every man which he must change at least once; he must change his philosophy." He continued: "only in the discovery of some fatal threat to himself in the framework of his inheritance can he discover freedom." Volumes could be written with this dictum as a text, but here it will serve to indicate that he saw philosophy as an enterprise involving the whole man in inescapable ways. To change one's philosophy was no light matter, and he treated students in their turmoil with the most delicate respect.

With undergraduates he was no missionary for a Millerian point of view, and he was proud of his success in directing attention to problems rather than to his answers. Philosophy did not, he said, offer information about the world that could be proved or disproved and memorized, as one could prove or disprove and memorize Boyle's Law. Beginning students were therefore frequently puzzled. They were used to being told what to believe. In other courses they learned that the Corn Laws were attacked and defended for specific reasons that could be underlined in the textbook, that osmosis worked in a certain way, that Leonardo had unfortunately painted *The Last Supper* in something other than *buono fresco*. But Philosophy 1–2 provided no answers, only questions that, once raised, would not go away. He insisted only that the questions be faced and the consequences of one's answers deliberately accepted.

His devoted students did not fall into any predictable pattern of thought. They included men who became Anglican bishops, Roman Catholic priests, Protestant clergymen, and professional philosophers of several persuasions. At a Williams College colloquium in 1978, honorary degrees were awarded to five alumni who were presidents of other colleges. When they discussed what had meant most to them in their education, it turned out that all had studied under Miller and all remembered him vividly. "He was," one said, "a person who frightened me and thrilled me." Another said that his choice of a career came from Miller's "having challenged me and pushed me to the wall."

Miller was not in any way indulgent of his students' whims. Agreement was not compelled, but understanding was required. No one got a high mark for denying free responsibility and simultaneously asserting morality. At the same time no one got a high mark for regurgitating lecture notes. Miller gave very few high marks anyhow. He happened to preserve the record of one course's grades; it shows only five A's in two sections totaling seventy-five students, and this was a postwar class, when the "gentleman's C" was no longer fashionable.

The courses varied from year to year, partly because they were to some degree shaped by the problems brought by the students, and partly because Miller himself was always alert for new insights, always searching for new ways to express old ones. His bibliographical notes for Philosophy of the State, a one-semester course he offered to seniors, are on two hundred five-by-eight cards. His notes, queries, and more or less detailed studies of particular topics occupy several hundred pages in notebooks, in blank examination books, and even on the backs of cardboard posters (he cut these in half and found them convenient to write on when held in his lap).

In spite of his immersion in the history of philosophy, and although he was awesomely well read in all the humanities and the sciences as well, he was not a scholar in the ordinary sense and did not consider himself one. Of many of his contemporaries he read only enough to catch the drift of their thought. "It is," he wrote, "always difficult in dealing with the history of philosophy to demonstrate that a figure in a standard textbook ought to be in the textbook. There are those who would stop the story with St. Thomas, and others favor John Locke, holding, with James, that philosophy goes around Kant, not through him." As for himself, he was particularly impatient with the various analytic and positivistic schools. That their essentially ahistoric positions should be in the ascendant in his time no doubt aggravated the feeling of isolation to which he, like many undergraduate teachers, was prone. In any event, his study of the past was not in search of arguments or debater's points. To one correspondent he wrote: "Give me *your* views. I can quote authorities, too, but it won't get us anywhere because my authorities are your follies. Authority in thought means to me what must be taken into consideration, no more. But, I should say that I think anyone who ventures into thought must be taken into consideration."

The senior man in the department called himself a critical realist and had written several books on the subject. Miller had studied under Josiah Royce and with special intensity under William Ernest Hocking, and in defending their idealism against the realist attack came to a more comprehensive understanding of their weaknesses as well as those of the attacker. The result was a lifelong study of epistemology. He early came to the conclusion that the ancient problem of universals and the equally ancient problem of appearance and reality had no solutions on passive terms, that a passive observer was a self-contradiction, and that the consequences of active observation were profound and pervasive. Act, actuality, acting, action became central words in his lexicon.

A hasty reviewer of Miller's book *The Paradox of Cause and Other Essays,* noting this trend in his thought, oddly mistook him for a follower of Dewey's instrumentalism. But Miller was concerned with the conditions of action and with the self-maintenance of those conditions. His ethics considered how it was possible to do any deed at all. His logic considered how it was possible to make a meaningful assertion.

Though all of his students were exposed to his thought—for he lived by talking—it is fair to say that none of us came close to encompassing it. There were at least three reasons for this.

The first was that his thought was truly original. Nothing in our previous training or experience prepared us for it. We were predisposed to misunderstand, to fail to see. I still have my notes for Phil. I. His position is substantially there in those notes, which I thought I understood, and I didn't see it at all. I didn't even begin to see it until two years later, and now, forty-five years later, I still rediscover points I dutifully but uncomprehendingly made note of then.

He knew he was breaking new ground—there was no false modesty about him—but he did not appreciate how difficult it was for others to follow. It was difficult for professional philosophers no less than for laymen—and this quite apart from a professional's commitment to his own point of view. He said, no doubt overstating the case somewhat, that only Hocking, among professionals, showed interest in his essay "Accidents Will Happen" when it was first published in the *Journal of Philosophy*. Ten and fifteen years later he was puzzled and even hurt that "History and Humanism" and "The Midworld" seemed to meet considerable incomprehension when he read them before the Harvard Philosophy Club. In recent years he was, I know, sincerely offended that his dictum, "The universal is the form of the actual," did not find an immediate response. The first time I begged him for an elucidation, he impatiently changed the subject. He had no audience, he said, and I had to confess myself an inadequate one, though I could see that he was subtly distancing himself from Hegel.

The second reason why so much of his thought eluded us was that it was constantly developing. The admittedly clumsy term "the midworld," which will be central to a forthcoming book of his later work, was not used by him in my undergraduate days, and the distinction he made between artifacts and "functioning objects"—another clumsy term—was not defined until a few years ago. These are only two examples of many that could be cited.

Finally, none of us knew more than a part of him—because there were so many of us. He made, he said, a point of taking a man at his word. Taking each man at his word, meeting each student on his own ground, he had many grounds to cover. With one of us he would explore abnormal psychology; with another, the common law; with a third, existentialism; with a fourth, the philosophy of history; with three of us in my senior year, aesthetics. Sometimes this was done by way of directing honors work, and sometimes it led to formal courses in the catalogue, but more often it was done for the love of it. God knows we loved him for it.

In all this there was one thing he could not abide: debating.

In his essay "Idealism and History" (included in *The Paradox of Cause*), he writes: "The practice of teaching philosophy by argument is widespread. But any such procedure is the plainest evidence that nothing necessary can result. . . . There is no conventional philosophy, but only the free discovery by the individual of his own reality through a wholly free activity." Again, in "History and Humanism," he says, "For I do think it is at last a matter of exhibition rather than of abstract argument." Nietzsche's superman, he remarks in "Utopia and the State," "can be tamed, because he can be argued with." Any of us who tried quickly found that Miller himself could not be tamed.

Sometimes he expressed his aversion to debate with terrifying ferocity. I remember him once terminating discussion of a point by turning on the friend who had been arguing for it all evening. "No," he said abruptly. "No. It's no good arguing. I *hate* what you're supporting." I have been shown letters he wrote to others castigating their arguments in terms that make you gasp, and I have received one or two such letters myself. It is probable that some good men were thus driven away—to their loss, and no doubt to his, too. In a possibly autobiographical comment in "Accidents Will Happen," he writes, "There are beliefs, moods, conflicts, attitudes which seem impervious to modification." Certainly there were situations in which his usual tact and courtesy were unpredictably overridden.

It was not that he would not suffer fools. In my sophomore year I worked out a monstrous amalgam of Unitarianism with Hardyesque determinism. Aglow with foolish enthusiasm, I sought him out in his office and read him my manifesto. He listened gravely, managed to find something to comment on in the midst of my absurdities, and sent me away with the feeling I had been taken seriously. And indeed he would take seriously any student who showed even the most misconceived willingness to grapple with his own thought.

But of course Miller was not all solemn seriousness. He enjoyed laughter at his own expense. He told with relish how a camping companion, the then assistant dean (there were only one dean and one assistant dean in those innocent days), called him the Prince of Darkness. He appreciated the campus pun that identified him as the Phantom of the Apriori (like many who respect language, he enjoyed puns). His favorite actor was W. C. Fields, who could make him laugh until the tears came, his hand held over his mouth in a characteristic gesture. He loved Gilbert and Sullivan and could quote long passages from them. He himself had a secret talent for light verse and once recited for us a naughty ballad he had composed while in the ambulance service in World War I; so far as I know this has nowhere been reduced to writing. It was on a beer picnic in Flora's Glen (previously celebrated as the inspiration for Bryant's "Thanatopsis") that several of us first began to know him. Many years later he suggested that his book be dedicated "To the Williamstown Utopian and Beer Picnic Society." With some misgivings I suppressed the tribute.

For forty years I tried off and on to get him to let me publish a book of his writings. Several times I thought I had persuaded him, only to have him back away. Once he even signed a contract for his dissertation, but it was clear enough that his intention—and that, too, of the founder of my firm, the late Warder Norton—was merely to boost my morale as I entered the army. At the time of his retirement I put together, with the help of a friend, a collection that contained most of the essays he ultimately published; yet still he hesitated.

In a letter that became the essay "Functioning Objects, Facts, and Artifacts," he wrote, a year before his death, "I have promises to keep and cannot keep them all." Then he quoted the seventeenth-century poet James Graham:

> He either fears his fate too much
> Or his deserts are small
> Who will not put it to the touch
> To win or lose it all.

Having once put it to the touch, he was ready to do it again. Just before his death he was working again on the idea of nature. He remarked that there are only two "philosophies"— the philosophy of history and the philosophy of science. He had advanced far beyond his dissertation topic, The Definition of the Thing, but the problem was not fundamentally different—only greatly evolved.

He wrote incessantly, more often than not letters he didn't send or essays he never quite finished. Several of the latter were typed by his students and circulated in a sort of *samizdat* and eventually included in the one book he published in his lifetime. He was much concerned with style, sometimes contending (falsely) that he had none and sometimes that philosophical discourse had none. These contentions were variants of his notion that philosophy was a one-on-one affair. Nevertheless, Miller left at least a dozen drafts of the start of the first chapter of a book on the philosophy of history. He proposed a rough outline in a letter to me and made notes, sometimes extensive, for the succeeding chapters. These are brilliant and will be published, but they also intensify our regret for what might have been.

As I reread what I have written, I see that I have described the ideal teacher in the ideal undergraduate college. I'll not back away from that. I was awakened and stimulated by other great teachers—the late David Brown, then also of Williams, chief among them—but my life was permanently shaped by Bill Miller. I can name almost three hundred other students whose experience was similar, and for each one I can name there must be several I have not had contact with. Miller's influence on us was through his presence; his presence resulted from his taking us at our word and insisting that we take him at his word. He was generous, not merely with his time but with his thought. His thought was deceptively simple, but for anyone who can grasp it, nothing will ever be the same again.

Of all the men of his time whom I have known, he was the wisest, and justest, and best.

10

Ruth Benedict

VICTOR BARNOUW

IN THE SPRING of 1941, I took a course on Social Organization of Primitive Peoples given by Ruth Benedict at Columbia University. In those days graduate students in anthropology were not expected, as they usually are now, to have taken various prerequisite anthropology courses as undergraduates, for few such courses were then offered. Except for Ralph Linton's Introduction to Anthropology, I had no background in this field; so during my first semester in the fall of 1940 I was rather lost—learning phonetics in one course, archaeological methods in a second, bodily measurements and identification of bones in a third. I also attended the Linton-Kardiner seminar on Psychological Analysis of Primitive Cultures. None of these courses had any relation to any of the others, apart from the fact that they all had to do with human beings.

Consequently, in my second semester I had hopeful expectations for Professor Benedict's Social Organization course. Perhaps an authority on cultural integration, as she was, could help to pull these disparate fields together. It turned out, however, that much of the course dealt with the analysis of kinship systems. As homework assignments, the students were given lists of kinship terms from particular societies and were required to figure out the systems from the terms. I used to meet with a fellow student to draw up kinship charts and to prepare for the next session. We laughed helplessly over the outlandish complications of these systems, trying to figure out why an Omaha mother's brother's daughter should be called "mother." We did not enjoy these assignments, although they were, of course, educational. In later years I met anthropologists who were more interested in kinship systems than in anything else and for whom this field was an absorbing chess game. I doubt that Ruth Benedict had the same sort of enthusiasm for this specialty; she was not interested in intellectual puzzles for their own sake but saw kinship as part of the basic data we had to acquire.

Kinship, however, was not the only subject that Professor Benedict explored in her course, and in the long run I did, after all, get some of the sense of integration I sought. Not only did she relate social organization to other aspects of life, but she connected the study of primitive societies with the modern world. This was because part of the course was based on Emile Durkheim's *The Division of Labor in Society.* Durkheim had argued that as division of labor has increased in the course of sociocultural evolution, there has been a concomitant increase of social solidarity that binds together the interdependent units of the social order. The "mechanical" solidarity found in more primitive, undifferentiated societies tends to suppress individuality, while the "organic" solidarity of more complex societies, marked by division of labor, facilitates it. Law was Durkheim's index of solidarity. He claimed that primitive societies are governed by repressive law which keeps people in line through punishment, while in complex societies there is more emphasis on restitutive law, which seeks to restore order rather than to penalize its violators.

Ruth Benedict admired Durkheim's work but criticized him for overemphasizing law and ignoring other forms of social control. She was more aware than Durkheim had been of the great variation in primitive societies. She provided a rough typology and spoke of atomistic societies, corporate societies, and hierarchical societies. The first of these groupings included the simplest hunting-gathering societies with the least social and political integration. As examples Ruth Benedict cited the Eskimo and White Knife Shoshone, peoples who live in small bands with only a sexual division of labor and almost no political leadership.

Most primitive societies, according to Benedict, are corporate societies, which have more social cohesion than do atomistic ones. Corporate societies are often organized on a segmentary basis. Each unit in such a system has the same constituents as the others, such as a chief, a shaman, patrilineal kin, and so forth. When such homologous units are in interaction, there is a danger of conflict between them, but they may be bound together by periodic rituals such as the Sun Dance of Plains Indian societies. Benedict saw present world states as existing in a comparable segmentary system. Each homologous unit has the same institutions—a central government, its own legal machinery, monetary system, and so forth—but the relations between the units are anarchic.

In hierarchical societies, as in the caste system of India, there may be organic solidarity in Durkheim's sense, for there is a division of labor which allows the society to capitalize on unlikenesses, whereas social responsibilities are often tied to higher status.

Although I was stimulated by all this, I found Professor Benedict's course very confusing; there was so much that was new to me. And while Benedict was an impressive teacher, she was not a particularly good lecturer. She spoke hesitantly and uncertainly; there was no drama in her lectures. But she was fascinating to watch because of the beauty of her face, with her reflective, dreamy-looking eyes. She was gray haired, tall, and thin. Her hands were surprisingly large and rough skinned, perhaps a heritage from her early years of poverty on a farm in upstate New York. When I became her student, Ruth Benedict was in her mid-fifties. She was famous, having published *Patterns of Culture* seven years before, but although she had great dignity, she had not altogether overcome the shyness of her earlier years.

Judging from the autobiographical sketch and journal selections which Margaret Mead published after her death, Ruth

Benedict (née Fulton) had a most unhappy childhood and adolescence. She frequently gave way to violent temper tantrums and bilious attacks throughout childhood, and these were succeeded in later years by fits of depression. Despair, stoicism, and ambition are expressed in many passages of her journal. The ambition was first directed toward poetry and literature, and she planned to write a series of biographies of gifted, restless women—Mary Wollstonecraft, Margaret Fuller, Olive Schreiner—a project never completed. Between 1911 and 1914 Ruth Fulton taught at girls' schools in California; in 1914 she married Stanley Benedict, a biochemist. It is said that she longed to have a child and was crushed to learn that she could not have one. After this discovery, at the age of thirty-two, she turned her energies to anthropology and began to study with Franz Boas, whose trusted colleague she later became.

Professor Benedict's reverence for Boas was evident to her students, for she often referred to him in her lectures and required us to read his rather dry theoretical articles. He had stopped teaching at Columbia a few years before I arrived, but he could often be seen in the corridors of the anthropology department, where he came to have tea with Ruth Benedict and other disciples. Seeing his scarred, ancient face made me feel that I was close to the historical roots of anthropology.

Another historical old-timer was Bronislaw Malinowski, who once came to address the anthropology faculty and graduate students at Columbia. Although he was a great man, he was a nervous chain-smoker, who made some poor jokes on this occasion and kept referring in his lecture to Linton and Benedict as Ralph and Ruth, as if he were trying to be very American. As he talked, he abruptly turned to me (I was sitting in the front row) and asked, "What was Bob's last name?" Somehow, I guessed whom he had in mind. "Do you mean Robert Lowie?" "That's right. Bob Lowie."

Lowie, and Alfred Louis Kroeber also appeared occasionally at Columbia. So those of us who were graduate students were able to feel some continuity with these pioneers. We knew

Ruth Benedict

that anthropology was a young field and that Boas had taught the first generation of professional anthropologists in the United States. We would be part of the next generation.

This was a time when the Columbia anthropology department gave emphasis to the field of culture-and-personality, or what is now called psychological anthropology, dealing with the relations between the personalities of individuals and their cultures. Franz Boas had given such investigations his blessing, having advised Margaret Mead on her choice of problem for her fieldwork in Samoa, while Ruth Benedict drew upon Boas's voluminous Kwakiutl data in describing Northwest Coast culture in *Patterns of Culture*. Boas wrote an introduction to that book and a foreword to Margaret Mead's *Coming of Age in Samoa* (1928).

In *Patterns of Culture* Benedict proposed to view cultures as wholes and expressed a philosophy of cultural relativism. For her, each culture was a special case, a unique configuration characterized by a particular set of values and world-view, although some cultures were held to be more integrated than others. Some have claimed that this relativistic approach is at odds with the analysis of cross-cultural regularities, since it does violence to institutions to take them out of context for comparative purposes. Characterizing Ruth Benedict's views in this way, on the basis of her published work, may be correct enough, but she never remained static. Her whole course on social organization involved cross-cultural comparisons, and, as I shall show later, her emphasis on these brought about a major change in the organization of my Ph.D. dissertation. I once talked about Benedict with Jules Henry, who had been her student at Columbia a few years before my time. He was pleasantly surprised to learn that she had discussed Durkheim's *Division of Labor*, for she had never dealt with it when he was there.

Another new development was Ruth Benedict's concept of social synergy, put forth in the same course and also in a course on Primitive Religion. Social synergy refers to the combined effects of social institutions within a society, when they reinforce one another and lead to greater social cohesion and to the release of a greater than purely arithmetical sum of energy. Benedict argued that atomistic societies are low in social synergy, while more corporate societies have high synergy. This concept of hers was presented only a few years after the publication of *Cooperation and Competition Among Primitive Peoples*, edited by Margaret Mead. Ruth Benedict preferred to speak of high and low synergy rather than of cooperation versus competition, for competition may be valuable in stimulating high synergy. Ruth Benedict never published anything on this concept, but it illustrates her continually inquiring, speculative tendency.

I remember one bit of advice she gave her students in this course. She wanted us to read ethnographies with empathy, to project ourselves into the culture being described, and to imagine what that life must be like. I suppose we all do that to some extent, but normally we are too lazy when we read to make the extra effort that Ruth Benedict urged upon us.

Apart from Ruth Benedict's courses, the field of culture-and-personality was also represented at Columbia by the Linton-Kardiner seminar. Ralph Linton came to Columbia in 1937 after Boas's retirement and became chairman of the Anthropology Department. He was said to get along badly with Ruth Benedict, but their interests were similar in many ways. Linton collaborated in the seminar with Abram Kardiner, a psychiatrist who had been analyzed by Freud and who coined the phrase "basic personality structure" to refer to the personality patterns shared by members of a particular society as the result of passing through a common gamut of childhood experiences. This Freudian emphasis on childhood distinguished the Linton-Kardiner school from Benedict's more culturological approach in *Patterns of Culture*. Another new characteristic, in keeping with the clinical background of Kardiner's training, was the use of the Rorschach test and other projective techniques in fieldwork. (The Rorschach test involves showing subjects ten semistructured inkblots in a particular sequence; the subject tells what he or she sees in the blots.)

The usual practice in the Linton-Kardiner seminar was for an anthropologist who had recently returned from the field to give an ethnographic account of the community where he or she had worked, including the presentation of life history materials. After brooding over this information, Kardiner would present an analysis from a modified Freudian viewpoint, particularly noting relationships between the society's institutions and the basic personality structure. If there were recurrent personality patterns among the members of the society, there should be some evidence of such patterns in the Rorschach protocols, which would supplement the impressions of the fieldworker and the deductions of the psychiatrist who analyzed the life history material. Then, if these different kinds of evidence appeared to converge, as in Cora Du Bois's study of Alor, that would greatly strengthen the validity of the conclusions reached.

Since I was enthusiastic about this approach, I was happy to learn in 1944 that the Columbia Anthropology Department planned to send me to northern Wisconsin for a summer's fieldwork on Chippewa (or Ojibwa) Indian reservations. One session of the Linton-Kardiner seminar had already been devoted to the Chippewa, and Ernestine Friedl had presented the ethnographic picture, including information about child-rearing practices. However, Kardiner felt unable to come up with his usual analytic synthesis, since he thought there was not enough life history material to draw upon. My assignment, then, was to collect some Chippewa autobiographies and more Rorschach protocols to add to those already acquired. Before going to Wisconsin in the summer of 1944, I accordingly took lessons in Rorschach administration. Ruth Benedict was assigned to be the chairman of my thesis committee.

Although she supported my efforts in other respects, Benedict did not approve of my giving the Rorschach test. When

I mentioned studies which had made productive use of the Rorschach, she was not impressed. "They are not testing the *people,*" she said severely. "They are testing the *test.*" From her point of view, it was no doubt useful to test the test by giving it in different cultural contexts, but that would not lead to better understanding of the people involved—which could only come from soaking oneself in the culture, so to speak. However, I did give the test to Chippewa subjects in the summers of 1944 and 1946.

I still consider the Rorschach test to be a useful instrument, but I must admit that this has become a minority view. Benedict's adverse judgment has since prevailed. Many psychologists assert that the test lacks validity and reliability, and anthropologists have generally stopped using it in their fieldwork. One of the first anthropologists to use the test in a non-Western culture was Jules Henry, who collected Rorschach protocols in the native language from Pilagá Indians in South America in the late 1930s. But he was one of the first anthropologists, in a symposium in 1955, to claim that the test is a waste of time, echoing much later the view of his former teacher.

From 1944 to 1946 Ruth Benedict was on leave from Columbia. After my two summers of fieldwork I had a thesis committee which lacked my major professor. However, I started writing my dissertation, occasionally showing chapters to the two other committee members, who were encouraging enough. The model I chose for imitation was *The People of Alor* (1944) by Cora Du Bois, about half of which consisted of eight autobiographies. The rest contained an ethnographic description with emphasis on the life cycle and analyses of the biographies, Rorschachs, and children's drawings.

My dissertation about acculturation and personality among the Wisconsin Chippewa started off with about fifty pages of ethnohistoric data based on the reports of traders, missionaries, and Indian agents in northern Wisconsin before the modern period. Then there were an ethnographic account and four life histories, which made up my principal field data.

Ruth Benedict

Rorschach analyses were also included. All told, the manuscript ran to nearly six hundred typed pages. My two committee members seemed to think well of my efforts, but we had to await the return of Professor Benedict for a final assessment. I felt quite pleased with what I had done.

The meeting with my adviser, when it came, was therefore a shock. Ruth Benedict looked up from my manuscript and said gravely, "You have to write a *thesis*," emphasizing the word. "We all have to type up our notes when we come back from the field. You've done that. But now you have to write a *thesis*." She went on to say that my dissertation lacked a comparative focus. It dealt with the Chippewa Indians and how they had responded to acculturation and contact with the whites, but there was no information about how other American Indian groups had adjusted to contacts with whites and faced comparable situations. Hence one could not tell whether there was anything distinctive or diagnostic about the reactions of the Chippewa. Finally, Professor Benedict said to me, "Your manuscript is much too long; it should be only half its present length."

I was stunned. Later I was able to see that Ruth Benedict's advice to me was excellent, but at the time I was mainly aware of the fact that I had to begin all over again. In those days I had the use of a cubicle in the Columbia Library. I began to work there, going through the literature about such Plains tribes as the Dakota and Cheyenne. From my reading I could see that the Cheyenne had responded quite differently to white contact than had the Chippewa. Chippewa social organization was atomistic, in Benedict's terms, in contrast to the much more cohesive, corporate social order of the Cheyenne. In summertime the large Cheyenne camp circle sometimes included as many as two or three thousand persons. There were a council of forty-four chiefs, soldier societies with policing functions, and collective activities like the buffalo hunt. In Benedict's terms, this was a society with high social synergy. The Chippewa social order, on the other hand, was more scattered and decentralized, and their acculturation proceeded in a more gradual, piecemeal fashion than that of the Plains tribes where the organic social order was disrupted by white contact and the decimation of the buffalo. In contrast to the situation on the Plains, I argued that there had been continuity in Chippewa personality patterns from the past to the present, for the atomistic social order had not changed very much on modern reservations.

I sometimes visited Professor Benedict's book-lined office to discuss these matters. On the walls were two framed photographs of stern old men with lined faces. One was her mentor, Franz Boas; the other was a Blackfoot Indian chief. She had spent the summer of 1939 with a group of graduate students doing fieldwork among the Blackfoot. This gave us some common ground, for I had come to know some Blackfoot Indians while attending the Winold Reiss Art School in Glacier Park, Montana, for three summers in the 1930s. Blackfoot Indians served as our models, and between poses I sometimes wrote down lists of Blackfoot words elicited from them. I also went to sun dances at Fort Browning and across the border in Canada.

"The Blackfoot always dance on a knifeedge," Ruth Benedict once said to me with a smile, as if we shared a common secret. It was a curious, vivid remark that remained in my mind. I didn't know exactly what she meant by it, and couldn't decide whether it was a profound insight or just an odd comment. Unfortunately, I lacked the courage or initiative to pin her down further. Another time she remarked seriously—indeed emphatically—"The Chippewa cannot kill the father!" She suggested that they could be contrasted with the Eskimos in that respect. In trying to understand cryptic remarks like these, I told myself that Ruth Benedict was a poetess as well as an anthropologist (between 1928 and 1930 she had published some poems under the name of Anne Singleton), and although she had the disciplined mind of a scientist, she sometimes spoke in the Delphic language of poetry.

When my revised dissertation (half the length of the original draft) was submitted to my adviser, she gave it her qualified approval. The comparisons of the Chippewa with the Plains

Ruth Benedict

tribes had strengthened it, and much unnecessary exposition had been deleted. My Ph.D. thesis was later published as Memoir 72 of the American Anthropological Association. I doubt that my first draft would ever have seen print.

It is clear that I owe much to Ruth Benedict. Later, in my book *Culture and Personality* (1963), I wrote in criticism of *Patterns of Culture*. Some might see this as disloyalty or impertinence on the part of a former student, although it was in keeping with the critical tradition of the Boas school. After I began to teach anthropology, I used to give lectures on the Pueblo Indians, including the Hopi and Zuni, drawing upon that marvelous document, *Sun Chief: The Autobiography of a Hopi Indian* (1942) and on the writings of people like Elsie Clews Parsons and Dorothy Eggan, who had worked in the Southwest. I found many discrepancies and contradictions in Ruth Benedict's account of the Pueblo Indians. She depicted the Hopi and Zuni as mild-mannered Apollonian people who prefer an orderly, predictable round of life, in contrast to other American Indians, who share a Dionysian set of values and seek unusual psychic states in vision quests, hallucinogenic drugs, and alcoholic intoxication. Benedict claimed that Pueblo repugnance to liquor was so strong that drinking had never become a problem on their reservations. But there is much evidence of excessive drinking among them, especially around the time of the Shalako festival. Benedict stated that Pueblo Indians never whip their children, but contradictory testimony about that is found in Sun Chief's autobiography and elsewhere. To point out these discrepancies—and there are others—does not necessarily invalidate Ruth Benedict's generalizations about the integration of Pueblo culture, but it seemed clear to me that she had tried too hard to find evidence for a consistent world-view underlying all aspects of Pueblo life. The same may be said of her description of Kwakiutl culture, which overemphasizes the violent, Dionysian tenor of Kwakiutl life.

More recently, I was brought back to Ruth Benedict's work, this time to her two-volume *Zuni Mythology* (1935), when I used the Zuni material for comparative purposes in my *Wisconsin Chippewa Myths and Tales and Their Relation to Chippewa Life* (1977). Contrasts between Chippewa and Zuni mythology are particularly interesting, since they involve contrasts between an atomistic social order and a corporate one, between a hunting-gathering and a horticultural people. Chippewa origin myths recount the wanderings of a lone culture hero, Wenebojo, and his episodic encounters with different animals, while Zuni mythology concerns the movements of groups and migrations of clans, which are never mentioned in Chippewa narratives. In keeping with the Zunis' horticultural subsistence basis, their emergence myth tells how the first people made their way from below the earth up to the surface, aided by the sons of the Sun. It is characteristic of this settled farming people that particular localities—mountains, rivers, and villages—are often mentioned in their narratives, while Wisconsin Chippewa tales hardly ever mention specific places. Thus the Chippewa tales are expressive of a nomadic hunting-gathering way of life. Moreover, their casts of characters are small. Many of these stories are about two or three people living alone: a man and his nephew, a boy and his grandmother, a brother and sister. The Zuni dramatis personae is larger and more complex. Also, the Zuni also have an abundance of courtship tales. In volume I of *Zuni Mythology* there are thirty such tales, which make up nearly 180 pages, and courtship themes also occur in eleven other stories. By contrast, there are very few courtship tales in the Chippewa collection. Moreover, there is a mildness in the Zuni narratives, as Benedict points out, with some exceptions in witch tales and stories of violent revenge. In general, the folklore does support Benedict's claim for the Apollonian character of the Zuni.

There are many kinds of relationship between a teacher and student. Ruth Benedict's response to Franz Boas was one of worshipful commitment. In a moving letter to him, toward the end of his life, she wrote: ". . . there has never been a time since I've known you that I have not thanked God all

Ruth Benedict

the time that you existed and that I knew you." More often, I think, a student's response to a teacher is marked by currents of resistance or rejection as well as by the willing acceptance of guidance. Even in Ruth Benedict's case, the kind of work she did turned out to be quite different from that of Boas. It may be agreeable for a student to have a teacher whose views are the same as his or her own, but in that case nothing fundamentally new can be learned. When their outlooks differ, it may be unpleasant for the student to reexamine things from an unfamiliar perspective. In such cases the relationship between teacher and student, like that between parent and child, is marked by ambivalence.

I was aware of some ambivalence in my feelings toward Ruth Benedict. I was awed by her knowledge and by her beauty and graciousness, but I was often puzzled by her lectures and mystified by her occasional cryptic remarks. To me she was an enigmatic person, not easy to assess. Yet her influence has been long lasting. I have criticized some of her writing, but when I return to her work, I find that I still learn from it.

11

John Crowe Ransom

ANTHONY HECHT

I HAVE NEVER, except in childhood, belonged to a secret society, though I was to learn much about the thrills of initiation from *Tom Sawyer* and *War and Peace*. And if those novels had not supplied my needs I might have divined a good deal one spring in New Haven, coming home with my wife from a party on the very night the Yale clubs had chosen to induct new members. There were the blindfolded postulants, robed in mortuary black, standing at well-spaced intervals, pale, mute, and submissive, occasionally moved to a new position along the street by wordless, solemn-faced members. The awe! The fatuity! And the whole, soundless spectacle closely observed by a small group of black teenagers, children who would never go to Yale, much less be invited to join such an elite. I was that evening no more than an outside observer, certainly more like the blacks than like the members or initiates. But during one year of my life, in my early twenties, I was a sort of adjunct member of a group, the more exclusive for having no formal shape or membership, its exclusions determined by instinct and a high destiny, like those that once characterized Calvinist New England. We few, we happy few, were English major students of John Crowe Ransom at Kenyon College.

I was a special student, not a degree candidate, having al-

John Crowe Ransom

ready obtained my B.A. but feeling, after nearly three years in the army, by no means ready to take up graduate studies. It had been in the army, and from Robie Macauley, a fellow soldier and a Kenyon graduate who was later to take over the editorship of the *Kenyon Review*, that I first heard of Mr. Ransom. And when at length I applied for admission on the GI Bill, it was Robie who suggested that it would assist my acquaintance with and understanding of Mr. Ransom if I read some of his work before heading for Ohio; and he especially recommended *The World's Body*. As an undergraduate I had read literary criticism—Eliot, Richards, Empson, Wilson, Winters, Blackmur—and I thought I knew generally what it was like in its best, as well as its most trying, features. Its aim was not only to be persuasive but definitive, and its tone therefore at times assumed the stiff and constipated grandeur of "objectivity." To have come to Mr. Ransom's prose with such expectations was to be completely undone. What was I to make of such paragraphs as these, from the preface to *The World's Body?*

It is my impression that the serious critic should serve a sort of apprenticeship with his general principles. But the studies can scarcely afford to be pursued in any way except in the constant company of the actual poems. About ten years ago, when I did not know this, I wrote out and sent to a publisher a general aesthetic of poetry, a kind of Prologomena to Any Future Poetic, thinking that the public needed one, as perhaps it does. The intelligent publisher declined my project politely and returned my mansucript, which the other day I had the pleasure of consigning to the flames.

But for the animating idea which informed my little effort of that time I have no repentance. I was concerned with urging that it is not a pre-scientific poetry but a post-scientific one to which we must now give our consent. I suppose I was rationalizing my own history, for I came late to an interest in poetry, after I had been stuffed with the law if not the letter of our modern sciences, and quickly I had the difficulty of finding a poetry which would not deny what we in our strange generation actually are: men who have aged in these pure intellectual disciplines, and cannot play innocent without feeling very foolish. The expense of poetry is greater than we will pay if it is something to engage in without our faculties. I could not discover that this mortification was required.

When T. S. Eliot, in his second Milton essay, begs of us that "it will, I hope, be attributed to me for modesty rather than for conceit if I maintain that no one can correct an error with better authority than the person who has been held responsible for it," we are led to expect an acknowledgment of error, but are to learn in due course and by splendid, sophistical devices that there has never been any error at all; that there has merely been a "person who has been held responsible" for one: poor, calumniated Mr. Eliot. In telling us in Milton I that it was dangerous and "unwholesome" to read Milton, and in reversing himself twenty-five years later in Milton II, he tells us, he was *right in both cases;* like the physician who first takes you off and then puts you back on carbohydrates. And we are asked to attribute this revelation to Mr. Eliot's modesty. Educated as I was in defensive strategies of this sort, I found the genuine modesty of Mr. Ransom's paragraphs startling. It was more than merely the candor of the anecdote about burning his manuscript; it was the unassuming personableness of this prose. The word "impression" in the first sentence, where virtually any other critic I had read would have inserted "assertion" if he had dared; the courtly, hyperbolic and ironic charm of "I could not discover that this mortification was required," allowed a subtle, recognizably personal voice—gallant, old-fashioned, deliberate, witty, self-mocking, and generous—to appear right there on the page where I had come to expect nothing but inexorable proofs or *ex cathedra* declarations. And my first reaction was to wonder whether such stuff could possibly go into the making of literary criticism. Over the years it has been my growing impression (you see how valuable such influences can be) that Mr. Ransom's prose most nearly resembles the prose of George Santayana in its rhythmic and rhetorical elegances, its quirky delight in the unexpected word, its worldly and

John Crowe Ransom

polished skepticism, and its warmth of spirit. I never met Santayana, but these traits were native to Mr. Ransom in person as in print.

To have become one of that little group of Kenyon students in the mid-forties was not merely to have joined them under Mr. Ransom's remarkable tuition; it was also to have been assimilated into a hieratic tradition, a select branch in the great, taxonomic structure of the modern intellect, in which we were the direct and undisputed heirs not only of Mr. Ransom himself but of all our distinguished predecessors who were his former pupils. These ranged from legendary young men of stunning mental powers who had graduated just too soon for any of us to have met them (about one of these it was affirmed that he wandered the campus reading extremely difficult texts in philosophy from which he tore out the pages and threw them away after a single, hasty, but sufficient perusal) to such as Peter Taylor and Robert Lowell, who were just coming into their fame, and beyond to Allen Tate, Cleanth Brooks, and Robert Penn Warren, who had discernibly changed the course and character of American letters. We were aware that Mr. Warren's nickname was "Red," and took the liberty of so referring to him. The responsibility of following in so august a procession we regarded as a difficult, historic burden, just sufficiently mitigated by our private sense of being among "the anointed."

Let it be said at once that Mr. Ransom was altogether innocent as well as ignorant of our fatuities. And even had he known about them, his natural courtesy would probably have forbidden him to notice them. He was, I believe, the most courteous man I have ever known, and not a little of what I learned from him I learned through his supreme and kindly tact in ignoring my follies. Mr. Ransom's silences and omissions of comment were triumphs of educative eloquence, and no small part of their triumph lay in the fact that no more than his verbalized comment were they ever allowed to wound if that extremity could be prevented. I'm sure such prevention was not always possible. We were all either secret or confessed poets, as well, of course, as being close readers, exegetes, speculative aestheticians, and literary ontologists. And Mr. Ransom found himself exposed to our compositions from time to time. He had no formula for dealing with our ineptitudes, but he had a little arsenal of critical words of great subtlety that must often have stood him in good stead. Of these, one of the most powerful was the word, "bold," usually incorporated in the phrase, "that's mighty bold," applied either to an entire poem or some central detail or metaphor in it. A young poet, hearing Mr. Ransom comment thus upon his work, might easily feel that his poem exhibited a breath-taking and unprecedented originality of so striking a sort as to reorder the whole tradition of Western literature, as Eliot suggested in a famous essay when he wrote, "what happens when a new work of art is created is something that happens simultaneously to all the works of art that preceded it. The existing monuments form an ideal order among themselves, which is modified by the introduction of the new (the really new) work of art among them." Naturally such newness, such novelty, such flying in the face of established expectations and received procedures required a rash intrepidity, a last-ditch faith in oneself and one's own poetic instincts upon which all poets must surely rely in the end. Still, it often happened that late in the afternoon after an audience with Mr. Ransom in which he had pronounced on the boldness of some poem, and after the understandable euphoria had abated, one came to realize that a possible meaning of "bold" might be "impudent," and that one's work might be not so much a reordering of the great tradition as an affront to it.

He was rather short in stature, and when I came to know him, in his late fifties, his hair was already white as swan's down. When the first warmth of spring arrived in Gambier, Mr. Ransom would sometimes turn out in a powder-blue sports jacket with matching socks with white clocks in them, and white shoes. He was by no means a dandy, but he was a dapper and sprightly dresser. He was also a pipe-smoker, but used a rather sweet-smelling, aromatic tobacco such as

John Crowe Ransom

I suspect a true smoker would find lacking in seriousness, though it could not fail to be agreeable to those around. And as part of his smoking paraphernalia he always carried with him in his right-hand trouser pocket a thick clutch, a sort of beaver-dam, of strike-anywhere kitchen matches. It seemed to me that some grace or special providence never allowed these matches to ignite as they rubbed constantly against one another in that pocket. But I was often anxious in his behalf. He had an especially beautiful and gently modulated tenor voice, with the special delicacy of his regional Southern speech to which he brought a lilt of his own, characterized by his tendency to end his sentences on a rising inflection, as though they were more questions than statements, and conveying thereby a considerate tentativeness. This highly personal, idiosyncratic, and musical mode of speech he employed both in normal discourse and in the reading of his own poems. And we, his students, vied with each other in imitating Mr. Ransom's readings—especially of "Captain Carpenter." There was something wonderfully incongruous about the gentleness of Mr. Ransom's voice and the martial bluster of that poem.

And his effect in class was naturally colored by the singularity of that voice. His class behavior is difficult to describe except to say that I first mistook it for diffidence. Mr. Ransom did not lecture, he inquired, and he invited the class to join in his inquiry. This was nothing so symmetrical, so antiphonal as a Socratic dialogue; nor as manifestly stacked in favor of the teacher. Neither can I remember his uttering any "memorable pronouncements," or even point with accuracy to a particular thing I learned in my studies with him. But I soon began to see that what I had first taken for diffidence was his firm and principled refusal to usurp our interests from the primary position of the poetic text under consideration. He had neither the need nor the inclination to exhibit himself, to parade his learning or his perspicuity. And with characteristic generosity he was curious enough about us to suppose that we might, any one of us, discover something in the text that had escaped his notice. He was almost always disappointed in that hope, but it had the healthy pedagogical effect of inviting us to be diligent, cautious, and thoughtful.

Mr. Ransom was exceedingly fond of games, and in recalling this fact about him I am struck by the recollection that Frost, Wilbur, and Auden all have found in game-language apt and useful metaphors for the art of poetry. More striking still is the fact that in the first chapter of his highly suggestive work, *Homo Ludens*, the great Dutch historian, Johan Huizinga, describes play and games in terms no reader of Ransomian critical prose could fail at once to recognize.

> Play is superfluous. It is never imposed by physical necessity or moral duty. It is voluntary, free. It is disinterested.
>
> It stands outside the immediate satisfactions of wants and appetites, indeed it interrupts the appetitive process. . . . It thus has a place in a sphere superior to the strictly biological processes of nutrition, reproduction and self-preservation.
>
> It contains its own course and meaning.
>
> It at once assumes fixed form as a cultural phenomenon. Once played, it endures as a new-found creation of the mind, a treasure to be retained in memory. It is transmitted, it becomes tradition.
>
> All play moves and has its being within a playground marked off beforehand either materially or ideally, deliberately or as a matter of course. Just as there is no formal difference between play and ritual, so the "consecrated spot" cannot be formally distinguished from the playground. The arena, the card-table, the magic circle, the temple, the stage, the screen, the tennis-court, the court of justice, etc., are all in form and function playgrounds, i.e., forbidden spots, isolated, hedged round, hallowed, within which special rules obtain.
>
> It creates order, *is* order. Into an imperfect world and into the confusion of life it brings a temporary, a limited perfection. Play demands order absolute and supreme. . . . The profound affinity between play and order is perhaps the reason why play . . . seems to lie to such a large extent in the field of aesthetics. . . . It is invested with the noblest qualities we are capable of perceiving in things: rhythm and harmony.
>
> It is an activity connected with no material interest, and no profit can be gained by it.

This final observation, as applied not to games but to poetry, would not signify in Mr. Ransom's understanding any sar-

John Crowe Ransom

donic comment on the social and economic status of the poet in the modern world but simply would indicate the absolute non-utility of the poetic object.

At the time I knew him Mr. Ransom was an avid baseball fan, an insatiable player of bridge, and if there was any fierceness at all in his character he was said to have expressed it in his playing of croquet. But I best remember being invited with other students to his home on a number of occasions to play a game then classically known as *The Game*, but more commonly called "charades." I remember it best because I was once forced into the humiliating admission that I could think of no way of representing some small, transitional word, some preposition or conjunction in the phrase or sentence that it had fallen my lot to enact. And in an altogether. unassuming way, without a hint of the pedagogue about him, Mr. Ransom briefly indicated that the categories of grammar perfectly expressed the names, nature, behavior, and relationship of things as they exist in the actual world. This correspondence had never occurred to me before. And for quite some time after, I was astonished to think of the parts of speech as the very ligaments and sinews of the world itself.

And at first I did not know what to make of his poems, their arrant archaisms, sophistications, and opulent Latinities that contrasted with such shameless, nursery-rhyme simplicities as:

> *To me this has its worth*
> *As I sit upon the earth**

An early taste for the witty lyrics of Cole Porter and Noël Coward had persuaded me that rhymes, like poems themselves, should seek to be original, and in any case avoid the obvious, unless in parody. And what was I to make of the phrase, "dainty youths," for God's sake, in a twentieth-century poem that had no homosexual or "campy" intentions?

---

* John Crowe Ransom, "Somewhere is Such a Kingdom," from *The Collected Poems of John Crowe Ransom* (New York: Knopf, 1963), p. 66.

One had to come to terms with such oddities if one was not to stint or mitigate one's loyalty. But of course it was always possible to point with delight and gratitude and, if necessary, with defiance, at *the real thing:*

> *The larks' tongues are never stilled*
> *Where the pale spread straw of sunlight lies.**

To follow those matchless lines with the remorseless abstractions of the next two:

> *Then what invidious gods have willed*
> *Him to be seized so otherwise?†*

at first seemed to me an exercise in perversity, but gradually came to be seen as a poetry of high rhetorical flourish. All of us in that little group grew to be very touchy about Mr. Ransom's fame and reputation, and this was perhaps partly due to the smallness and isolation of Gambier. One could so easily step off Kenyon's hill and out of the loftinesses that obtained in its halls into the quite unliterary cornfields and cow pastures of rural Ohio, that "other Thrace." We appointed ourselves Mr. Ransom's champions, of which he was mercifully unaware. He had, of course, no need of us, even though we thought he did when some particularly obtuse or literal-minded critic ventured to take him to task. And to this day the memory rankles of an especially foolish lady who once remarked to me that she found the lines about the cries of the geese in "Bells for John Whiteside's Daughter" sticky with tasteless sentiment:

> *Her wars were bruited in our high window.*
> *We looked among orchard trees and beyond*
> *Where she took arms against her shadow,*
> *Or harried unto the pond*

---

* John Crowe Ransom, "Man Without Sense of Direction," *The Collected Poems,* p. 79.

† John Crowe Ransom, "Man Without Sense of Direction," *The Collected Poems,* p. 79.

John Crowe Ransom

> *The lazy geese, like a snow cloud*
> *Dripping their snow on the green grass,*
> *Tricking and stopping, sleepy and proud,*
> *Who cried in goose, Alas,*
>
> *For the tireless heart within the little*
> *Lady with rod that made them rise*
> *From their noon apple-dreams and scuttle*
> *Goose-fashion under the skies!**

She thought it too adorably cute that there should be a "goose-word" which was the equivalent for "alas," and she seemed to suppose that the "alas" was the geese's complaint at being disturbed from their noon apple-dreams, and herded and marched so vigorously about. She was totally unaware that all the regret in that "alas" was not for the geese themselves but for the young girl, "For the tireless heart within the little/ Lady" which was not due to beat for very much longer. And the geese knew this because they are prophetic creatures. Their cries once awakened the soldiery of Rome at a moment when the invasion of barbarian hordes was imminent, decisively saving the city and civilization itself. Their divinatory faculties were ever after remembered with honor, at least until my interlocutor brought up the subject. On that occasion I ventured not a word in the poem's defense, and she may to this day rejoice in her faulty and trivial sense of it.

I find it very difficult in retrospect to say exactly what it was one learned from Mr. Ransom, to point to particular notions or propositions. One found it possible, and sometimes necessary, to disagree with him—private, interior disagreements about details in the interpretation of poems, even of general philosophic premises—without losing any respect for him by such silent dissent. For one learned from him, not facts or positions, but a posture of the mind and spirit, a humanity and courtesy, a manly considerateness that inhabited his work as it did his person. And one learned to pay a

---

* John Crowe Ransom, "Bells for St. John Whiteside's Daughter," *The Collected Poems*, p. II.

keen attention to poetic detail. Probably there were those moments when he indicated to us a truth so simple and profound it seemed not so much to be his own statement as the sudden, objective appearance of the truth itself, independent of its utterer; a truth so elemental and undeniable as to resemble the statement reported by Kenneth Clark in *Landscape Into Art:* "Constable said that the best lesson on art he ever had was contained in the words, 'Remember light and shadow never stand still.'" All the flux of history and Heraclitus, Demeter and Persephone, our jubilant triumphs and intolerable defeats are figured in that anonymous advice.

12

Hannah Arendt

PETER STERN & JEAN YARBROUGH

WHAT MADE Hannah Arendt a great teacher? She seemed to violate many of the canons that make for effective teaching. She had no special pedagogical methods and no set doctrines. She made no attempt to attract students through polemics or flattery, and she did not try to entertain them. In fact, the format of her lectures probably sounds quite dull: for the first hour or so she would read from a fully written set of notes; then, for the remaining forty minutes, she would answer questions.

This format—reading a prepared lecture and opening the class to questions for a prescribed period of time—can, in the wrong hands, discourage learning. A dense, closely argued paper on complicated, unfamiliar material can be difficult for students to follow, and Arendt's lectures were no exception. What was unusual was that she recognized this and made her lectures available to students after class ended, to reread and take notes from. Setting aside a large block of time for questions at the end of the lecture also presents hazards. For one thing, there is an inevitable loss of spontaneity: questions that seemed appropriate during the lecture may, by the time it is over, strike the student as not worth the trouble. Or this procedure can give rise to the opposite problem: students may ask questions simply because the time is available and they want to hear themselves talk. Even when the questions are germane, handling them one after the other, with no thematic link, can be difficult for the lecturer. Each answer must be specific enough to clear up a particular student's problem while remaining sufficiently general to hold the class's attention.

This rather old-fashioned method of teaching—formal, rigorous, and full of potential pitfalls—Hannah Arendt mastered and transformed. She did so not by any special technique, but through the sheer brilliance and originality of her ideas and the mysterious force of her personality. Although we tend to separate not only passion from reason but a person from his ideas, Hannah Arendt presented the spectacle of their union. So her lectures, despite their being read, were lively, exciting, and sometimes overwhelming in the power and insight they expressed.

In trying to explain what made Hannah Arendt a great teacher, we must, then, say something about her as a person. This, however, is no easy task. She seemed to be made up of many contradictory traits, each of which was so greatly magnified by her enormous intensity that it was impossible to conceive of them all existing in the same person. She was warm and friendly to her students, but could suddenly end a conversation with an abrupt but benign "So. . . ." Inside the classroom and out, she welcomed debate—a "free-for-all," she liked to call it, smiling, with a foreigner's delight at being able to use American slang in this unexpected way.

Yet she could become impatient. "But, my dear . . ." she would reply imperiously, and that was that. She was generous. Although there was something slightly chaotic, even eccentric, about her generosity, the combination never failed to charm. Mary McCarthy, her close friend, captured this quality perfectly in a eulogy address: "She would press on a visitor assorted nuts, chocolates, candied ginger, tea, coffee, Campari, whiskey, cigarettes, cake, crackers, fruit, cheese, almost all at once, regardless of conventional sequence or, often, of the time of day." Hannah Arendt was also a worldly person. She

Hannah Arendt

had been around and prided herself on knowing the ropes. She was famous, knew everyone, had many friends, and, in her writings, unfashionably celebrated the virtues of worldliness. Nevertheless, she often seemed uncomfortable, awkward, and somehow removed from the world. The reason for this awkwardness, which for a long time seemed so incongruous given her tremendous energy and forcefulness, eventually became clear. Contrary to our first, and indeed lasting, impression of Hannah Arendt as a toughminded, strongwilled, and entirely fearless person, we slowly came to see that she was also shy, modest, and strangely vulnerable, never quite convinced she deserved all the attention she received.

We studied with Hannah Arendt at the New School for Social Research, where, since 1967, she had held the post of University Professor of Political Philosophy. Her classes were always packed, although not everyone attending took them for credit. Some were official auditors, students who had completed their course work and were writing their dissertations; others were former students from other universities who were now in New York and were eager to reestablish old ties. Usually there were also a few outsiders, unconnected with either the New School or Miss Arendt, who, impressed by her writings, were curious to hear her in person. But the majority were regularly enrolled students taking the course for credit, most of them in the philosophy department. The fact that a fair number came from other fields, especially political science, reflected the interdisciplinary nature of Hannah Arendt's thought.

Certain rituals surrounded her classes. About ten minutes before the lecture was scheduled to begin, the room would start to fill up. By the time Miss Arendt actually began lecturing, all the chairs were taken (room size being designated on the basis of *official* enrollments), and students who came late would have to sit on the floor or raid nearby classrooms for more chairs. On the table in the front of the room were her props: a lectern, a glass, and a pitcher of water (from which she would pour a glass when she wanted to pause for emphasis, when a new thought suddenly occurred to her, or when she was just plain thirsty). Usually she came into the room escorted by her teaching assistant and sometimes, especially during her last several semesters, by her student secretary as well. As she entered, she seemed curiously apprehensive, as if deeply troubled, and the presence of her assistants seemed necessary to reassure her. Walking slowly to the lectern, still preoccupied, she would suddenly stop, turn to the class, and nod, smile, or wave to students she recognized—her usual cheerfulness returning. She then continued to the front of the room and, reaching the lectern, would remove the manuscript of her lecture from its folder, remind us where we had stopped the week before, and then begin reading from her notes.

One of the qualities that made Hannah Arendt a great teacher was her ability not only to make ideas come alive and seem important (all good teachers possess this gift), but, going beyond this, to handle them in such a way that they evoked a vivid, tangible sense of reality—of a specific, concrete situation and man's confrontation with it—so that the ideas she discussed became one with the realities they described. What she analyzed conceptually conjured up a world of experiences we recognized even when they were not our own. In her hands, ideas were not simply steps in an argument, or abstractions divorced from experience, but the very essence of experience distilled into the language of conceptual thought.

This achievement stemmed in part from the combination of an immense literary gift with a powerful philosophic mind—always a rare blend of talents. Literary sensibility is usually concerned with capturing meaning through imagery and narrative, according to a vision of the beautiful; while philosophy, by way of logical argument, aims at what is true. It was Hannah Arendt's genius to combine these two modes. Uniting logical rigor with the use of metaphor, example, and a clear sense of the shape of a story, she helped us to grasp the central concerns of philosophy and the concrete contexts

Hannah Arendt

out of which these arose. Part of her success as a teacher, then, lay in her "gift of thinking poetically," an expression she herself used to describe Walter Benjamin's mode of thought.

Hannah Arendt's uncanny way of handling ideas so that they evoked a dramatic sense of reality also sprang from her conviction that ideas grow out of our everyday experience and they are its conceptualization, the way in which thought—as opposed to, say, poetry, or painting—attempts to discover meaning. For her, understanding an idea required discovering the concrete experiences out of which it arose and to which it referred. These experiences, while remaining ever present possibilities, usually included a historical dimension. They first occurred in the past and were noticed by thoughtful men who tried to understand and explain them. In later times, these explanations, if compelling, may become part of the general storehouse of ideas that we take for granted as simple common sense. This subtle process of transformation from theoretical discovery to common sense—everyday knowledge, broadly speaking—leads to two results. On the one hand, experience becomes more abstract and less natural, since to an ever greater degree it is shaped by previous interpretations. On the other hand, to the extent that these interpretations preserve important experiences that in later times are ignored, or no longer clearly understood, they help orient us in the midst of confusion when we seem to have lost our way. In either case, whether emphasis falls on the present or on the past, understanding ideas demands tracing them back to their roots in experience.

Thus, for example, Hannah Arendt attempted to pin down what authority means—a central concept in political philosophy that has gradually fallen into disfavor—by analyzing contemporary and past experiences where its use seems most plausible and by reexamining what philosophers, both ancient and modern, meant by it. Authority, she argued, signifies the voluntary acceptance of rules that are more than advice and less than commands. It necessarily implies obedience, yet—and this is the crucial point—obedience that is not coerced but is willingly accepted. In the political realm, which was the focus of her concern, authority manifests itself in those institutions where legitimacy is sustained without recourse to instruments of force or violence. In the United States, the Supreme Court is the outstanding example of this phenomenon. As Alexander Hamilton put it in *Federalist* No. 78, the Court "has neither the power of the purse or the power of the sword."

However important a role the concept of authority plays in politics and political theory, several factors have helped make its meaning increasingly problematic: the liberal insistence upon absolute freedom, the conservative adherence to obedience as such, and the tendency of political philosophers to derive their standards of authority from nonpolitical realms of fabrication (the artisan fashions his product according to a pre-given model) and of the family (the male household head rules paternally without consent). To restore the integrity of authority, Hannah Arendt returned to the past, showing how Greek political experience and thought obscured the true nature of authority and how, by contrast, the Roman and American experiences illuminated it. In this complex examination, going from present-day politics to the political situation of the past, and from ideas to experience and from experience back to the realm of ideas, she vividly brought to life the significance of a much-disputed notion, the way it has changed, and why.

Her last lecture course on the will formed part of her final series of philosophical investigations aimed at elucidating man's mental faculties: thinking, willing, and judging—what she chose to call the Life of the Mind. There Hannah Arendt revealed another quality, one closely connected with "the gift of thinking poetically," that made her a great teacher. This was her talent for finding the perfect sentence, the perfect saying and passage—those that were almost epigrammatic, containing, in the fewest possible words, the core of a philosopher's meaning, and then unraveling their significance. Han-

Hannah Arendt

nah Arendt carefully collected these sayings, treating them as if they were cryptic utterances of a divine oracle, rich in meaning and embodying profound clues and lessons that indicated, if properly interpreted, the right way to think and act. They guided her reflections on every kind of issue, and she used them in various ways. Sometimes they served as illustrations, other times as steps in the proof of an argument, much as we use the multiplication table when we do math. In her writing, they often inspired and served as the connecting thread for an entire essay or a section of one. Thus her paper "Truth and Politics" analyzes the complex relation of the political realm to truth telling by exploring the old saying, "Let justice be done though the world perish." Her famous essay on Bertolt Brecht examines the political role of the poet in terms of the Roman adage, *"Quod licet Iovi non licet bovi"* ("What is permitted to Jove is not permitted to an ox"). And her acceptance speech for the Lessing Prize was concentrated on Lessing's concept of humanity in the light of his own statement, "Let each man say what he deems truth, and let truth itself be commended unto God."

Of course it was not simply Hannah Arendt's finding relevant passages or sayings that made her classes so exciting, but her analyses of them. In her discussions, she accomplished several tasks at once. She explained what the thinker meant in a particular passage, and showed how it related to his thought as a whole. But to help us understand the larger implications of the passage, she frequently went beyond the philosopher in question, contrasting his view with the opinions of other philosophers and finally with her own. Her point was not to refute but to present the greatest variety of perspectives that could be brought to bear on an issue. Not that she believed that all these positions, taken together, added up to the truth, or that they were all equally valid. On the contrary, she seemed convinced that no final answers were likely, but attempts to shed light on the perennial philosophical questions remained important nonetheless. They demanded, she told us, evoking the spirit of Kant, the highest kind of thinking, that which went beyond the limits of knowledge.

Hannah Arendt liked to use the image of Penelope's weaving to capture what was for her one of the most striking aspects of this kind of thinking: that it never reaches its goal, and so must return to its starting point and begin again. These starting points are either our own pre-philosophic experiences or the reflections of philosophers on such experiences. Both were important for her, but in the classroom the philosophic sources predominated. She was at home with the great works of philosophy, reading and teaching them over and over with undiminished enthusiasm, convinced that they still had important things to tell us; she did not believe that these writings had been superseded or had become outdated by the mere passage of time. To her the notion of philosophical progress— that we understand the fundamental questions of human life better today than they were understood in the past—was a myth, and a dangerous one at that. It bred an unhealthy neglect of the past and an unjustified confidence in the future. Having seen through the dangerous illusions engendered by belief in philosophical progress, Hannah Arendt succeeded in accomplishing the first essential task of the philosophical scholar: establishing a living relation with the old philosophers.

However, it was not only because she refused to be lulled by the false hopes the idea of progress inspires that her reading of the great philosophic texts was suffused with new life. With her teachers, Martin Heidegger and Karl Jaspers, she held that the tradition had broken down, so that it was no longer possible to transmit the teachings of the past intact and to submit passively to their authority. What this meant for her she told us in her own commemorative essay on Heidegger, "Heidegger at Eighty." Describing his effect on the post–World War I generation of German students, she wrote:

. . . thinking has come alive again; the cultural treasures of the past, believed to be dead, are being made to speak, in the course of which it turns out that they propose things altogether different from the familiar worn out trivialities they had been presumed to say.*

Seen in this light, the interpretation of old texts becomes both a sobering and a creative experience. At the same time that we can now genuinely learn from them, we are also inspired by them to think for ourselves.

Hannah Arendt's own interpretations were dazzling exercises, drawing out from a passage, sometimes from even a phrase, an unexpected wealth of meaning. From the *Gorgias*, she discussed Socrates' statement, "It is better to suffer wrong than to do wrong," and suggested this was based on Plato's view that thinking is a silent dialogue with oneself where the self splits in two. But for the two interlocutors to trust each other in the give-and-take of their joint search for the truth, there must be mutual respect, the essential precondition for which is that neither acts unjustly. Because Plato believed that thinking is man's highest activity, it follows that this mutual respect, which requires that both partners be just, is the most important consideration—more important than being admired by others, even more important then self-preservation—especially if either of these involves acting unjustly. Thus, according to Hannah Arendt, Socrates argues that it is better to suffer wrong than to do wrong because committing injustice corrupts the soul and destroys the ability to philosophize. On the other hand, Arendt wisely pointed out that this Socratic argument against acting unjustly would only convince someone who already wanted to be a philosopher. Its appeal, therefore, would be strictly limited.

In discussing Epictetus's statement, "You will be harmed only if you think you are harmed. No one can harm you without your consent," she made clear the fateful consequences of the Stoic doctrine of the will: that men can be considered absolutely free when they are in worldly bondage and, conversely, that they can be regarded as enslaved when

---

* Hannah Arendt, "Martin Heidegger at Eighty," *New York Review of Books*, Vol. XXV, No. 16, Oct. 26, 1978, p. 51.

they are politically free. Hannah Arendt showed us that this strange conclusion is not just a peculiarity of Stoicism, but comes about whenever subjectivity is celebrated without giving worldly concerns and responsibilities the philosophical recognition they deserve. To her way of thinking, Epictetus's statement has the very opposite meaning from the one he intended; rather than affirming man's freedom from the world, it stands as a constant warning against the all too human desire to want to escape from it.

Taking Cicero's saying, "I prefer before heaven to go astray with Plato rather than hold the true views of his opponents," she showed how, from a worldly point of view, a genuine sense of humanity might take precedence over even the love of truth. A cultivated mind, Arendt explained—developing Cicero's thought—eschews absolutes and extremes that endanger prudent judgment and the limited horizons men need in order to be at hime in the world. In her discussion, she emphasized Cicero's essential sanity and common sense; at the same time, however, she also made us aware of the incompleteness of this view.

In her interpretation of a particular text, in her treatment of a philosophical problem, and in her overall manner as a teacher, Hannah Arendt succeeded in the difficult art of saying something definite—taking a stand, so to speak—and yet preserving an atmosphere of openness. This is a rather unusual achievement. Although everyone celebrates the virtues of open-mindedness, especially in philosophy where the example of Socratic ignorance stands as a permanent warning against the dangers of becoming dogmatic, few teachers succeed in practicing it. And this is readily understandable, all high-sounding appeals to tolerance notwithstanding, for a teacher generally knows more about his field than his students.

Hannah Arendt held strong views, defended them vigorously, and never liked being wrong. When challenged, she could become impatient and testy. During the question period following her lecture, disagreement often became sharp, and we occasionally sensed there was a point beyond which it was useless to argue. Yet a spirit of openness prevailed, in part because of her and in part in spite of her.

Ultimately this openness was the result of Hannah Arendt's essential honesty and courage. She never failed to discuss all the alternatives, presenting them with such passion and clarity that they could seldom be entirely dismissed. Moreover, we could never forget that, according to her own understanding of philosophy, the kind of questions she chose to discuss precluded giving final answers. After Socrates, she found her favorite examples of open-mindedness among the Greek historians and poets: Homer, Herodotus, and Thucydides; even in war they knew how to praise the virtues of the Greeks or Athenians, as well as their enemies.

As Hannah Arendt's last course on the will brought out her extraordinary interpretive gifts, so too did it highlight this open-mindedness, which preserved the genuine complexity of a difficult problem. During the semester, she sympathetically examined various theories of the will, slowly and carefully developing her own position and yet all the while keeping before us the central theme of her inquiry: the question of how there can be such a thing as the will at all. For the very notion of the will seems to contradict all we know of the internal world, governed as it is by desire on the one hand and intellect on the other. And the status of the will is made still more problematic by the difficulty we have in pinning down unambiguously those moments when the will is at work. Yet the fatalist argument that denies the existence of an independent will, and argues instead that all our actions are determined, makes judgment and responsibility meaningless. Hannah Arendt pointed her own way out of these dilemmas, but she stated the problems so forcefully that no answer, not even her own, seemed entirely convincing. It was a testimony to her teaching and her extraordinary mind that she allowed this uncertainty to reflect back on her own position.

If, then, there is a criticism to be made of Hannah Arendt's teaching, it is not that she simply read her lectures verbatim or that she was dogmatic. The problem was rather that her interpretations were sometimes so idiosyncratic, so noticeably and even obviously departing from the text, that it was difficult to take them seriously as textual interpretations. Ironically, this was the other side of her interpretive genius—her ability to relate, in surprising new ways, the general and the particular, the familiar and the obscure. As we became better acquainted with her own point of view, we saw clearly enough what, perhaps, should not be surprising: her explanation of a particular passage seemed much closer to what she herself thought about an issue than it did to what the text actually said. What was curious was that her own ideas were always so fresh and illuminating that we wondered why she did not say they were her own instead of, in effect, attributing them to others. For example, she discussed Augustine's theory of the will but removed it almost entirely from its religious context, endowing it with a political relevance Augustine never intended. She brilliantly explained Kant's theory of the enlarged mentality in the *Critique of Judgment*, but then used it to argue, albeit cautiously and with reservations, that Kant intended it as part of his political as well as his aesthetic philosophy. Or she analyzed at great length the Founding Fathers' concept of happiness, which they seldom explicitly discussed, arguing that they meant *public* happiness, the joy that comes from participating together in public affairs. In so doing, she minimized their emphasis on privacy and divorced their view of happiness from the natural-rights doctrine, despite the explicit statement to the contrary in the Declaration of Independence.

For the graduate student this procedure has obvious drawbacks. Less familiar with the texts, the unsuspecting young scholar who uses these rich but idiosyncratic interpretations as a guide to a philosopher's thought can easily be misled. But as he advances, this defect is usually remedied. And the method—if indeed it is a method—has its unexpected rewards. Hannah Arendt's interpretations, original and provocative, shocked us out of our complacency and forced us to consider anew what we thought we understood. It happened that no

Hannah Arendt

matter how novel, even outrageous, her analysis appeared to us at first, we discovered after much reflection that she was never entirely wrong, that even if the philosopher in question had not explicitly developed an idea in the direction she suggested, her use of it was not simply arbitrary. She had uncovered an aspect of an issue that had been overlooked and deserved further study. The special virtue of her interpretations, then, was that they always cast fresh light on a problem, either by approaching it from a different perspective or by emphasizing elements of it that more conventional scholars had neglected. Nevertheless, this was a procedure her students could rarely imitate, since it depended so much on Arendt's own intuitive genius. Thus, as far as interpretive method was concerned, we were left to ourselves to discover the best way to approach the text.

There is, however, another explanation, one we have already mentioned in a different context, for Hannah Arendt's taking liberties with the texts. This strategy stemmed from her conviction that because the tradition had broken down, we could freely appropriate the great works of the past. Indeed, this is the only way the past can be preserved. If we do not use the past in new ways to think creatively about the future, it will simply die of neglect, having been ignored and forgotten. This, she thought, would be the worst calamity; we would lose the depth and stability that are necessary to sustain the present and guide the future. Although Hannah Arendt celebrated the human capacity for novelty, she was no destroyer. On the contrary, she wished to preserve all that was worthwhile in the past so that it might spark the desire to create greatness anew.

Paradoxically, then, Hannah Arendt's liberties with the texts grew out of her deep love of the philosophers who nourished her and for whose chances of survival she so greatly feared. In these precarious times, when genuine thought is corroded by the pedantry of experts as well as by the fear, contempt, and indifference of the masses, the interpreter's responsibility is enormous. He must explain the thoughts of the wise men of old—a difficult enough task in itself—and in such a way that the future is not stifled by excessive veneration for the past, or the past destroyed by the boredom of empty repetition, breeding impatience for the new. Hannah Arendt fully recognized this problem. When she departed from the letter of the text, her departures were never frivolous; they were informed by a profound sense of intellectual crisis and the need to foster a culture worthy of being remembered.

II

A graduate student soon learns that a great teacher is more than someone who gives memorable lectures. For if a teacher remains aloof or inaccessible to students, his lectures, no matter how brilliant and polished, eventually become somewhat tedious. Rather than being a means of sparkling intellectual curiosity and debate, they become virtuoso performances, and the teacher is transformed into a star, primarily concerned with dazzling his audience and attracting a circle of admirers. Whether a student actually learns something, and develops an abiding passion for the subject, becomes largely irrelevant. Of course Hannah Arendt was a celebrity—a scholar of international repute, surrounded by a special aura—yet in the classroom she remained first and foremost a teacher, dedicated to introducing students to the world of thought.

She demonstrated her concern for her students in ways that may sound rather pedestrian, but that were actually quite helpful and none too common. First of all, she was accessible. Despite enormous demands on her time, getting to talk to her was never a problem. She regularly held office hours after class, and would stay as long as there were students waiting to see her. Before class, we could usually catch her in her office or in the hall, and even if there was nothing particular to discuss, she would always stop and inquire, "So—how's it going?" On special occasions, such as passing an oral exam or a dissertation defense, she would treat us to dinner at one of the nearby Italian restaurants.

She was also uncommonly efficient. Letters of recommendation usually went out within a week; dissertation chapters were read in two weeks. If something was pressing—say, a fellowship deadline suddenly closing in—one could call her at home. And she was always accommodating when it came to scheduling tedious chores like an oral exam or a dissertation defense. Almost every graduate student knows, either by first-hand experience or by word of mouth, how irksome the handling of these routine matters can be when professors are not so considerate.

Finally, and perhaps most important, Hannah Arendt was encouraging. Although she did not gush, she was not afraid to compliment. She expected her students to work hard, and when she was pleased with their efforts she told not only them but her colleagues and other students as well. In reading student papers, she was never begrudging or petty; if she had criticisms, they were constructive and to the point. Here too, however, her comments could be quite idiosyncratic. She had her pet dislikes, and it was best to stay clear of them. We learned the hard way, for example, that she could not abide anything having to do with Freud. If his name was mentioned in connection with writing a paper, she would sit up, fidget, and become a bit short. Then a mischievous smile would cross her face as she quoted Karl Kraus: "Psychoanalysis is that disease of which it considers itself the cure."

Even after studying with her for several years, we found it difficult not to be nervous before seeing her. There was a certain intimidating formidableness about her, a combination of her great intelligence, experience, and learning. Moreover, she was not a calm, even-tempered sort of person who could put a student at ease. On the contrary, what was so odd was that, though forceful, she was also high-strung, uneasy, and quite unpredictable. In fact, we had to find a way to put her at ease—no easy task, especially when we were already jittery, worrying about her reaction to term papers or dissertation proposals. But after we got to know her better, she seemed to become more relaxed (as did we), and we usually found her warm, witty, and generous. Whenever we visited her in her office, she would smile, offer us a seat, and then eagerly ask about the progress of our work or our thoughts on current political events. She was an excellent storyteller, and a good, if somewhat disconcerting, listener. While a student was talking, she would hunch forward and stare straight at him, eyes intent, her forefinger curled slightly, moving back and forth against her upper lip like a metronome measuring the rhythm of her thought as it absorbed, then weighed, what he had to say. Though she listened carefully, she certainly did not mind interrupting if some thought suddenly occurred to her. What was striking in these meetings was the expressiveness of her face, which reflected her quick changes of mood; in rapid succession she might be humorous, grave, accommodating, expansive, brusque.

At the end of the semester, Hannah Arendt always invited the students in her seminar to her home. Sitting in her living room, we would spend the first hour or so in a last free-for-all—tying up loose ends and arguing with her about the issues she had raised in the course. As soon as the official discussion had ended, platters of finger sandwiches stuffed with ham, roast beef, and tongue suddenly appeared, followed by trays of deviled eggs, relishes, and cheese. Across the hall in the dining room, which housed her enormous library, a bar was set up. Little groups formed, and she scurried from one to the other, joining briefly in the conversations, then leaving to return with still another platter of food, seemingly convinced that no matter how much we had eaten it was not enough.

These gatherings brought out two of her most memorable eccentricities: she always insisted that the men tend the bar and the women serve the food, and that the men's coats go to the far bedroom while the women's hung in the front closet (where, to our surprise, she had hung a giant Kafka poster on the door). No one was ever offended by this rather old-fashioned division of labor, nor by the oddness of her banishing the coats of one sex to the other end of her apartment. In fact, it helps explain the special affection we all felt for her. For while she was at once a powerful and commanding figure, grappling in profound and startling ways with the perennial themes of philosophy, sure of herself, with the courage to say what she thought no matter how unpopular, she was also a bundle of small quirks that betrayed how strangely ill-suited she was to deal with the more routine aspects of life. Like her parties, she was a charming, wonderful blend of the conventional, the unconventional, and the old-fashioned.

III

Although officially a member of the philosophy department and although her final book, *The Life of the Mind*, was to be a work of straight philosophy, Hannah Arendt was primarily known as a political philosopher, and rightly so. Her earlier works dealt directly with political themes, and her chief intellectual aim, spelled out in her most theoretical book, *The Human Condition*, was explicitly devoted to politics. What she attempted there was nothing less than a total reevaluation of the meaning and significance of the political realm.

Now, while the goal of political philosophy—the search for the essential character of political life and the best political order—sounds respectable enough, the field is nevertheless eyed with suspicion by most political scientists. Examining the raw world of politics from the rarefied heights of philosophical speculation, asking such questions as what is justice, what is freedom, what is authority, political philosophy is open to two different dangers, which political scientists are quick to point out. On the one hand, it may become so abstract as to lose all connection with the realities of political life as we commonly know it; on the other hand, it may, under the benign guise of philosophical inquiry, of disinterested search for truth, degenerate into mere ideology, subtle special pleading for a particular political position. In other words, it runs the risk of becoming irrelevant—or of becoming too relevant, sheer propaganda.

Yet even when the philosophical approach to the study of politics steers clear of these temptations, political scientists have objected to it for three reasons. First, they argue that the study of politics must be rooted in science, not philosophy, because only science is truly objective—that is, value free. Second, political philosophy is no longer necessary because social science itself tells us what politics is all about—who gets what, when, where, and how. Finally, we no longer have to concern ourselves with abstract questions such as "What is justice?" since its meaning is now deemed to be clear: justice is equality, or freedom in equality.

In the past, the study of political philosophy suffered not only from these objections made by scientifically minded political scientists but also from the mechanical way it was taught by political theorists themselves. Students seldom read original philosophical sources and, if they did, were assigned only snippets, badly excerpted, in dull, gray, heavy anthologies, with an inadequate introduction to each selection. But in either case, rather than seriously exploring the questions these philosophers raised, the teacher presented the class with a brief synopsis of the main ideas of ten or fifteen "great thinkers" that, by the end of the semester, had become an endless catalog of meaningless arguments to be memorized for the final exam. The distinctive character of each thinker was entirely lost. Further, the political philosophers were almost always studied from a narrowly historicist perspective. It was taken for granted that present political ideas were unquestionably superior to past positions; thus the views of older

Hannah Arendt

philosophers were criticized or dismissed simply because they did not anticipate, or agree with, contemporary views. By method and example, these teachers suggested that the wise men of old no longer had anything important to teach us. Without really intending it, they had reduced political philosophy to a lifeless history of ideas.

Hannah Arendt was part of a disparate group that reacted against the deadweight of these assumptions and against the fashionable criticisms of political philosophy put forth by modern social science in general, and by behavioral political science in particular. She did so not by directly criticizing the behavioralists—she seldom attacked head-on the sterile assumptions underlying much of their research—but by force of example; that is, by doing political philosophy. In this way, its worth could be judged by criteria social scientists themselves agreed on: results. One could read Arendt's work and see if she had anything new or important to say about the great political issues of our time—revolution, totalitarianism, the welfare state—or about the perennial problems of politics: freedom, authority, law, civil disobedience, and the like, the understanding of which decisively colors, whether we recognize it or not, our opinions concerning the more immediate issues of the day. This, she believed, is one of the reasons why political philosophy is so important and deserves continued study. It sheds fresh light on issues and opinions we tend otherwise to take for granted, by exposing and examining their unacknowledged presuppositions. Moreover, political philosophy proceeds on the assumption that the fundamental political questions have not been definitively answered and concludes, unlike scientific social science, that the centrality of these questions must be acknowledged and addressed. For it insists that ultimately these questions cannot be methodologically excluded, and that, moreover, social science itself unconsciously embodies a partisan political preference and a particular philosophical standpoint.

Aware that the fundamental questions of politics were still open, and shocked by the horrors of totalitarianism, Hannah

Arendt set herself the enormous task of reexamining and clarifying the nature of the political realm, and the ways in which it had been depicted by earlier philosophers. What is unique and startling in her work is her attempt to provide a defense of politics against its critics, beginning with Plato and continuing through the nineteenth century and up to the present day. Not that she was unaware of the limits of politics, for she was quite aware of them. Yet she still believed that the typical critique of politics misses the mark because it judges the political realm by inappropriate standards, thus obscuring the profound possibilities for fulfillment that political life holds out to both the individual and the community.

Hannah Arendt's principal point, first hinted at in *The Origins of Totalitarianism* and later fully developed in *The Human Condition,* ran like a red thread through all her courses. Politics, she believed, is not simply or even primarily the domain that holds the monopoly of force, or the sphere that determines who gets what. Rather, it is the arena of excellence and responsibility where, by acting together, men can become truly free. It transcends the domains of interest and power in the usual sense by providing citizens with the opportunity of achieving a greatness and nobility that may be revered and remembered forever. Thus, for her, politics established the context for tradition and authority as well as culture and judgment in the widest sense. In developing this view, she was inspired by those relatively brief moments in history when politics achieved its purest expression: classical Greece, republican Rome, and America during its founding. During these crucial moments, men recognized the importance of the political realm and chose to take direct responsibility for it. With great insight and passion, Arendt explained her position and, in so doing, reassessed the traditional distinctions between public and private, labor and work, power and violence, freedom and authority. The simple question guiding her investigation into these complex matters was always: How do these phenomena relate to politics? Politics was her touchstone. It illuminated all aspects of society, even those usually regarded as being independent of politics, or at least politically neutral.

Because of the uniqueness of her interpretation, Hannah Arendt has been attacked from every political corner. To radicals and liberals, she was a conservative in the tradition of Aristotle and Edmund Burke. To conservatives, her critique of the status quo seemed grounded in the radical politics of Rousseau or Marx. In fact, she was not a radical, a liberal, or a conservative because none of these positions recognizes the validity of her controlling insight, the primacy of the political realm. Although she did argue that the preservation of republican government depends upon promoting greater political participation, she was not a radical because she believed that the social question is not amenable to a political solution. While she held that certain institutions, such as the press, and certain rights, such as speech and association, must be free from governmental interference, she was not simply a liberal because she opposed liberalism's emphasis on private freedom. And finally, although she remained sensitive to the need for tradition to act as a bulwark against the uncertainties of the future, she was not a conservative in the usual sense because she believed that traditional categories tend to obscure what is genuinely new, making us complacent, unable to face creatively the fresh challenges that inevitably arise. If, then, she was not a radical, liberal, or conservative, what label can we ascribe to her? The answer is—none; hence, for her, each issue must be judged on its merits and from diverse perspectives, independent of party program and platform.

In eschewing a doctrinaire position, and by opening up new horizons for thought, Hannah Arendt taught us, by her example, to think for ourselves. This included, of course, the freedom to disagree with her, however testy she might become if we did. That was a difficult lesson to learn, and perhaps it is never fully mastered. For the sensitive student, in the course of his studies, discovers that the philosophers are far greater thinkers than he. Thus he is caught on the horns of a dilemma. Either he is overwhelmed by a thinker's brilliance and submits to his authority, or, convinced that thinking for oneself and expressing one's own opinions is the true point of education, he glibly or too quickly criticizes the philosophers of old. As a teacher, Hannah Arendt pointed to a sane middle way. She taught us to respect the great tradition of philosophy even as it appeared to be crumbling under the combined weight of its many antagonists; at the same time, she helped give us the courage to come to our own conclusions.

IV

Not all great teachers are also important writers. Hannah Arendt was both, and we are fortunate that we can reread her books to recall, rethink, and reexamine what she had to say. Since she was also a prolific writer, there is an ample body of work from which to draw.

Hannah Arendt was fond of saying that man's humanity lay in the recognition that who one is—a person's unique character and manner—can transcend one's gifts and achievements. Maintaining this perspective guaranteed that the creator would not be overwhelmed by his creations, thus preserving what, in her essay on Jaspers, Arendt called *humanitas:* the sense that each individual represents an aspect of humanity with a dignity of his own. It seemed to us that she occasionally drew too sharp a distinction between the individual and his work, since the work—be it a book, a painting, a building, a piece of sculpture—often reveals something of the unique quality of its creator. Hannah Arendt's own writings are certainly a case in point; her distinct voice is always unmistakably present. Still, it was in her teaching more than in her writing that her distinctive character seemed most manifest. There her gaiety, wit, and passion, her testy impatience, her love of debate, her shrewd common sense, and her joy in communicating her knowledge to others be-

Hannah Arendt

came most clearly visible. This combination of qualities, along with her brilliance and learning, is what made her such a remarkable and inspiring teacher. Her books, including her posthumous work, *The Life of the Mind*, can never fully compensate us for our loss. We shall always feel that, although she died suddenly and painlessly at the age of sixty-nine after a long and brilliant career, she died much too soon.

13

The Education of
a Scientist

JEREMY BERNSTEIN

IF ONE IS LUCKY, great or at least extremely significant teachers appear in one's student life at about the time that one can appreciate them. But too much of a mismatch in sophistication leads to the sort of mutual frustration that was expressed by the late E. U. Condon, a very distinguished physicist, who, when I met him, was just emerging from a class at Washington University in St. Louis. He remarked, probably more in sorrow than in anger, "I have just been casting false pearls before genuine swine." It was my incredible good fortune to encounter three remarkable teachers of physics at just the most appropriate moment. They were—working backwards in time, the sequence in which I will describe them—J. Robert Oppenheimer, Julian Schwinger, and Philipp Frank. It was Philipp Frank who first convinced me that learning modern physics was about the most exciting thing that a sentiment human being could do. It was Julian Schwinger who taught me in detail what modern physics was, and it was because of what I learned in his courses that I could begin the research that I later continued at the Institute for Advanced Study at Princeton in 1957–1959, when Oppenheimer was its director.

The Education of a Scientist

A great deal has been written about Robert Oppenheimer.* I will not review here his career, his work in physics, his role in the atomic bomb project, or his subsequent encounter with McCarthyism, which ended his career as a government adviser. I will, rather, concentrate on the impact that Oppenheimer had on me as a teacher.

In 1957, I finished a two-year appointment at the Harvard Cyclotron Laboratory, where I was what was called the "house theoretician," meaning that I was available to assist experimental physicists with theoretical questions, if any arose. But since the Harvard experimental physicists knew as much theoretical physics as I did, or more, I do not recall having been asked anything, and so I simply did my own work. After two delightful years spent like this, I was looking for a job. I do not have a very clear recollection of what the job situation was in 1957; very likely, if one was looking for a proper teaching job in a university, it was not very good. But teaching was the last thing in the world that I wanted to do. I was having much too good a time doing full-time research. Indeed, after having spent four years working my way through graduate school as a teaching assistant, not having to teach seemed like a splendid vacation. One of the young Harvard professors then held what was generally assumed to be the record for the number of years of postdoctoral appointments without having to teach: I think it was seven years—an inspiration to us all. I later managed to break his record by one year; but by that time money was flowing into physics because of the post-Sputnik surge in government support for science, so his was a vastly more significant tactical achievement.

One of the few places that seemed to offer just what I was looking for was the Institute for Advanced Study, so I applied. Among the happiest days of my life was the day I received a letter from Oppenheimer announcing my acceptance—with a stipend of four thousand dollars a year, a financial advance-

* Two of the best recent books are *Disturbing the Universe*, by Freeman Dyson, and *Robert Oppenheimer: Letters and Recollections*, edited by Alice Kimball Smith and Charles Weiner.

ment for me; I was then twenty-six. The appointment was nominally for one year, but the problem of finding a job at the end of *that* period was a bridge I would jump off when I came to it.

My first encounter with Oppenheimer was not in Princeton but in Cambridge. He had come to Harvard that spring to give a series of lectures for the general public. I don't recall the precise subject on which he spoke, but I do have a vivid recollection of two wonderful, white-gloved, blue-haired, flower-hatted elderly Boston or Cambridge ladies who sat in front of me clutching each other's arms for reassurance when, at one point in the lecture, Oppenheimer actually wrote down an equation. In any event, after the first lecture I made my way to the podium to introduce myself since I was about to spend the next year, at least, at his institution. I recall that when I first approached him he was not very friendly. I imagine that, as a sort of celebrity, he had had enough of people coming up to him asking foolish questions. But I managed to explain who I was, and said that I would surface at Princeton in the fall—at which point his entire demeanor changed. He began listing the people who would be there, sounding like a who's who of modern theoretical physics. He ended by telling us that Lee and Yang (Tsung Dao Lee and Chen Ning Yang), who were instrumental in the discovery that parity symmetry—the symmetry between left and right—was violated, for which they would, that fall, win the Nobel Prize, would be in Princeton to teach us about parity, and promised that "we are going to have a ball." At this point noting his use of "we" I think I would have gone through a flaming hoop for the man.

Eventually I spent two years at the Institute, and during that time I never heard Oppenheimer give a technical lecture. I do not think he was actually doing research in physics, and we used to speculate whether he ever put pen to paper to calculate anything. But, remarkably, he seemed to have a total and immediate comprehension of everything, a phenomenon manifested in the weekly seminar.

The Education of a Scientist

Oppenheimer sat in the front row of the small seminar room with the *Geheimrats,* local and visiting. (A Viennese physicist once told me that in the great days in Vienna, seating assignments in the colloquium were determined by the assignment of a number called the *"bonze-moment"* which was defined as the product of the intrinsic importance of the visitor times the distance he had come.) He smoked incessantly, and from time to time would offer a cracking cough to the general ambiance. The junior members—like myself—cowered in the back row. But after a few months I came to the conclusion that, given the incredible talent assembled at the seminars, it was unlikely that anyone would be interested in hiring me for anything in physics so I had little to lose by relaxing and enjoying myself. I began to ask questions. By and large Oppenheimer tolerated these interruptions, although he could, when he thought either the speaker or a questioner was talking nonsense, be incredibly cutting. In fact, I remember once, after asking an astronomically stupid question and being told so by Oppenheimer, that my colloquium neighbor whispered in my ear, "Bernstein, this is a good day to stay down in the trenches with the rest of the troops."

The kind of science teaching (if one wants to call it that) at these seminars was the dialogue of professionals. As Oppenheimer once put it, "What we don't understand we explain to each other." An undergraduate—even most doctoral students—would have been lost. In fact, we postdoctorals had to work extremely hard to keep up, and usually tried to read and discuss the relevant papers before the seminar. In these seminars Oppenheimer was more than a kind of master of ceremonies; he was more like an orchestra conductor—clarifying, challenging, and refining. Sometimes his technique would get out of hand, especially when he had some fixed *a priori* notion of the importance of something or someone. But this, at least as I saw it, was far outweighed by his ability to focus ideas and to convince us, by some indefinable quality of his personality, that these ideas were terribly precious.

The most difficult step in the education of a scientist is

that which takes the young person from being a student to being a professional. In my case, the teacher who played the decisive role at this point was Julian Schwinger. The first course I took with Schwinger was in quantum mechanics in the fall of 1950, my senior year. But even before I set foot in the class, I knew that Schwinger was a legend among the scientifically-oriented students. He was in his mid-thirties, but by then he had been doing original theoretical physics for some twenty years. A few years ago, in the course of writing a *New Yorker* profile, I interviewed I. I. Rabi, the distinguished Columbia University physicist who had, in fact, discovered Schwinger. He told me, "It was sort of romantic in a way. You can fix it to a year—1935." Rabi, at that time, was trying to understand a celebrated paper by Einstein, Boris Podolsky, and Nathan Rosen, involving an apparent paradox in the quantum theory. He said, "I was reading the paper, and my way of reading a paper was to bring in a student and explain it to him. In this case the student was Lloyd Motz, who's now a professor of astronomy at Columbia. We were arguing about something, and after a while Motz said there was someone waiting outside the office, and asked if he could bring him in. He brought in this kid. (Schwinger was sixteen.) So I told him to sit down some place, and he sat down. Motz and I were arguing, and then this kid pipes up and settles the argument . . . and I said, who the hell is this?"

Schwinger was failing a number of courses at City College where he was enrolled, but Rabi got him into Columbia anyway, and under Rabi's firm hand Schwinger blossomed—even making Phi Beta Kappa. By the time he graduated, he had completed his research for his Ph.D. thesis, but spent two more years fulfilling the doctoral requirements. Rabi then sent him to California to Oppenheimer. During World War II, Schwinger, young as he was, became the guiding theoretical genius behind the development of radar. He went on to Harvard, where I believe he was the youngest full professor ever named.

The Education of a Scientist

I believe that there is an element of theater in all great teaching. One may well wonder what drama could possibly occur in a course on quantum mechanics, and I will explain. The nominal starting time for the class was 11 A.M. That's when the classroom began to fill up with the forty or fifty people who were taking, or auditing, the course. This group included not only graduate students in physics and mathematics, along with a few undergraduates like myself, but many of the junior—and occasionally the senior—faculties in these disciplines, with a few chemists tossed in for good luck. Schwinger, who in those days drove a light-blue Cadillac, would arrive sometime between 11 and 11:30, someone would spot the Cadillac, and we would all rush for seats in the classroom. Schwinger had certain verbal mannerisms, characteristic phrases such as "we can effectively regard," that became part of the student *lingua franca*. A friend of mine once concocted a model Schwinger sentence, which began, "Although 1 is not perfectly 0, we can effectively regard . . ." Schwinger, at least in those days, pronounced "nuclear" as "nucular," and some of his students acquired this pronunciation as well. That was the superficial theater. The real theater was the content of the lectures.

Schwinger would lecture nonstop for well over an hour, doing the most intricate calculations imaginable *without notes*. Formulae appeared and disappeared, melted into other formulae as if by magic. Whenever Schwinger taught one of these courses, he simply recreated the subject. It was as if he were presenting three original research papers a week—and indeed many of these lectures were eventually published. During this period, it was a sort of "in" joke among physicists that Schwinger had solved nearly every problem in his unpublished lecture notes. I still have my notes and now, thirty years later, still find revelations in them. The simplest imaginable problems were done several ways, each of them novel. I recall that at one of the lectures I sat next to Abraham Klein (now a professor at the University of Pennsylvania), who was then a Junior Fellow at Harvard and who became my thesis advisor. He was advanced enough to appreciate what Schwinger was up to, and at one point he said to himself, "It's like poetry."

Schwinger's lectures were frequently quite difficult to follow for relative newcomers to the subject like myself, so we would sometimes go down to MIT where Victor Weisskopf taught quantum mechanics. Weisskopf, also a great teacher, was a mirror image of Schwinger. His classes had a marvelous homespun quality. All the students called him by his nickname "Viki," and felt free to interrupt him frequently. Whereas Weisskopf rarely got any formula quite right on the blackboard (I have been told that this was also true of Oppenheimer.), Schwinger almost never got anything wrong on the blackboard, and questions from the audience were rare. Each man in his own way illuminated the mysteries of the subject: Viki by bringing it down to earth, Schwinger by pushing mathematics and its physical meaning to its limits. When I became a graduate student, and later a postdoctoral fellow, I audited Schwinger's course—which changed constantly—at least three times. No one was surprised when, in 1965, he won the Nobel Prize. It had only been a question of time.

The sequence of events that led to my taking Schwinger's course was far from obvious, but in it Philipp Frank played the decisive role. I entered Harvard, in 1947, with absolutely no intention of becoming a scientist. The one science course I had taken in high school had been a disaster; I had learned nothing. Mathematics, at which I was proficient, was then taught in the same spirit as Latin—as something that would "improve your mind." (Whatever *that* means.) One never got a glimmering of the notion that mathematics might be a creative discipline.

The only skill that I thought that I had was writing, and, as I remember it, I once thought that I might become a journalist. In those days Harvard had just begun its general education program, which I understand has now been abandoned. Everyone was required to take one of the general education courses in science—courses which were to science what the Harvard requirement that each undergraduate be able to swim one or more laps of the pool was to the sport of swimming. There were various levels of difficulty among these courses, and, needless to say, I chose the easiest. This course produced an amiable tedium until sometime late in the fall, when we touched on relativity and the quantum theory, ideas that for me, meant love at first sight. In retrospect it is hard to understand why. I did not have the remotest background to help me appreciate what these theories were trying to achieve, but the notion that lengths could shrink and time could expand set me off. I decided I would try to teach myself the theory of relativity, undaunted by the prevalent myth that only sixteen, or maybe twenty-eight, people in the world were said to understand it. My idea was that I would get a solid book in the subject and read it very slowly.

I went to the Widener Library, looked in the catalogue under Einstein, and took out his book *The Meaning of Relativity.* That was the worst possible choice, since the book is an extremely technical series of lectures that Einstein delivered at Princeton in the 1920s. I understood essentially not one word. It was the first time in my life, I think, when I had tried with every neuron to understand something and totally failed. I went to the professor of my course—the noted historian of Science I., Bernard Cohen—and explained my dilemma. He told me (and for this I owe him an eternal debt) that that very spring Philipp Frank was teaching another general education course devoted to these matters and that, while it was a bit irregular, there was no real reason that I could not take both courses, his and Frank's, at the same time. Moreover, he explained, Frank was a good friend of Einstein's, having been his successor at the German University in Prague. Nothing short of an atomic bomb explosion in Cambridge would have kept me from enrolling in that course.

Apart from this, I knew nothing about Professor Frank and I remember, as we gathered on the first day of the class

in the large lecture room in the physics building, wondering
what the great man would look like. As I write this I have
in front of me two photographs of Professor Frank. The first
one is on an announcement of a lecture series that he was
to give in the summer of 1938, at several American universities.
(As the series began, the Nazis invaded Czechoslovakia, and
Professor Frank and his wife remained permanently in America.) The photograph shows Professor Frank as he appeared
in early middle age. Then, as later, his scalp was unperturbed
by the presence of hair. But in his first photograph he has
an odd brush-like mustache. He is also wearing those small,
round, dark-rimmed spectacles that I have always associated
with central European intellectuals. His expression is unchar-
acteristically severe. The second photograph adorns a pam-
phlet which contains memorial addresses given by a group
of us at a service at Harvard Memorial Church in October
1966. (He had died on July 21 of that year, at the age of eighty-
two.) I like this photograph much better. The mustache has
vanished, and the spectacles are now rimless. His expression
shows the beginning of the extraordinary smile that always
preceded an anecdote or a joke. First would come the smile,
usually followed by "I remember very well really. . . ," an
understatement since Philipp had almost total recall of everything he had ever learned—to say nothing of entire conversations, some of which had taken place fifty years earlier. It
was crucial not to say anything and distract him while Philipp
reminisced, smiling, and resurrected his memories; a meeting
with Einstein during the first World War; a classroom encounter with Ludwig Boltzmann; a dialogue with Ernst Mach; a
description of a trip taken on the River Don with P. A. M.
Dirac; the details of the assassination of Moritz Schlick by
a student whose girl friend had been having an affair with
Schlick; or his impressions of Kafka in Prague.

I came to know Philipp Frank, and his stories, much later.
But in the spring of 1948, there he was, walking into the
classroom with a slight limp that I think was a souvenir of
a childhood encounter with a streetcar in Vienna. He began

his lecture by describing the organization of the course. We would meet once a week for about three hours, a period that was to be broken in the middle where Professor Frank said he "would make a certain interval." The interval was to be followed by a lengthy question period. His accent was a little difficult to place. It was predominantly characteristic of his native Vienna, but I later discovered that he had a fluent command of French, Italian, Spanish, Russian, and Czech. He also read Persian, Arabic, Hebrew, Latin, and Greek, and could write in these languages as well. I finally decided that his present language, English, had been built like the foundation of the seven cities of Troy: it contained the ruins of all the preceding languages in which he had lectured and taught. He once explained to me that he had studied English in Prague. At that time, the middle thirties, he said there were three factions in the University: the Nazis, who feared that the Russians would invade Czechoslovakia; the Communists, who were sure that the Germans would; and the Jews, who were sure that either step would be a disaster. The only thing they all agreed on was that the University should hire an instructor to teach them English and thus facilitate their emigration to the United States.

Professor Frank's course began in what, for me, was an entirely unexpected way—with a discussion of Euclidean geometry. We learned that there were two kinds of geometry: an empirical geometry—earth measure—in which the propositions become statements that can be tested experimentally, and a mathematical geometry in which the propositions are merely relations among abstract entities and therefore without empirical content. We learned (and for me this was a revelation) that from a mathematical point of view there were alternate geometries to that of Euclid, and that, in particular, the geometry of great circles on the surface of a sphere was one in which the sum of the base angles of triangles added up to *more* than 180 degrees. We learned that Einstein's theory of gravitation made it plausible that the empirical geometry of space and time was one of these non-Euclidean types. Professor Frank then discussed the evolution of the ideas of motion again, beginning with the Greeks. He traced the history of the concept of inertia through the Middle Ages to Galileo, and he carefully explained the theological element in Newtonian mechanics: Newton's conviction that absolute space and time were the *sensoria* of God. Then he told us about Ernst Mach's devastating critique of Newton in Mach's *Science of Mechanics.* (Mach had been one of Professor Frank's illustrious predecessors at the German University.) He explained to us the influence of Mach on the young Einstein. Professor Frank had just written his biography of Einstein, *Einstein: His Life and Times.** This was the first time I heard what has now become the standard version of how Einstein was led to the theory of relativity. Einstein had explained to Professor Frank (as later explained in Einstein's *Autobiographical Notes,* now once again in print), that when he was sixteen he tried to imagine physics from the point of view of someone who could ride on a light beam. He realized that to such a voyager, light would no longer appear to be an oscillatory wave motion, hence he would have a criterion by which he could decide that he was moving with the speed of light in empty space. This, Einstein apparently reasoned, was a violation of the principle of relativity, which asserts that by no observation can one decide whether one is moving uniformly or is at rest. But Newtonian mechanics allow one to move at any speed, so it led to a violation of the principle of relativity that also embraced electromagnetic phenomena. I wish that, during the nearly twenty years when I knew Professor Frank, I had gone into this with him more critically. Why did Einstein have such a firm belief in the principle of relativity at the age of sixteen? And if he did have it, why did it take

* One of the numerous absurdities that festoon the world of publishing is that this book not only is out of print, but was never properly published in English at all. Knopf published an abbreviated version of the German edition, which inspired Einstein to the pun *"Herr Knopf hat geknopft"* (Mr. Knopf has buttoned it up). No one has troubled to take the original German edition and translate it into English. I would do it myself if I knew German well enough.

The Education of a Scientist

him ten years to produce the theory of relativity? Perhaps when, and if, Einstein's complete papers are published one may find further clues, or perhaps not—in which case, at least for me, the creative leap will still remain mysterious.

Next, in Professor Frank's course, we came to the quantum theory: the wave nature of matter and the uncertainty principles which express the ultimate limitations on measurement on the atomic scale. All this involved mathematics no more complicated than what I had learned in high school. But to teach this course Professor Frank had to have an absolute mastery of the subject matter. Nothing is simpler in physics than to conceal one's confusion over fundamental principles behind a smoke screen of mathematics. It was in this spirit that Professor Frank once explained to me his criteria for good popular science writing. Not only must it instruct the layman, it should also instruct the professional by calling his attention to the general principles so often taken for granted. After the "interval" Professor Frank would sometimes go into more detail for those—and I was not one— who knew "a little of mathematics." These sessions made clear to me what I did not know, and by the end of my freshman year I decided that, no matter what, I would learn mathematics. I began a crash program that encompassed summers and resulted in my majoring in and taking a master's degree in mathematics before eventually switching, full time, to the physics department. It also convinced me that, whatever else, I must continue to study with Professor Frank.

Somehow I managed to persuade my adviser to allow me to take a reading course with Professor Frank in my sophomore year. This was an eccentric thing to do as a sophomore and the greatness of Harvard—as it was and as I hope it still is—was that someone like myself was allowed to wander serendipitously through the curriculum. I think I changed my formal major about four times: physics, philosophy, history of science, and finally mathematics. *I* knew where I was going, and somehow knew that, given my inadequate preparation and my lack of confidence, to become a scientist I needed to take a strange and often circuitous route. Through all of this intellectual wandering, however, working with Professor Frank remained a constant. In my sophomore year, we read many of the classics in the philosophy of science. Beginning with Aristotle, we studied Medieval philosophers like Aquinas and William of Occam. We read Hume, Locke, and Mill. We read Mach, and we also worked our way through the *Tractatus* of Wittgenstein. I also learned about the early days of the Vienna Circle—the group of Logical Positivists of which Professor Frank was a founding member. We read Bridgeman and even, from time to time, would descend to his basement laboratory to discuss something with him.

In later years, when I was working full time in physics, I would visit the Franks at their home. Once on a roasting summer day, I went there with my parents. Professor Frank's wife, Hania, was dressed in a wool shawl and, after offering us a spectrum of benign liquids of various colors, she drank something that I naively thought was water. She announced, "I drink slivovitz to keep me warm." (I believe she had been his student in Prague, and would often say that Philipp "knew a great deal for a physicist.") As a Viennese, Philipp Frank loved the ambiance of the coffeehouses. The closest approximation to them in Cambridge was the Hayes-Bickford cafeteria, where many of our discussions took place. One evening I recall telephoning Professor Frank at home and being answered by Hania. In her monumental accent she said, "We are here singing English folksongs. Philipp has gone away." I had no trouble locating him at the Hayes-Bickford.

In 1954, Professor Frank retired from Harvard, and I helped him clean out his office. It was unbelievable chaos. He had, as I remember, a rolltop desk, and from it he extracted letters, some of which he had never opened, and which dated from the 1930s. He opened a few and observed, "you see, they were not so important anyway." He also had a treasury of letters from Einstein, Schrödinger, and other notable physicists. (Somehow this collection disappeared after his death.) He read me a number of Einstein's letters, and from them

The Education of a Scientist

I learned that Einstein could be exceedingly sharp and severe in his criticism of work that he did not like. This also came as a revelation, since I had the naïve idea that Einstein was a saint. I once asked Professor Frank whether the young Einstein, with whom he had contact as early as 1907, had appeared to be bright. He laughed, but he knew what I meant, since some very great physicists (like Bohr) are not so much "bright" as deep. He told me that the young Einstein was very bright and much given to what Professor Frank referred to as "cracks"—spontaneous jokes. From out of the innards of the desk he pulled a dusty, rolled-up piece of drawing paper on which there was an etching of Einstein, done in 1931. It was signed by the artist and by Einstein. Professor Frank gave it to me and it hangs in my living room.

I saw Philipp Frank for the last time a year or so before his death. Gerald Holton, who had been a colleague and close friend of the Franks' throughout this period, told me that the Franks' had reached a stage in their lives where they would be much better off in a retirement home where they would have help in caring for their needs. He told me that he had found a desirable place, and we went together to tell the Franks about it. I recall that Professor Frank said that he was surprised to "somehow have lived to more than eighty years." He also said that when he read things he had written long ago they no longer seemed to have been written by him, but by someone else. He seemed to view old age and death with the same clear-eyed objectivity with which he had viewed life. The memory of that visit haunts me still.

Someone once remarked that the difficulty in writing about teachers is that the life of a teacher, as a teacher, is written on water. How can one recreate, even for oneself, the ambiance of a classroom? I was eighteen when I first attended Professor Frank's course. I am fifty as I write this. In my mind I think that I can trace a continuous thread that leads from here back to there. But in writing about these three great teachers I also recall how unlikely such continuity seemed to me then.

14

I. A. Richards

HELEN VENDLER

I. A. RICHARDS was the most extraordinary teacher of poetry I ever encountered, and this essay, in dwelling on Richards as a teacher, must necessarily present an incomplete view of a many-sided man.* I audited two of Richards' courses at Harvard in the fifties; one was an undergraduate course in poetry, the other a graduate seminar in Shelley and Plato. A little later, I saw Richards appear in two television series: in the first, he repeated parts of the undergraduate poetry course; in the second, he presented excerpts from his Basic English version of the *Iliad.* Videotapes were made of both series; one set burned in the fire at Boston's Channel 2; the other set, Richards told me, was deposited, but then misplaced, at Harvard's Carpenter Center for the Visual Arts. That set may yet reappear to corroborate memories of Richards as a teacher. Until then, personal reminiscence must attempt to convey some sense of his magical presence.

Richards entered the hall in Harvard Yard where the large poetry course was to be held, saw the overcrowded room with undergraduates seated on the floor, heard the fire sirens shrieking from the Broadway fire station, and pronounced

---

* A biography is being written by John Paul Russo, whose comprehensive annotated bibliography of Richards' writings in *I. A. Richards: Essays in His Honor*, ed. Reuben Brower, Helen Vendler, and John Hollander (Oxford University Press, 1973), offers a rapid overview of Richards' interests and work.

I. A. Richards

emphatically (quoting Arnold's Callicles), "Not here, O Apollo, are haunts fit for thee!" Those were the first words I heard him speak, and they were spoken in that voice, of unforgettable depth and emphasis, which gave words a luster they usually possess only in the mouths of remarkable actors. (When Richards, in 1971, took the role of the Trojan rhapsode in a dramatic version of his *Iliad*, it was, one could say, type-casting). But quite aside from the eloquence with which they were spoken, Richards' first words in that class surprised in themselves; they were not concerned with class lists, or syllabi; they were addressed to Apollo as though he existed still (and to Richards, a thoroughgoing believer in Platonic forms, Apollo was an eternal Being), and they assumed that our classroom would become (if a fit one could be found) a haunt of Apollo. I cannot emphasize too much the utter absence of irony in Richards' quotation. Many of us, as teachers, might make some such remark ironically, and then subside into our geographical lot. Richards moved the class to the quiet of Radcliffe Yard, and Apollo, or so it seemed to me, consented to frequent Longfellow Hall.

There were other surprises. The room was totally dark. The undergraduates were thereby prevented from doing their calculus homework, writing each other notes, or indeed taking notes on what Richards said, all admirable results. On a screen up front, high and very large, were projected, by a slide projector, the words of a poem—always, without exception, a great poem. (Richards never condescended to students.) The poem appeared a stanza or so at a time. Richards stood below the screen, his back to us, a long pointer in his hand. We saw the back of his head, and its halo of floating white hair. He was *not* interested—at that moment—in us; he was absorbed in the poem, as, it was expected, we should be. (We had scarcely any choice, since, in the dark, it was our only possible object of attention.) The large words took on an aura they cannot possess on the page—"as if a magic lantern threw the nerves in patterns on a screen."

I still think this the ideal way to teach poetry without distraction, but it requires help—to make the slides, to project the slides, to darken the room—which not all of us have. But this method served, at most, to fix attention; it alone did not account for Richards' spectacular effect.

That effect arose from two root causes. The first, of which the reference to Apollo is an example, was Richards' compelled and compelling belief in the absolute reality of the world of poetry, which was not, for him, parallel to the world of life but was coextensive with it, and the means of deepest penetration into it. In that belief, he was Arnoldian and Ruskinian; poetry had replaced religion as the source of a culture's deepest self-insight. In beholding Richards, one beheld the last of the great Victorians (or so I felt); he had their buoyancy in crisis, their resilience of inquiry, their appetite for knowledge, their confidence in the soul of man, their indomitable will. He also showed their overmastering sense of doubt— doubt of the most sacred and of the most conventionally hallowed beliefs, doubt of the relation between the active and the contemplative life, doubt of the function of empire. It was his most attractive personal quality, his mixture of assertion and query, his exhibition of what one might call dogmatic doubt; it had the charm of the magisterial combined with the charm of the speculative, a heady mixture for his students, who envied his certainties while ensnared in his speculativeness.

Richards read us the whole poem, complete as it passed before us on the screen. It made no difference that there may have been scarcely a soul in the room who could understand Donne's "Extasie" on first seeing and hearing it: we had a right to the whole poem, and to what Richards always referred to (borrowing the word from Donne), as the mutual "interinanimation" of its parts, before we began to take it in more slowly. Though there was great simplicity in this view, there was also great cunning; Richards-as-reader-aloud was quintessentially Richards-the-interpreter, casting the poem into the guise he saw it wear. No one hearing Richards read "The Extasie" could ever subscribe to the vulgar reductiveness

I. A. Richards

which makes it simply a libertine poem of seduction. No one hearing Richards read "To His Coy Mistress" could think the mistress the center of the poem, not with the "desarts of vast eternity" and the "slow-chap't" power of time resonating in the room. In one sense, Richards' work was done, once his powerful interpretation-through-enunciation had lodged itself in our ears.

But that was only the beginning and here I come to the second cause of Richards' success as a lecturer. Richards worked less by paraphrase than by collocation. On one occasion, next to the "Ode on a Grecian Urn," by Keats, he placed passages from earlier Keats, the Old and New Testaments, Porphyry, Yeats, Sir Thomas Browne, Milton, Marvell, Swinburne, Wycliffe, Blake, Shakespeare, Eliot, Byron, Spenser, and Plato.* He bestowed a considerable bounty on us as we listened; tantalizing fragments of the two great Byzantium poems by Yeats (my first acquaintance with them), two stanzas of Spenser's "Hymne of Heavenly Beautie" (also, to me, ravishingly new), a brief flash of Swinburne:

> *And soft as lips that laugh and hide*
> *The laughing leaves of the trees divide,*
> *And screen from seeing and leave in sight*
> *The god pursuing, the maiden hid.*

The "interinanimations" were, as the fashionable word now has it, intertextual as well as intratextual. What we were seeing was the Ricardian mind launching out filament, filament, filament, like Whitman's spider, creating before us a replica of his radiant verbal universe, in which no word stood lonely.

Most teachers of literature lack Richards' tenacious memory, and could not hope to range, as he did, without books, without notes, from the Greeks to the moderns. But there is a great deal to be said for straying, in any class, beyond

---

* This class—later a television program—has also been published under the title "Beauty and Truth," in *Complementarities*, ed. by John Paul Russo (Harvard University Press: 1976). Interested readers may also deduce from it something of Richards' method.

the confines of the author of the day, to make students feel how wholly a mind that admires Keats will also admire the *Symposium*, or the psalms, or Spenser. It was a world, not a text, to which Richards introduced his students.

If placing a single word or image in juxtaposition with its appearance elsewhere was Richards' first way of conveying its "meaning," he did not evade pursuing "meaning" to more ample reaches. He never failed in delicacy in this most difficult of tasks; I think it was for this delicacy that I revered him. We have all, in teaching, heard our own failures in tone—exaggerations innocently enough meant, perhaps, in an effort to persuade young readers or enliven a dull day—indicating a lapse in trust that the poem can do its own work. Richards was never less than exquisite, at the same time never less than firm. He never vulgarized; he never condescended; he was never reductive; he never patronized his author; he never underestimated his students. How he gained this heroic equipoise I cannot imagine. Why he thought well enough of us—if he thought of us at all, his mind so wholly on the poets—to address us as if we understood the mysteries of life and death, is to me a mystery. Perhaps he learned his manner from Socrates. Or Confucius. I will give only one example of a serious remark (again, from the class on the Urn, which I recall as the single best class he gave, and from which I draw still when I approach Keats). Richards is speaking of the way Keats passes, in illustrating his urn, from scenes of love and music to a scene of sacrifice:

It is by this sacrifice that the other side of the Urn as we turn to it becomes so poignantly fulfilling. We need though to remind ourselves of how central to men's hopes and fears his ritual sacrifice of his best has been.*

It may be risky to speak to twenty-year olds in such Orphic terms. But for me, Richards' classes were classes in perception as well as art. There was a great deal I did not, in my youth,

* Ibid., p. 221.

I. A. Richards

ignorance, and innocence, understand; but I understood that Richards knew, and the poets knew, things about sacrifice, renunciation, hopes, and fears that I did not yet know, but could hope to know. "In brief," as Richards put it, "the way of Love and the way of Knowledge meet."*

It is important to distinguish Richards' manner of enunciating moral remarks, such as the one on sacrifice, from comparable remarks made in a religious vein. Richards' vein was unalterably polemic, not hortatory. He was in every case defending his poet against misinterpretation. "The prose of discussion," Richards remarked in an early essay—in a remark which perfectly expresses his own lively critical practice—"is grounded, if not in an instinct, at least upon a tradition of combativeness." He said this in explaining his instinct to mount "a major assault" on certain positions of Middleton Murry. "The cannon, in fact, are itching to go off," he added with a certain joyful candor.†

Richards' classes, in consequence, never had a lugubrious seriousness. There was an éalan about them that emerged in his Puckish delight in making critical mischief. His chief targets were those who affected a wisdom greater than the poets'. I give an example from the Urn class, on the line "Beauty is Truth, Truth Beauty":

> Of these lines an authority writes: "But, of course, to put it solidly, that is a vague observation—to anyone whom life has taught to face facts and define his terms, actually an uneducated conclusion, albeit pardonable in one so young." The Urn isn't exactly "so young"— is it? But, of course, this critic carelessly supposes that these concluding lines are uttered by Keats, not by the Urn.‡

Richards' same elfin relish in others' misreadings glitters through *Practical Criticism* (1929); no one has ever so enjoyed, while deploring, the grotesque misunderstandings of texts.

---

* Ibid., p. 225.
† Ibid., p. 39.
‡ Ibid., p. 222.

The Cambridge undergraduates who produced the famous "protocols" on set texts, exhibiting their stock responses, moral inadequacy, sentimentality, and simple illiteracy, became the prototypes of all those whom Richards wished to—it is not too strong a word—save. "Our purpose, which was Plato's, is saving society and our souls," he said in wartime (1942).*

All Richards' work—writing and teaching alike—may be summed up as a lifelong campaign against illiteracy. The first, and worst, illiteracy is an inability to read—to decode letters assembled into words. Against that illiteracy, Richards developed with Christine Gibson the stick-figure books in language teaching, the Language through Pictures series. He thought that film and television could teach the world's illiterates to read; without him, we might not have seen a program like "Sesame Street" on television. He worried about the illiteracy, in large world languages, of people who spoke lesser-known languages; he believed, all his life, that Basic English, if it were mastered as a world language, could eliminate potentially disastrous misunderstandings between cultures. To that end, he wished to present, in Basic, the chief cultural documents of the West—Homer, Plato, Job—because he knew that the East does not understand the West by learning its vocabulary; it must also become acquainted with its cultural ideals and norms.

Richards once told an amusing and horrifying story of the "illiteracy" of the "literate," to illustrate the need, if true "literacy" were to be achieved in a foreign culture, of something more than language mastery. He was teaching, in China, a group of Chinese teachers of English. They had mastered English vocabulary and English grammar in literary and spoken form; the set text for the class was *Tess of the d'Urbervilles*, and they had reached the end of the novel. Richards read them the harrowing close with Tess's execution: "The President of the Immortals . . . had ended his sport with Tess." The class, with every appearance of satisfaction, burst into

* I. A. Richards, "The New Republic," *Nation* (March 28, 1942), p. 371.

approving applause. Richards was taken aback, and asked them why they clapped—"Because she was a wicked girl who had disobeyed her elders, and was suitably punished." Every word had been understood, but their Chinese cultural respect for elders had prevented them from understanding the Hardy ethic.

For Richards, tradition and context were the controlling factors enabling us to distinguish, as he said, misreadings from variant readings. Among the New Critics, no one was more sensitive to the resonances among texts—and not only the reverberations among literary texts, but between literary texts and those others—historical, philosophical, and religious—which influenced the poets. In that sense, Richards' campaign for literacy reached toward the education of his fellow-critics: woe to the critic who had no sense of the wider context.

In a public lecture Richards once said, with entire sincerity, "Think of the planet!" I was, in my twenties, quite unaccustomed to any such focus. It may be that students raised in an atmosphere of political awareness had a wider consciousness than the bookish one I possessed; but I was shocked into interior protest. How could I think of "the planet?" It was too difficult! But it was evident that the planet—and not England, not America, not Cambridge, not Harvard—was Richards' sphere of reference. In some inchoate way, I sensed that his masters—Plato, Milton, Coleridge—may have been thinking of the planet too, if not quite in Richards' very practical and up-to-date ways. For a young woman, whose sphere was expected to be the kitchen or at most the classroom, it was invigorating to be expected to think of the planet.

Richards' dismay at illiteracy may have grown out of his philosophical studies with G. E. Moore, when he did moral sciences at Cambridge, or out of his work in *The Meaning of Meaning* (1923) with C. K. Ogden, or out of his reflexive meditations in *Interpretation in Teaching* (1938). His interest in intercultural understanding (and incomprehension) grew from his visits to China and his long residence as a foreigner at Harvard, where, as University Professor, he interested himself in theories of education and in the possibilities of electronic aids to literacy (from television to computers), all the while teaching literature.

In his last two decades he became a poet. The poetry was gnarled, intellectual, angular, unsparing. Richards was perhaps too conscious of semantic instability to use words with heedless instinct; nonetheless, the books of verse came to seem, for me, ratifications of what his students, if not his readers, sensed in Richards—the poet manqué. His acute sense of the tactility of language, his ear for nuance in the spoken word, his kinesthetic catching of a subtle rhythm, his learnedness in what we might call "Poetic" (a language like "Basic"), were all those of a poet. Though his writing, perhaps in deference to his century, aspired towards a scientific accuracy, his teaching was that of a Welsh evangelist—fervent in seriousness, deep with belief, stern in fidelity to the word, and rich in celebratory language. He *saw* language, and heard it too; it is not surprising that in 1926 he wrote one of the first articles on Hopkins, a poet who heard and saw language in a way that would have seemed instantly congenial to Richards. Coleridge, Richards' true master, represents the other side of Richards—the side that yearned after universal knowledge, an all-encompassing system. The two aspects of his mind, poetic and philosophic, were never quite reconciled. He admired "philosophical" lyric poets (Shelley, Coleridge, and Hardy among them) and this admiration led him to a prolonged inquiry into the function of statement in poetry; it is unfortunate that the term he invented ("pseudo-statement") to cover the peculiar truth-value of statements in poetry was widely misunderstood; he meant it scientifically, as in "pseudopod," but it was taken as contemptuous. Nonetheless, his courage in investigating the function of symbolic statement was matched only by the utter absence of sentimentality in his discourse on the worth of poetry. It should be recorded that he never, not once, in my experience, brought into the classroom his own critical quarrels. The class time belonged not to him, but to the poets. He served the poets not self-effac-

I. A. Richards

ingly—his self was too original and assertive to be effaced—
but cooperatively: his mind and memory were at the service
of the poem. The more powerful the mind and memory devoted to them, the more worth devotion the poems appeared.

At the end of his life, in the summer of 1979, Richards
had the great pleasure of reentering China and teaching classes
to university students. It was to be the last act of his intellectual life: he fell ill there and died on his return to England.
Photographs taken in China show him seated at a desk in a
classroom; on the blackboard is written, in large letters, *A
Warm Welcome to Dr. Richards.* The students, in the stifling
summer heat, are excited and smiling in one picture, bent
in concentration in another. That taxing effort to be yet once
again a bridge between East and West was Richards' last en-
deavor in teaching. His "gratuitous rashness" (a trip to China
in his mid-eighties) and his "serpentine hesitation" of
thought—both phrases are Robert Lowell's about Richards*—
remained in dialectic to the end of his life. To those who
thought him over-ingenious, we can offer his own reply (from
a poem called "Sunrise"):

> *You make broad day your house;*
> *My mind moves with the bat, the owl, the mouse.*

In the "dark passages" of art, Richards moved with the wisdom of the owl, the instinct of the bat, the soft inquiry of
the mouse. In his classes, the dark places of poetry were explored for us who had made broad day our house; it was
not by accident that it was in the dark, where only the words
of the poets glowed on a screen, that Richards awoke new
exploratory instincts in us.

* I. A. Richards, *Essays in His Honor* (Oxford University Press, 1973),
p. 13.

15

C. S. Lewis
as a Teacher

JOHN WAIN

ONE'S ESTIMATE of C. S. Lewis as a teacher, as a critic of literature and ideas, and perhaps as a literary artist, is bound to be influenced—probably, in the end, to depend outright—on whether one agrees with the proposition that civilization ended in 1914.

I write that sentence and then sit back and look at it. The opinion that civilization did not survive the First World War, like any opinion, is true from the point of view from which it is uttered. On its own terms it is incontrovertible; what are its own terms?

In the early summer of 1914, Western Europe was a much bigger place than it is now, because it dominated the earth; it was also a much smaller place, because it was more homogeneous. It was largely impervious to influences from outside, and its intellectual and artistic life was in the hands of an educated class that was very much the same from one country to another, being produced in every country by the same training. Literature, music, the visual arts, and the theater ruled supreme with no competition from cinema, television, radio. In literature, the foundation of educated taste was still to be found in the Greek and Latin classics, which also provided one half of its framework of values. The other half, Christianity, still enjoyed solid institutional respect, though it was beginning to show structural cracks. It was a middle-class world, not dominated by courts and aristocracies but firmly in the hands of the property owners; "socialism" was a word on the lips of a few cranks, or at best licensed entertainers like Bernard Shaw. It was likewise a man's world; women were just beginning to appear, in tiny numbers, in higher education and the professions, but the vengeful goddess of Feminism had not begun to do more than stir in her sleep. Ethnic minorities offered no cultural challenge that need to be considered for a moment. English people; Welsh children who were heard to speak Welsh at school were punished by having a slate hung round their necks, and Ireland, not yet partitioned, was treated more or less as a colony. The unique musical sensibility of the black American, already noticed for a century as an idiom apart from that of Europe though related to it, was not yet accorded any importance; it was safely corralled in a kind of childish entertainment to be found on piers in the summer time, called "the nigger minstrels." In art, in thought, in politics, dress, cooking, in every detail of life, Europe was entirely European, and off its northwestern mainland, England was Entirely English.

The changes which brought about the disappearance of that world were, in some instances, disasters; in some, benefits; in others again they were just changes, about which we are free to make up our minds according to the framework of our general beliefs and preferences. When I was young, there was a popular philosopher, C. E. M. Joad, who used to maintain, among other things, that the greatest misfortune ever to befall the human race was the invention of the internal combustion engine. I agree with this proposition (if you take it for a triviality, think about the matter for five minutes by your watch), but doubtless there are people (car salesmen and highway engineers, for instance) who would dissent from it, and once again one can only say that all opinions are valid from the point of view from which they are uttered.

To C. S. Lewis, the values and customs of the world in which he grew up remained those he lived by, and the changes that eroded his world—before he finally died at sixty-five, more or less abolished it—were a matter for regret. This caused a permanent bias (using the word neutrally, as it is used on a bowling-green) in his criticism and in his conversation. He enjoyed standing against the tide of nailing fashionable cant. To a lady who wrote to him asking his opinion of psychoanalysis, he replied (March 26, 1940): "In talking to me you must beware, because I am conscious of a partly pathological hostility to what is fashionable. I may therefore have been betrayed into statements on this subject which I am not prepared to defend." That admission, in its bluntness and candor, is characteristic of Lewis. It is also characteristic that he goes on to make some valuable and interesting distinctions between what psychoanalysis can expect to achieve and what it cannot, which shows that he had considered the matter very fairly.

Clive Staples Lewis was born in 1898 in a suburb of Belfast, where his father was a solicitor. The date is significant because it means that his school education fell entirely within the confines of that epoch before 1914 when the world was substantially as I have described it above. Had it not been for the interruption of the First World War, in which he served in the trenches and was wounded, Lewis would have been securely launched on his Oxford undergraduate career by that fateful date of 1914—which, of course, in that case would not have been a fateful date.

Lewis's mind, then, was formed in Edwardian England. This was the case with virtually all the men who fought in 1914–1918, but most of them, and certainly most of the intelligentsia among them, came back radically altered: embittered, twisted perhaps, disaffected, sceptical; the modern arts were born out of their mood. Lewis, and it is useless to speculate why, seems to have come back with no change except a greater relish for the peaceful pleasures of reading and thinking, a

C. S. Lewis as a Teacher

greater need to work hard and make up for lost time, a greater belief in the values and attitudes of the settled world whose last days of golden peace he remembered, even though (and this is a puzzle I cannot offer to explain) they had not been particularly golden or peaceful for him. Most of the things that the typical modern man of the mid-twentieth century looked back on with distaste when he remembered his own and the century's earlier years—a large, stuffy, convention-ridden family, systematic ill-treatment at school, a rigid intellectual discipline administered by severe dominies—Lewis experienced in their full force, and, as his letters to his brother make plain, he was not docile by nature; but he acquiesced, and, when that world disappeared, he mourned it and harked back to it. He remained content throughout his life, with the framework of values that had seemed natural to him during his upbringing. Of course he learnt lessons from life, of course he weighed his experience and shed various illusions, but he remained an Edwardian in all essential particulars. Most of his controversies, and he engaged in a good few, were basically motivated by a wish to defend beliefs and attitudes which were usual in his boyhood and became more scarce and more threatened as his life went on.

It is usual to represent the First World War as a powerful explosive which suddenly went off amid a peaceful setting, and caused immense havoc to settled beliefs and calm attitudes. Certainly this is how I have always seen it, and still do. Causes of unrest were there, in the society of those first years of the century, and the more sensitive minds had begun to register them; in the arts, and in social thinking, there are marks of upheaval and radical innovation, any time from 1912 or thereabouts. But the surface of life was remarkably placid and it must have seemed likely to stay placid for ever. Culturally, as I have roughly indicated, there was no serious challenge to the recognized corpus, the body of information which was handed from generation to generation, very much as old birds teach young birds to fly.

The youthful Lewis was remarkable for the eagerness with

which he swallowed this mixture. His early reading was evidently a series of golden discoveries; as a child he was reveling in Spenser, Chaucer, and Malory; his school years were grim, but in mid-adolescence he escaped and went to live in the house of a private tutor, who put him in front of the Greek and Latin classics: he seems to have dived into them like a young bear getting into a tub of honey. No complaints about overwork, no sighing for a more active life away from all these books and papers—it was his world and he knew that from the start. "Outside a life of literary study, life has no meaning or attraction for him," his tutor, W. T. Kirkpatrick, wrote to his father: "he is adapted for nothing else. You may make up your mind to that."

The war, when he was taken from his books and pitchforked into it, meant mud and blood and bloated corpses and barbed wire and bombardments; but in some curious way it seems to have passed over Lewis like a dream. He hated it, of course; he was frightened, of course; but he seems to have accommodated the experience in some region of his mind where he could hold it separate. Perhaps, being a dreamer by nature and inhabiting a variegated dream-landscape, he could assign the experience of actual war to a nightmare section of that same landscape and thus stop it from running amok within his mental world as a whole. Certainly he remarked to me once that when he first approached the front line and heard gunfire, actual gunfire directed against human beings, a voice in his head said, "This is war. This is what you've read about in Homer." By putting it on the same plane of reality as Homer (for Lewis, a very important plane and a very vivid reality) he somehow contained it; perhaps we are here in sight of an explanation of the curious fact that unimaginative people go raving mad more often than imaginative people; once the ultimate horrors break loose into our experience, it is only the imagination that can contain them, and in this way the dreamers can survive better than the planners and doers.

The point is no mere triviality, because Lewis was, in fact, faithful all his life to the dreamer in him. As an original writer, as a critic, as a teacher, he labored always to get better understanding for that side of literature which concerns itself with the waking dream. On realistic literature he had nothing to say that went beyond the bounds of ordinary sensible comment; he would have been no more than average as a critic of Crabbe or Balzac or Gissing or Arnold Bennett or even Tolstoy; but he could expound Spenser or William Morris or George MacDonald, he could find what there was to say for Rider Haggard or Tolkien, he could move with ease from Malory and Chrétien de Troyes to Charles Williams.

Perhaps Lewis's preference for romance to realism, his willingness to inhabit a dream-landscape, was something to do with his being Irish. Though, in accordance with his general formative ethos, he presented the exterior of an Edwardian English gentleman, something in his innermost being was as Irish as Yeats or James Stephens; certainly he remained always "the man who dreamed of fairyland," even, in his more heroic moments, that Cuchulain who "fought the ungovernable sea." Because the Romantic in art and literature came under attack during his lifetime, his defense of them could seem like a general feature of his cultural conservatism; a generation who attacked the authority of Milton, exalted a poet like Dryden above a poet like Shelley, turned away from Spenser, and debunked romantic mythopoeia in the name of psychoanalysis, probably seemed to him merely "modern"— a catchall word for everything he opposed. I believe it lay deeper than that; I believe it was the suppressed or neglected Irishman coming out in Lewis's literary taste; but it certainly cemented in well with his general position of harking back to the days when the world was sane.

Like most people who are basically satisfied with the order into which they have been born, satisfied despite a clear-sighted view of its failures and shortcomings, Lewis took no interest in politics and regarded the impulse to change as a mere symptom of restlessness, an antlike scurrying about on the part of people who would do better to sit still. Thus he writes to his brother (March 22, 1940):

Why should quiet ruminants like you and I have been born in such a ghastly age? Let me palliate the apparent selfishness of this complaint by asserting that there *are* people who, while not of course liking actual suffering when it falls to their own share, *do* really like the "stir," the "sense of great issues." Lord! how I loathe great issues. How I wish they were all adjourned *sine die*. "Dynamic" I think is one of the words invented by this age which sums up what it likes and I abominate. Could one start a Stagnation Party—which at General Elections would boast that during its term of office *no* event of the least importance had taken place?

His ideal, in fact, was a quiet life of literary study; since he was an energetic controversialist, this sounds like a failure of self-knowledge, but I do not think it was a serious one; men of letters find plenty to dispute about, without going any further than their desks, and Lewis would have fitted into this pattern contentedly enough.

During the years when he was growing up, Lewis accepted the study of the Greek and Latin authors as the essential business of his life, and the reading of English authors, of every epoch since the English language made its appearance, as his chief recreation. Nothing that happened to him in his life disturbed this view. As a young graduate, seeking employment, he made several attempts to get a post in classical studies; his decision to enter the English faculty was motivated principally by the fact that that was where he found an opening: though he had, to be sure, no objection to teaching English literature nor to treating it, on his own terms, as an academic subject.

These terms he explained in two essays that sum up the opinions he had arrived at during some dozen years of teaching. One is "Our English Syllabus," addressed to an undergraduate audience, and the other "The Idea of an English School," addressed to the Classical Association in London; both are to be read in *Rehabilitations* (1939), a book of essays that does not in fact show Lewis at his best. These two pieces, however, are perfectly satisfactory as statements of the position Lewis never basically abandoned, though he elaborated on them several times, notably in *The Abolition of Man* (1943) and his inaugural lecture after moving to Cambridge, *De Descriptione Temporis* (1955).

"Our English Syllabus" is an attempt to present the *rationale* of English studies as practiced in Oxford at the undergraduate level in those days; it is a hard sell and a skillful one, with Lewis's inherited forensic instincts well to the fore. His main argument is that studying a literature is like working over a piece of natural woodland and seeing what actually grows there, what the climate and the soil, left to themselves, will foster; the vegetation, the insects, the birds, and mammals, even the parasites and the diseases. Not all of it is equally good, but the total experience is a real one because it confronts the enquirer with something that has actually happened, has come into being of its own accord and not because someone thought it would be desirable and improving. There must have been in those days a strain of opinion that wanted to study "great books" and famous names, and grudged spending time on the minor and the local; Lewis's defense has his characteristic pith and lucidity:

> The composite school, as its very name implies, has been composed by some one. Those little bits of various subjects are not found lying together in those quantities and in that order which the syllabus shows. They have been put together in that way artificially by a committee of professors. That committee cannot have been following the grain and joint of reality as reality discovers itself to those actually engaged in the pursuit of learning. For the life of learning knows nothing of this nicely balanced encyclopaedic arrangement. Every one of the suggested subjects is infinite and, in its own way, covers the whole field of reality. The committee would in fact be guided by their idea of what would do the students good—that is, by a purely educational idea. In reading such a school, therefore, you would not be turned loose on some tract of reality as it is, to make what you could of it; you would be getting selections of reality selected by your elders—something cooked, expurgated, filtered, and generally toned down for your edification. You would still be in the leading strings and might as well have stayed at school.

The address to the Classical Association is more subtly argued and more impressive in its display of a wide learning both classical and modern; but it makes what is essentially the same point:

> The English School as it stands has chosen unity and continuity: that is to say, taking a given area of reality, it has chosen, so far as possible, to explore it thoroughly, following the natural structure of that area, and neglecting all the interesting and delightful things over the frontier. The alternative school which is suggested, with Greek, Latin and perhaps French classics side by side with the greatest English writers, would be based on a different principle—the principle of selection. In the one you turn the young out into a single, untidy country to make what they can of it; in the other you take them to what their elders think of the five or six most interesting places in a whole continent. It is the difference between knowing, say, Worcestershire inside out, while remaining ignorant of the rest of the world, and knowing four or five European capitals while striking no roots in any single European soil. The choice is a very difficult one. On the one hand we have Arnold's ideal—"the best that is known and thought in the world"; on the other *Spartam nactus es*. Embrace the latter and you may become insular and provincial; embrace the former and you may be a mere tourist, glib in all countries and rooted in none. Which is the more deeply ignorant, the shepherd who has never left the Cotswolds, or the Peripatetic millionaire—the tap-room of the "Red Lion," or the lounge of the Palace Motel?

A few weeks ago (March 21, 1980) I read an article in the *Times Higher Educational Supplement* by a member of the Oxford English Faculty which contained this passage:

> "I suppose we can't do Brecht until next year?" a first-year undergraduate asked me gloomily the other day. Her gloom deepened considerably when I broke the awful news that *English* language and literature meant exactly what it said. The rampant chauvinism which bulked large in the original establishment of English as a university discipline is alive and well in Oxford, even if it has been modified elsewhere.

I read the passage with an obedient chuckle, assuming that its author was joking, though the irony seemed to me rather heavy-handed—"the awful news that English literature means English literature," etc. But the rest of the article alerted

C. S. Lewis as a Teacher

me to the fact that the author, Mr. Terry Eagleton (Fellow and Tutor of Wadham College) was perfectly straight-faced; that whereas the corresponding person in 1939 thought that a concentration on English literature was parochial and provincial, to him it is "chauvinism" to try to do one thing at a time.

I laid down the paper and tried to imagine what Lewis would have thought of such an attitude. It was not difficult. His preference for a solid understanding of local landscapes rather than a globetrotter's Instamatic click-click would have led him, I'm afraid, to be rather stony-hearted about the suffering of the damsel who yearned to "do" Brecht as part of (presumably) a course in English, but was prevented by "chauvinism" from doing so. One can imagine a few of the questions he would have asked: Has the student signed on in a department of English? Or are we to conclude that in the enlightened future, purged of chauvinism, such distinctions will be abolished? If so, will schools of Modern Languages be abolished as well as schools of English? And will everybody simply mill around in a glorious hotch-potch, "doing" whatever they think will turn them on? If so, a student who really wants to study Brecht carefully and understand him fully will have to make detailed inquiries in advance, because study will necessarily start with a thorough grounding in the German language and an acquaintance with German history and institutions; or is the "English" school supposed to offer these as well as everything else?

Another question Lewis might have been provoked to ask is: Does the English School in its chauvinism tell the girl what to do in her spare time as well as in her working time? If she has a notion that Brecht might interest her (and it must be a prior notion, formed on the basis of at most a nodding acquaintance with Brecht, since a cruel world has not yet allowed her to "do" him), are there no theater clubs she can join, and take part in productions of his plays? Are there no discussion groups that talk about his ideas? Are there no introductions and popular guides on sale at the bookshop?

The answer is, of course, that these things exist in plenty; but in the mysterious world inhabited by the party-line modern academic, students are not supposed to have any spare time—nor, for that matter, any subsequent part of their life after they cease to be students. The notion seems to be that they come to the university for three years, come to it from a background of mass media and mass entertainment, that they never opened a book or pondered an idea before they came and will never do so after they leave, so that their three-year course becomes a breathless, hurried pit stop in which they must be fueled with such knowledge and such ideas as they can carry. If Brecht (or whoever else is in fashion) attracts you, then the university has a duty to teach you about Brecht, and without the tedious formality of enrolling in a modern German course and learning something solid—because if it doesn't, when your university course comes to an end, some mysterious process will intervene and Brecht and all his works will be blown like a puff of smoke, utterly beyond recall.

I bring in this example of modish absurdity as a convenient way of highlighting one important feature of Lewis's thinking about University teaching and learning. He had in one sense less faith in it than the Eagletons of this world; in another, much more. He believed in the university study of English without ever being in danger of overestimating what it would do for people. He approved of it, assented to its main objectives and values, and worked hard in its interests, but he never thought, or said, that it was enough on its own. He did not belong to a school of thought that could regard any one discipline as enough on its own. He himself, for instance, saw English literature through the eyes of one who had started in life with a sound classical education—as had most of the authors who had written what he was reading—and he was convinced that no other approach was really valid. This was, at bottom, the reason for his distrust of the "research" convention; he saw it as wasting a golden year or two in which students who intended to take up academic work might have been filling in gaps in their reading of the classics, while

C. S. Lewis as a Teacher

they were young and energetic enough to tackle the hard work this involved. As he put it to the Classical Association:

> Need I say that I should like English students to know Greek and Latin? But they must not come to an English school to learn them. If they have not learned them before they come to me, I should like them to learn them after they leave me. Any proposal which enables them to do so in those postgraduate years which are increasingly spent at the university will always have all the support I can give it; and to that end I am ready to sacrifice any amount of what is called "Research."

This attitude, naturally, put him out of step with the modern attitude towards the academic study of English as it took shape in his lifetime. He had no belief that two or three years spent in learning the methods of scholarly research were any substitute for the filling of linguistic and historical gaps. ("If a man wants to find something out," he said to me once, "he'll find it out.") He never took a research degree himself, and he regarded the products of the research schools as overtrained in some ways and undereducated in others. In this, as in most things, he swam against the current; all his life, in spite of the weight of his learning, the force and freshness of his critical writing, and the capacity crowds at his lectures (or possibly because of these things?), he was regarded with a certain sourness by members of the research-obsessed orthodox body of academia, a sourness that was certainly not sweetened when in his hours of ease he made quips, inevitably reported back to H.Q., such as, "There are three kinds of reader—the literate, the illiterate, and the B.-Litterate."

Lewis saw learning as something that needed to start with a broad base—the appropriate languages, the appropriate areas of history and philosophy—which alone prevented parochiality, faddishness and general loss of perspective. But he knew that if this broad base does not exist, its lack cannot be supplied by hasty little side excursions ("doing" Brecht, etc.) divorced from any linguistic or historical discipline.

In short, the quality Lewis worked hardest to instill in

his pupils was intellectual integrity. Your three years in the English School (or the Modern Languages, or History, or any other School) taught you the patient observation of one form of life; and the rest of your intellectual development, which lasted your lifetime, consisted of applying that observation and that patience to everything that came within your attention. For this reason he was not in the least put off by the argument that some of the works prescribed for study in the English Syllabus were not first-rate when judged by the standards of literary masterpieces generally. One university teacher of Lewis's generation, or only a few years younger, used to comment scornfully on the folly of making undergraduates read "parish-pump stuff" when the peaks of world literature were there to be scaled. But Lewis liked the parish pump. He saw it as a good meeting place between equals and a good reminder of down-to-earth necessities— one must have water and a bucket to carry it home in, and a home to carry it to for that matter. And peaks, he would doubtless have argued, can only be scaled if you start at the bottom, among much more humdrum scenes. To take in the peaks and nothing else is akin to flying over them in an airplane, a method of travel which teaches one nothing about the nature of the existence that goes on below.

This acceptance of the ordinary, the cheerful recognition that to acquaint oneself with the literature of a nation in anything like completeness means having time and patience for a good deal that is not absolutely of the best quality, is a clearly recognizable element in Lewis's published criticism as it was in his teaching. His Oxford History volume *English Literature in the Sixteenth Century* (he always referred to that series as the "Oh hell"), in which he dealt with the nondramatic literature of the sixteenth century, shows a wonderful relish for that epoch, a delight in the byways as well as the main routes, and a detailed acquaintance with half-forgotten— even, in some cases, almost totally forgotten—writing. But he never overestimates what he finds. Thus, after writing an interesting paragraph about William Warner (1587–1609),

C. S. Lewis as a Teacher

and quoting some good lines, Lewis adds, "But no one should be deceived by these quotations into reading Warner. The good things in *Albion's England* are as far divided as the suns in space." He was the opposite of the kind of critic who is always trying to astonish us with beauties and profundities that he has been the first to perceive, and to convince us that the latest work to engage his attention is a neglected masterpiece. To Lewis, reading books was like meeting people; he found it a normal and interesting activity without having to pretend that it was a constant source of astonishing illumination and inspiration. People are worth meeting even though not many of them are very original and some are actively unpleasant; only by meeting a lot of them, by making a habit of it, does one build up a knowledge of humanity. Books are the same. That was why Lewis never had any sympathy with a fastidious view of literary taste, anything that made a virtue of exclusiveness. When (before I knew better) I quoted to him T. S. Eliot's opinion that the amount of good poetry in the world is very small, he replied at once, "The amount that can be read with pleasure and profit is enormous."

That was typical of the man—a certain rough-and-ready quality, a willingness to be as generous and charitable with books as he was with human beings. It is not the only possible approach to literature and literary teaching; I am not even quite certain that it is the best one; but it was, in that time and place, an excellent corrective to the arcane intellectual disciplines of an Eliot or the acrid solemnities of a Leavis. Leavis once said to someone that Lewis "hated literature." When I first heard this, I thought it merely an absurd remark to make about someone so devotedly literate, so seldom found without a book in his hands, as Lewis. But of course from Leavis's own specialized point of view it is a meaningful judgment; it means, basically, that Lewis was content to enjoy literature and take it as he found it, without trying to make literary study into a priestcraft.

Thus, in his book on Milton, Lewis skirmishes for some

pages against T. S. Eliot, then adds as a kind of afterthought that he has no wish to attack Eliot personally. "Why should I? I agree with him about matters of such moment that literary considerations are by comparison trivial." This would be rank heresy to Leavis, to whom a literary judgment involved the whole personality; the way one responded to literature was an indication of one's whole response to life, so how could it be trivial? I am of Leavis's mind here, but I think these things must sometimes look very different to those who have an over-arching metaphysical religious belief. To a humanist like Leavis or myself, great literature will inevitably come to occupy something like the place of a body of scripture— a record of what mankind has found worth living and worth dying for—and to be flippant about it begins to look like chewing gum in church. But Gerard Manley Hopkins, in one of his letters to Bridges, says something like, "When we met the other day we had no time to speak of serious topics— our talk was all of literature." (I quote from memory, but that is certainly the gist of it, and it was a consistent attitude with Hopkins.) So perhaps to "hate literature" in company with a man like Hopkins is not so disgraceful after all.

All this time, I have been describing Lewis's mental configuration in general, without getting down to the task of describing his method as a teacher. In fact, it does not take much describing. It was, quite simply, forensic and disputacious; I suppose "Socratic" would be a loftier term for it, but the exchanges between Lewis and his undergraduate pupils did not often rise to Socratic heights; they usually smacked more of the courtroom. Lewis's father was a lawyer and he had inherited an aptitude for the weighing of evidence and for cross-examination. I never heard him formulate his philosophy of teaching, but it was obviously based on the conviction that we clarify our opinions most fully, and possess them most securely, when we are forced to defend them. It follows that the duty of a tutor is to subject the pupil's ideas to a vigorous attack which will either scatter them like chaff or,

C. S. Lewis as a Teacher

if they have any real substance, root them more strongly.

This duty Lewis performed with relish. He himself enjoyed a good argument and he had no innate sympathy with the kind of mind that shrinks away from dispute and develops its ideas best in an atmosphere of encouragement. After a year or two of being tutored by Lewis, one developed the mentality of a fighter pilot: *Get him before he gets you.* That is, if you survived at all. There were pupils of Lewis's who decided, after being repeatedly floored in these contests, that they had no gift for the kind of discipline he was trying to teach them, and went down from the university and took up something else. (Example: John Betjeman.)

Lewis of course taught graduate seminars now and then, and supervised research, but in the Oxford of his day "teaching" meant, overwhelmingly, the teaching of undergraduates; and, of course, lecturing, which he did with obvious enjoyment and great success. His lectures were not, like those of his admired friend Williams, rhapsodic; nor slyly humorous and solipsistic, like those of Tolkien; they were above all *teaching* lectures; he set out to impart information, and many parts of his discourse, heavily loaded with precise references, had to be taken more or less at dictation speed. This had probably evolved in response to the situation at Oxford, where the undergraduate has (or, in his and my day, had) no formal teaching whatever except an hourly "tutorial," two-thirds of which was taken up by his reading his essay aloud. There were no classes, no group discussion work of any kind, no formal sessions which the teacher could use to make sure that some solid information got into his pupil's heads; lectures there were, but they were not compulsory, and (in fine weather or toward the end of a term) very sparsely attended. So Lewis stood there patiently, his big voice booming out (nobody ever said they couldn't *hear* him), his bulky body standing solidly in the one spot (he wasn't one of those lecturers who march up and down the platform, or jingle coins in their pockets, or make asides which are only heard by three people in the front row), until the hour struck and then he would abruptly snatch up his papers and run out of the room, as if pent-up impatience to be finished with this routine task, or fear of being detained by some persistent questioner, had suddenly mastered him. (We undergraduates used to speculate, facetiously, at to whether he might have a weak bladder.)

Going to a lecture by Lewis was an enjoyable occasion; but then, meeting Lewis on any terms was an enjoyable occasion, for he liked cheerfulness, and congenial company, and he thought literature was something to rejoice in. I am glad of all the hours I spent with him, sitting in his rooms, or on the steps of the New Building at Magdalen, looking out into the deer-haunted grove, or drinking beer in humble taverns ("the taproom of the Red Lion"), and I am glad to have been his pupil.

16

Leo Strauss: Becoming Naïve Again

WERNER J. DANNHAUSER

SINCE HIS DEATH on October 18, 1973, at the age of seventy-four, Leo Strauss has become an ever more well-known figure. His fame is spreading slowly, but it is spreading. For a long time before 1973 he was not, to be sure, unknown, but his work tended to be neglected, misunderstood, ridiculed. In other words, he was controversial—and he still is. Now, however, his critics can no longer take refuge in scoffing and contempt; they are faced with the more rigorous task of refuting him before the bar of reason.

No doubt controversy will continue to rage around this thinker who produced interpretations of political philosophers from Plato to Nietzsche that were a mysterious combination of the strange and the simple. Yet one thing about him is conceded by both his friends and his enemies: he was an altogether extraordinary teacher. That assertion needs no more proof than that he founded a school of sorts, that he had a number of students so devoted to him that they became known as his disciples, and that today there are a number of teachers referred to at "Straussians."

Now, what is a Straussian? Since Leo Strauss reached the height of his power as a teacher at the University of Chicago, where he was a member of the department of political science during the fifties and sixties, his students most typically teach political science, though one can also find them in classics and philosophy departments. They hold positions at a goodly number of universities, and a goodly number of other universities expend considerable amounts of energy keeping them out.

The label Straussian is one affixed to certain people by those who are not Straussians. The motives for labeling anyone a Straussian can range from a neutral wish to describe, or benevolent skepticism, all the way to outright hostility. The reactions of those who are so described also show great variations. Some do not deny their affiliation but are hesitant or reticent; some claim that a case of mistaken identity has been perpetrated. And some —I am among them—wear the label with pride, knowing that to follow Leo Strauss is to be committed to genuine open-mindedness in regard to the perennial questions of political philosophy.

Not everyone, it is true, looks at it that way. From an outsider's perspective, a Straussian is likely to appear dogmatic, disputatious, and given to defending himself even when he is not attacked. His influence on academia has been described as "the dead hand of scholasticism," though it is not certain whether the man who used that phrase knew what scholasticism was. Presumably he meant that when others cite Lukács and Arendt, Straussians quote Plato and Aristotle; when others mention Tillich and Buber, we are more likely to refer to Averroës and Maimonides.

A Straussian, from this perspective, is someone who reads secular books religiously, Talmudically, cabalistically, but above all perversely. So intent is he on finding the message "between the lines"—Strauss articulated esoteric communication in *Persecution and the Art of Writing*—that he neglects to state what is on the lines; the resulting interpretations can be a haze of mumbo jumbo pierced by an occasional insight. Moreover, while he read secular books religiously, a Straussian reads religious books impiously, or at least in so obscuran-

Leo Strauss: Becoming Naïve Again

tist a fashion that one is hard put to say whether he is an antheist or a secret agent of the Vatican. To top off all these slightly unsavory characteristics, a Straussian may well be politically to the right of center. As the spectrum is defined at the universities these days, that may mean no more than that he supported Humphrey in 1968 and worked for Jackson in 1972. No matter—right of center is a bad place to be for professors.

Yet notwithstanding all their infirmities and iniquities, Straussians have, to put it quite simply, become a force with which even the most sensible and progressive university administrators must reckon. The reason is obvious: on the average, Straussians are teachers whose quality is far above average. And that is very important, for as the universities try to weather their finanical crises a Straussian who can attract students in droves is worth his weight in gold. What is more, the era of student power is by no means over; for example, while the grades teachers are giving students are becoming less important, the grades students are giving teachers on what are euphemistically called evaluation forms are becoming more significant. Straussian teachers regularly earn very high marks, a fact that is all the more curious when one considers they are prone to be strict with students and to abstain from kissing their feet—not to speak of other parts of the human anatomy.

The explanation the whole phenomenon calls for is not all that hard to find. Straussians attract students because they are able to address the souls of students, and they are able to address the souls of students because they were schooled by an altogether incomparable teacher: Leo Strauss.

So we are back at the beginning—Leo Strauss as teacher. Since teaching is a profoundly personal activity, I know no other way to try to describe Leo Strauss as teacher than by recourse to personal reminiscences, it being clearly understood that I was never his closest or best student. And since there is something ineffable about teaching and its effects, I must recollect in a manner completely nonscientific.

Once upon a time—the fall of 1956, to be exact—I wandered into one of Strauss's seminars at the University of Chicago. I had just arrived there as a graduate student and I was awestruck. For many of us who went to high school in the forties, the University of Chicago had an aura about it that not even Harvard could match; it was *the* place to go. (To this very day I cannot visit there without realizing that for me it will always be *the* university.)

I was a student of the social sciences and, like most of the students of Leo Strauss, at the time I began my studies I was a relativist ill at ease in his relativism. I took for granted the validity of the fact-value distinction, although I was pained by its implications. I somehow knew that Hitler was not merely one man's meat and another man's poison, but I really thought one would have to say I "knew" that. I believed that scientifically (which also meant rationally) one could not get behind or beyond the multitude of values people espoused. I had read *Natural Right and History* by Leo Strauss, a book attacking that very position. It left me confused, excited, mildly stunned, and determined to look for Leo Strauss as soon as I could manage to attend the University of Chicago.

He was not hard to find in 1956, being probably one of the three most well known—and certainly most notorious—professors in the Division of Social Sciences. That quarter he was giving a lecture course and a seminar, but I was told, correctly, that one could get the true flavor of the man only in his seminars. These were always held in the same room in the social science building (I believe it was 302) and always twice a week at the same hour. The catalog scheduled them from 3:30 to 5:00 P.M., but while they started punctually they usually lasted until 6:00 or even 7:00 P.M.

I had been admonished to come early, and that was good advice for a room holding thirty comfortably and holding fifty or sixty uncomfortably for a Strauss seminar. The class was about equally divided between newcomers like me and old-timers for whom it was a fall reunion. I was nervous but I did not have long to agitate, for Leo Strauss walked

Leo Strauss: Becoming Naïve Again

in punctually. In the middle of the 1950s he was a man in the middle of his own fifties, but my first impression was not that he was middle-aged, or old, or young, but small. (He had been described as an intellectual giant, and I suppose I am too literal-minded.) My second impression, when he began to speak, was that he had a high, soft voice bordering on squeakiness. I had been told to sit near the front of the room; that too was good advice, for one had trouble hearing him.

In the physical sense, he was a bit unprepossessing. Over the years I have often marveled at how little he had going for him, in the ordinary sense, as a teacher. For example, now that I am myself a teacher I frequently catch myself using histrionics, or trying deliberately to be charming, or striving after magnetism. Strauss, by contrast, operated with a quiet and undramatic kind of good cheer, a shining and pristine simplicity.

That simplicity is one of the first and most lasting impressions I have of the man. We were to read Hobbes in the first seminar I attended. Strauss began without further ado to say that we would read only the first two parts of the *Leviathan*, that this was "disgraceful" but that we would have our hands full doing justice to even that much. Then he spoke with a kind of childish seriousness about requirements: those wanting credit must prepare a twenty-minute presentation on a few chapters; long experience had taught him that seven double-spaced typewritten pages could be read aloud in twenty minutes.

After that, he turned unceremoniouly to some introductory remarks. The first question he considered surprised me: Why should one read Hobbes today? It was a question I had been asking myself, for I had read Hobbes previously in a survey course, and the only parts I did not find boring were those I found incomprehensible. I had come to study with Strauss; I had not come to study Hobbes, but Strauss firmly directed our minds to Hobbes (only much later were we to realize that the director was himself a great mind). He showed us that Hobbes was—relevant. One uses that term with some embarrassment today, but no other word will do. He exposed our opinions as *mere* opinions; he caused us to realize that we were the prisoners of our opinions by showing us the larger horizons behind and beyond them. Thus we all believed in watered-down teachings derived from Marx, Freud, and others; but buttressing our views was modern thought as such, and one of its towering giants was Hobbes. To understand the true nature of our beliefs, it was necessary to undertake an arduous journey back in time, a journey that would not even end with Hobbes, for modern thought at its best was a rebellion by giants like Hobbes against men perhaps even more gigantic—Plato and Aristotle. But the conversion, the turning to light he tried to effect in us, did not necessarily terminate in Platonism. Not the least remarkable of a number of remarkable suggestions—or commands—which Leo Strauss produced that day was that we simply must begin with the assumption that Hobbes's teaching was true—not relatively true, not true for Hobbes, not true for its time, but *simply true.* That was why we had to read him with all the care we could muster, and that was why (I was to hear him say this again and again) one ought not even to begin to criticize an author before one had done all one could do to understand him correctly, to understand him as he understood himself. What is more, we were there not only to learn *about* Hobbes, but to learn *from* him.

I write about Strauss badly because I write about him and his methods too abstractly, because I make it all sound very somber. I wish I were a poet, so I could do him justice. I wish I could recapture now, even as I wish I could relive, the atmosphere prevailing in the many seminars of his that I attended. They were not somber at all: what remains most shining and vivid in my memory is the great amount of laughter that punctuated those classes. They constitute some of the best and happiest memories of my life.

Leo Strauss talked a great deal during his seminars. He knew more about Socrates than any man I have ever known, and yet—and therefore—he did not act as Socrates is supposed to have acted. He did not answer questions with questions, nor did he play the midwife in the conventional sense. Nevertheless, he encouraged questions, and I suspect he would have agreed with Heidegger that questioning is the piety of thinking. His response to questions was amazingly thorough, patient, and good humored. I remember the first time I asked him something about Hobbes. I thought I was being stupid and I was afraid of exposing my stupidity, but he set up situations where one learned not to be afraid to admit that, or what, one did not understand. So I asked, and he astonished me by raising my questions to a stratospheric level. I had not known what I was asking, but I was wrestling with a genuine perplexity. I remember his leaving his desk, as he did at times, and coming over to my chair, talking to me personally about some knotty problem in Hobbes. I soon grew dizzy, for he was giving me more food for thought than I could digest; but before he was through I had learned something about what it meant to think.

He enjoyed himself hugely during those question periods, and the obvious fun he was having was contagious. His good humor was almost unfailing. Only once in the years I studied with him did I see him abandon that sunniness, and it was during that very seminar on Hobbes, when the questioner accused him of not taking Hobbes seriously enough. He icily informed the student that he had spent more time studying Hobbes than had anyone he knew. Urbane and polite, he deplored rudeness but loved to be challenged, and his response was almost unfailingly witty. What is more, it was unhurried, so that we learned most specifically the importance of leisure for learning.

In fact, most of what we learned was invested with the charm and potency of specificity. We did not so much talk about the larger aspects of the *Leviathan* as about certain difficult sentences or obscure passages. Since that seminar I have heard a great deal about Hobbes's absolutism, Hobbes's doctrine of political obligation, and the like. Such topics received due attention, but what I recall much more vividly is the way we entered into Hobbes's universe of discourse by thinking about what it meant to be afraid, what it felt like to give orders and to take them, and kindred matters.

Leo Strauss told us once that he doubted whether a book could be a good book if it contained no examples. Under his benign tutelage we began to think that we had not understood a general maxim until we could examine it in a specific instance. Everything called for illustration, and his own illustrations were a mixture of the apt, the eccentric, and the fantastic. They were fantastic, paradoxically enough, because they came from the world of our most immediate experience. It took me and my fellow students a while to get used to his habit of quoting Ann Landers, or of referring to scenes from movies (usually westerns or gangster films), or of quoting Groucho instead of Karl Marx, but our habituation to his procedure was always pleasant. Every class was, as I have suggested, rich in detail; I know he was familiar with Warburg's great saying that God resides in the minute detail.

As one became accustomed to his classes, one became accustomed to one's classmates. When I arrived at Chicago I was scared by the loneliness most graduate students know at one time or another. It was not only that I was in a strange place; it was that I no longer knew what the proper basis for lasting association was. It was in Leo Strauss's classes, as we were together pondering all those details with the exactitude he encouraged, as we were thinking and laughing (so much laughter in his classes!) that I found myself "becoming a member of a true community," as one fashionably puts it today: in those primitive days we thought of it as making friends. We argued long and brashly and wittily about matters that had come up in class. We talked and ate and drank together, and to this day most of my closest friends are those who shared with me the experience of being in the classes of Leo Strauss. I would not deny, in fact I would assert, that he had his share of obnoxious students: prigs, snobs, fools who thought they could successfully be Athenian gentlemen in

Leo Strauss: Becoming Naïve Again

Hyde Park, dogmatists in search of dogmas. But Leo Strauss snared more than his share of good souls, students one began to love. I had never before known personally that deep and abiding bonds can be forged around a book, when it becomes more than a book, when it turns into a world. Today I know that books and Leo Strauss, who turned books into a cosmos for us, are responsible for much of the happiness in my life. It is, of course, a knowledge that carries with it the realization that what I, and others, owe to Leo Strauss is beyond repayment. Perhaps it is not beyond gratitude, and not only to him. Years later, after I had stopped attending classes, someone very close to me, to whom I had given the transcript of Strauss's Spinoza seminar, said, "You ought to thank God for having had a teacher like that," and went on to bemoan her own bad luck. I knew what she meant.

When all is said and done, teaching turns out to be a rather occult activity. In moments of despondency we teachers think that teaching makes nothing happen, but evidence abounds to the effect that this is not the case. Leo Strauss changed those of us who took him seriously—but how? What did we learn from him? It is a difficult question, but since it is also a legitimate one, it requires an answer, no matter how fumbling that answer must of necessity be.

To begin with something apparently simple: Leo Strauss taught us how to read a book (his mastery of that art is dimly but definitely reflected in the masterliness of his book reviews). We learned that books were wholes, and that it was safest to assume that they were perfect wholes; for while even Homer may nod, he nods very rarely and not when we can see him. He knew the dangers of overinterpretation but that it has a cure because the house of cards one builds in such cases topples when either the interpreter or his well-meaning friends show it up as a house of cards. Underinterpretation, by contrast, is an irretrievable loss; one departs from a book without getting from it all it has to give, perhaps without getting from it the best it has to give. So we would read books carefully, line by line if possible, and we found that a great book is indeed a magic structure. It is wonderful—literally full of wonders, a house of many mansions, secret rooms, labyrinthine passages. Moreover, it is incredibly beautiful. By teaching us to see beauty, he elevated our taste, and we became a bit more pure without exerting any of the self-defeating straining-after-beauty that merely distorts.

Second, he taught us how to look at political things correctly. We had been staring at them long enough but not with understanding, at least not with *our* understanding. As Allan Bloom has put it, to study with Leo Strauss was an exercise in the restoration of the natural consciousness. He trained us to see things as they come to sight, to let them appear without the distortions modern opinion imposes upon them, and, yes, to let them *speak* to us. That meant we had to divest ourselves of many habits, including the habit of viewing things as budding social scientists. We learned what is, perhaps, hardest of all to learn: to become a bit more naïve again. Leo Strauss taught us to begin by considering political things in the perspective of the common citizen, though he also urged us to try to see further. So we learned to trust the superiority of proverbs again; we learned to talk in simple words again. Instead of "values," we talked of good and bad; we discussed unhappiness rather than alienation, and things ceased to be dysfunctional—they just did not work. Gradually we realized that Hegel was right when he insisted that, contrary to opinion, it is nonphilosophers who think abstractly, while only philosophers can do justice to the world in its marvelous particulars. In teaching us to see reality—and to understand that it was far richer than what so-called "realism" considers—he edified us in spite of, or because of, his repeated reminder to us that Hegel had excluded edification from the tasks of philosophy.

Some will say that what Leo Strauss did was to teach us to look at political things in a new way, *his* way—and they will be wrong. It is true that his own views were conservative, and that when all is said and done he preferred the ways and thoughts of Socrates to the thoughts and ways of any

Leo Strauss: Becoming Naïve Again

modern thinker. It is also true that he could be quite critical of the opinions of the Left, but that is because the highest education consists in an attempt to ascend from opinion to knowledge, and nobody can deny that the predominant opinions in the universities today are those of the Left. Those of us who came to know him knew that he was the very model of genuine open-mindedness (not to be confused with empty-headedness); his insistence that each book be approached on its own terms implies as much. As for the rest, I must bear personal witness. He advised each of us to do our dissertation on a great political thinker; this would mean that one was, as it were, going to spend several years living with a great man, which in turn was an education in itself. I chose Nietzsche for the shaky reason that he was the only philosopher I had ever read who had absolutely never bored me. Now, Nietzsche is the most vehement, eloquent, and profound modern opponent of Socrates. I remember an early discussion with Leo Strauss about my dissertation. In the course of our talk I finally found the courage to blurt out that I often felt that Nietzsche was right in his quarrel with Socrates. He replied he should hope I felt that way. I am by no means the only one of his students to whom he taught open-mindedness.

How did he do it all? For a long time I was mystified by the force of his effect on others and myself. After some years of teaching, that mystification increased because I realized he had violated many of the rules for good teaching that I had found useful and to which I continue to adhere. Thus, like many of *his* students, I believe in being somewhat severe with *mine*; yet he was most permissive, demanding almost nothing one did not feel like doing. (He never even collected the seven-page papers we prepared.) I believe in entering the life of my students not only by way of their minds but by socializing with them. He, by contrast, preserved his distance. He was always accessible if one needed help, but he was also a bit aloof. He almost never called a student by his first name, and it was unthinkable for us to call him by his first name, even after we had ourselves become teachers.

Nietzsche, to whom Leo Strauss brought me, has helped me to clear up the mystery. In aphorism 63 of *Beyond Good and Evil*, he writes, "Whoever is a teacher through and through takes all things seriously only in relation to his students— even himself" (Walter Kaufmann translation). Strauss took himself very seriously indeed, in the Socratic sense of "Know thyself"; he never ceased in his quest to understand the human things. Which is to say that he was a great teacher because he was more than a teacher: he was a philosopher. This, I think, accounts for that cluster of his characteristics which some have described as coldness but which is more justly called Olympian detachment.

Philosophers are difficult to understand because they bring back reports from regions most of us are not privileged to enter. We take our revenge on them for their agility and our clumsiness by freezing their teachings into doctrines. The more I studied with Leo Strauss, the more I came to realize he had no doctrine—or at least a most elusive one. That became strikingly clear to me at a party on October 13, 1973, in Toronto, at the home of Professor Allan Bloom, author of a masterful article on Leo Strauss in *Political Theory*. Among the guests were two most distinguished scholars, Professors Hans-Georg Gadamer of Heidelberg and Gershom Scholem of Jerusalem. The talk turned naturally to Leo Strauss, for he was to the end a very controversial man. The controversy was benevolent; there were no losers in the argument, only winners, but there *was* a good-natured argument. I will not say our side won, but Bloom, the others, and I were content not to lose. We were, so to speak, simultaneously defending Leo Strauss against the representatives of Heidegger and God.

Afterward we became aware that we ourselves disagreed as to the "position" of Leo Strauss. Not having seen him for several years, I decided to visit him within the next two weeks. But I was too late: he died a few days later. So I never had a chance to ask him where he really stood.

That was sad but not crucial. His books remain to be pondered. In a way he had taught me personally what is perhaps for me the most important thing: *reverence.* He showed me how to look up, and the things worthy of reverence. Education is a little weak on inculcating reverence today, but that was one of the trends of the time against which he was in combat.

A number of us were proud of Leo Strauss, and we are proud of him still. He does not need us to perpetuate his memory, for his books will endure. What we can do, and do do, is teach as well as we can; and that to some degree means we teach his teachings to those who will transmit them to another generation. Perhaps Henry Adams was right when he wrote: "A teacher affects eternity; he can never tell where his influence stops."